W9-AAC-104

ACTION
MOVIES

ILLUSTRATED REVIEWS OF THE CLASSIC FILMS

MALLARD
PRESS

Half-title page: *Errol Flynn as* **The Sea Hawk,** *a pirate-cum-adventurer preying on Spanish commerce in the 16th century.*

Title page: *Fantastic stunts were an integral part of* **The Cannonball Run,** *an actioner about a cross-country road race.*

ACKNOWLEDGMENTS
Editor: Julian Brown
Design Editor: Leigh Jones
Jacket designer: Ashley Western
Production Controller: Nick Thompson
Picture researcher: Jenny Faithfull

Photographic acknowledgments
The Ronald Grant Archive 1, 2-3, 9, 10 top, 11, 12, 19, 29, 30, 33, 36, 39, 40, 45, 46 right, 51, 54, 55, 57 bottom, 65, 68, 69, 72 top, 73, 75, 82, 84, 85 bottom, 86 bottom, 88 bottom, 94 bottom, 100, 105, 110, 111, 125; The Kobal Collection 6, 10 bottom, 13, 15, 16, 18 left, 18 right, 22, 24, 26, 27, 31, 32, 34, 35, 37, 43, 46 left, 47, 49, 52, 53, 56, 57 top, 58, 60, 62, 67 top, 67 bottom, 71, 72 bottom, 76, 77, 79, 81, 83, 85 top, 86 top, 88 top, 89, 90, 91, 92, 94 top, 95, 96, 98 top, 98 bottom, 108-109, 113 top, 113 bottom, 116 left, 116 right, 119 top left, 119 bottom right, 121, 122, 124 left, 124 right, 126, 128 top, 128 bottom; Octopus Publishing Group Ltd 20, 61.

MALLARD PRESS
An Imprint of BDD Promotional Book Company, Inc.
666 Fifth Avenue
New York, N.Y. 10103

"Mallard Press" and its accompanying design and logo are trademarks of BDD Promotional Book Company, Inc.

Copyright © 1992 Variety Inc.

First published in the United States of America in 1992 by The Mallard Press by arrangement with The Hamlyn Publishing Group Limited, a division of Reed International Books, Michelin House, 81 Fulham Road, London SW3 6RB, England

ISBN 0-792-45786-2

All rights reserved

Produced by Mandarin Offset
Printed in China.

GLOSSARY

The following is a guide to 80 years of *Variety* 'slanguage' as occurs in the reviews selected; it is not exhaustive and is intended especially for non-American and more general readers.

Variety's snazzy coinages are a goulash of publishing and showbiz/movie jargon, foreign words, Yiddish, street slang, contractions and acronyms that since the mid-1930s have since acquired a reputation and life of their own.

Many of the words have long vanished from use in the paper (along with the slang that inspired them); new ones are still being invented by writers. The only rule is that they sound 'right' and carry on the tradition of sharp, tabloid, flavourful prose.

As a further aid for general readers we have also included some words that are simple movie jargon or archaic slang rather than pure *Variety* language.

a.k.	ass-kisser	helm(er)	direct(or)
a.k.a.	also known as	histrionics	performance(s)
ankle	alcoholic	histrionically	performance-wise
anent	regarding	hoke	hokum
avoirdupois	weight	hoke up	over-act
b.b.	big business	hoofology	dancing
beer stube	bar	hotcha	excellent
belter	boxer	hoyden(ish)	tomboy(ish)
burley	burlesque, music hall	ink	sign
bow	debut; praise	i.r.	inquiring or investigative reporter
b.r.	bankroll; sum of money	jitterbug	(1940s) jazz dance(r); nervous person
cannon	gun	kayo	knockout
carny	carnival	legit(imate)	theatrical, theatre, stage
Chi	Chicago	legiter	stage play
chili	Mexican	legituner	stage musical
chirp(er)	sing(er)	lense(r)	photograph(er)
chopsocky	martial arts (film)	limn	portray
chore	job; routine assignment	lingo	dialogue
chump	crazy (in love)	longhair	intellectual; high brow
cleff(er)	compose(r)	lower case	minor (quality)
click	hit; success	manse	mansion
coin	money; finance	meg(aphoner)	direct(or)
contempo	contemporary	megger	director
d.a.	district attorney	meller	melodrama(tic)
dick	detective	milquetoast	meek man
doughboy	infantry soldier	nabes	suburbs
dualer	double-billed feature film	negative cost	production cost
femme	female; woman	nitery	nightclub
flap	flapper	oater	Western
flivver	car	ofay	white man
gat	gun	oke	okay
gob	sailor	one-shot	one-off
Gotham	New York	o.o.	once-over
gyp	swindler; cheat	opp	opposite
habiliments	clothing		

org	organization	stepping	dancing
ozoner	drive-in theatre	stew	drinking bout
p.a.	press agent	sudser	soap opera
pactee	contract player	super	super-production
Par	Paramount	switcheroo	(plot) twist
pen	penitentiary; prison	tab	tabloid
Pennsy	Pennsylvania	tapster	tap-dancer
photog	photographer	ten-twent-thirt/10-20-30	amateurish (acting)
pic	picture; movie	terp(ing)	danc(ing)
plat	platinum blonde	terpsichore	dancing
p.m.	professional model	thesp(ing)	actor, act(ing)
p.o.v.	point of view	thespically	performance-wise
p.r.	public relations	thespics	acting
prexy	(company) president	tint(ed)	colour(ed)
profesh	profession	tintuner	showbiz musical
programmer	B-movie fodder	topkick	boss
pug	boxer	topper	boss
quondam	one time	topline(r)	star
ridic	ridiculous	trick work	special effects
rod-man	gunman	trouping	acting
RR	railroad; railway	tube	TV
s.a.	sex appeal	20th	20th Century-Fox
sauce	alcohol	U	Universal
schtick	comic routine(s)	unreel	play
scripter	scriptwriter	unspool	play
sec	secretary	upper case	major (quality)
sheet	screen; newspaper	vaude	vaudeville
shutterbug	photographer	vet	veteran
slugfest	fight	vignetting	describing (romantic/sexual/ billing) partner
smokeater	fireman	vis-a-vis	
sock(eroo)	excellent; powerful	warbling	singing
solon	lawmaker	WB	Warner Bros.
speak	speakeasy	w.k.	well-known
spec	spectacle	yahoo	redneck
		yak	joke
		yclept	played by
		yock	joke

ACTION MOVIES
CONTENTS

INTRODUCTION

Variety is the world's premier entertainment newspaper. Founded in 1905, its film reviews run from 1907 and cover virtually the entire history of 20th-century cinema, with the freshness both of reviews written at the time of release and of *Variety*'s incisive house style.

Action Movies is a collection of over 300 reviews of some of the best action and adventure films of all time. Because of space, the selection has been limited to movies made in the English language. In editing the reviews down (often from many times their original length) much detail has unavoidably been lost. But we have tried to preserve the useful basics – a snappy intro, plot essentials, assessments of the main performances and technical merits, and any interesting background.

Reviewers' box-office predictions have been cut out, as well as plot revelations. Minor changes have been made so that the reviews 'read' from a modern viewpoint, and any now-meaningless contemporary references and prejudices (especially during the two world wars and the McCarthy period) have been toned down or deleted.

Any rewriting has been kept to the absolute minimum to preserve the flavour and opinions of the originals, although until the mid-1930s, when *Variety* reviews began to take on their current shape, editing has had to be considerably heavier.

American spellings and *Variety*'s 'language' have been retained (see Glossary); any annotations to the reviews have been put in square brackets. Although *Variety* recently began to include accents on foreign names, this book adheres to tradition by omitting them.

Assembling credits for each film has often involved extra research, and this in turn has been limited by the usual constraints of time and money. *Variety* only started regularly to publish cast lists and limited technical credits in the mid-1920s; fuller credits began from the late 1930s. Mistakes and misprints have been corrected where possible; real names put in square brackets after pseudonyms; and the latest version of people's names used throughout for consistency in the present format.

The following are the main criteria used:

★ **Film title** The original title in country of origin (or 'majority' country, in the case of co-productions). The form of the title is that used on the print itself, not that on secondary material like posters or press handouts. Subsidiary titles (a growing trend since the 1980s) are put on a separate line. Films are listed in strict A-Z order, letter by letter, ignoring all word-breaks and punctuation; those starting with numerals are positioned as if the figures were spelt out. All films included have received a theatrical showing at some time in their life.

★ **Year** The year of first public release in its country of origin (or, with co-productions, 'majority' country). Sneaks, out-of-town tryouts and festival screenings don't count; end-of-year Oscar-qualifying runs do. Establishing some films' opening dates is still problematical.

★ **Running time** The hardest nut to crack. Except when it's obvious the reviewer has been shown a rough-cut, *Variety*'s original running times are used. For silent films a very approximate conversion has been made, based on the number of reels or on information contained in the review. Films tend to get shorter over the years as they're trimmed, cut for TV and generally mangled; more recently there has been a trend towards issuing longer versions for TV or video. No running time should be taken as gospel.

★ **Colour** All films in colour, partly in colour, or tinted carry the symbol ◇. Some in the last two categories are now only shown in black-and-white but still carry the colour symbol as this denotes their original form,

★ **Silent** Where a film was made without sound it is indicated with the symbol ⊗.

★ **Video** A nightmare, Films which have been released on video (at one time or another) carry the following symbols: Ⓥ = available in both the US and the UK; ⬛Ⓥ = available in the US only; and Ⓥ = available in the UK only. But given the differences from country to country, and the rapid pace of deletions, don't necessarily expect to find a copy in your local store. Catalogue numbers are of little practical use, so have not been included.

★ **Director** The film's officially credited director or co-directors. Some productions are in fact the work of several hands (especially during Hollywood's studio era); only well-known uncredited contributions are noted in square brackets. Second unit or dance-number directors are occasionally included if their contribution merits it.

★ **Country of origin** The second hardest nut. The rule here has been where the money actually came from, rather than where a film was shot, what passport the director had, or what language the cast spoke in. With co-productions, the first country listed is the 'majority' one (which decides its official title – see above). In the case of many British and American movies, especially since the 1950s, deciding whether some are **UK/US, US/UK,** or even **UK** or **US** is virtually impossible.

★ **Cast lists** For space reasons, these have been limited to a maximum of six, not necessarily in their original order of billing. Early appearances by later stars are often included for interest's sake, even though they may only be bit-parts. For consistency, actors who later changed names are listed by their latest moniker.

★ **Academy awards/nominations** The date is that of the Oscar award not of the ceremony (generally held the following spring).

---

*Robin Hood (Errol Flynn) attempts to fight his way out of Nottingham Castle in **The Adventures of Robin Hood**.*

ADVENTURES OF DON JUAN

1948, 110 mins, ◇ ⊘ *Dir* Vincent Sherman   US

★ *Stars* Errol Flynn, Viveca Lindfors, Robert Douglas, Raymond Burr

The loves and escapades of the fabulous Don Juan are particularly adapted to the screen abilities of Errol Flynn and he gives them a flair that pays off strongly.

Plot depicts Don Juan adventuring in England. Opening has him escaping an angry husband, only to become immediately involved again with another femme. This time his wooing ruins a state-arranged wedding and he's shipped off to Spain to face his angry monarch. The queen assigns him to post of instructor in the royal fencing academy, he discovers a plot against her majesty, instigated by a conniving prime minister. Viveca Lindfors co-stars as the queen and she brings a compelling beauty to the role.

Top action is reached in the deadly duel between Flynn and Robert Douglas, the crooked prime minister, climaxing with a long leap down a huge flight of castle stairs.

THE ADVENTURES OF MARCO POLO

1938, 100 mins, *Dir* Archie Mayo   US

★ *Stars* Gary Cooper, Sigrid Gurie, Basil Rathbone, George Barbier, Binnie Barnes, Ernest Truex

A glamorous figure in history, which places him in the 13th century as the first European to visit the Orient, Marco Polo has been portrayed in as many different guises as imagination permits; as traveler, adventurer, merchant, diplomat. He probably was all of these and a first-class liar besides. Robert E. Sherwood, who penned the screenscript [from a story by N.A. Pogson], conceives him also as an ardent lover and politician. Gary Cooper fits the character to the apex of his six feet two.

The plot is strictly meller, starting with Ahmed (Basil Rathbone) as a conniving prime minister to the Chinese ruler, Kublai Kahn (George Barbier). Schemer has his eye on the throne and a desire for the dynastic princess for his queen. Into such a vortex of beauty and villainy come Marco Polo and his business agent.

Marco Polo is admitted to the court and there glimpses the beautiful princess, who is much taken with his six feet two and easy manner of love-making behind the Chinese fountain.

It is all played on the dead level by a fine cast. Rathbone is an excellent plotter, and Sigrid Gurie, a Norwegian actress who makes her American film debut in the picture, possesses beauty of a kind liable to start civil war in any country.

THE ADVENTURES OF ROBIN HOOD

1938, 104 mins, ◇ ⊘ *Dir* Michael Curtiz, William Keighley   US

★ *Stars* Errol Flynn, Olivia de Havilland, Basil Rathbone, Claude Rains, Patric Knowles, Eugene Pallette

Academy Award 1938: Best Picture (Nomination)

Warners revives the legend with Errol Flynn in the role in which Douglas Fairbanks Sr scored his first big success in 1922. It is cinematic pageantry at its best, a highly imaginative telling of folklore in all the hues of Technicolor.

Film is done in the grand manner of silent-day spectacles with sweep and breadth of action, swordplay and hand-to-hand battles between Norman and Saxon barons. Superlative on the production side.

Played with intensity by an excellent company of actors, an illusion of fairy-story quality is retained throughout. Michael Curtiz and William Keighley are credited as co-directors, the former having picked up the story soon after its filming started when Keighley was incapacitated by illness. There is skillful blending of their joint work.

Flynn makes the heroic Robin a somewhat less agile savior of the poor than Fairbanks portrayed him, but the Warner version emphasizes the romance. Teamed with Olivia de Havilland as Marian, Flynn is an ardent suitor and a gallant courtier. There are some convincing histrionics by Basil Rathbone, Claude Rains, Patric Knowles, Eugene Pallette, Alan Hale and Melville Cooper. Lighter moments are furnished by Una O'Connor and Herbert Mundin.

THE ADVENTURES OF TOM SAWYER

1938, 93 mins, ◇ ⊘ *Dir* Norman Taurog   US

★ *Stars* Tommy Kelly, Jackie Moran, Ann Gillis, May Robson, Walter Brennan, Victor Jory

Adventures of Tom Sawyer is in Technicolor and contains visual beauty and appeal in addition to a faithful and nearly literal adaptation of the Mark Twain story.

The story of the boy in an isolated Missouri community of the 1880s, who made fence-painting an enviable art, who attended his own funeral services, who was the cynosure of all eyes in the witness chair at an exciting murder trial, who teased and plagued his elders and melted in tears at the slightest kindness, is imperishable.

Casting of the picture was reported a laborious job, in the course of which hundreds of boys were tested before Tommy Kelly, from the Bronx, NY, was selected for the role of Tom. His early scenes show self-consciousness but in the final sequences when he is being pursued by Injun Joe, Kelly performs like a veteran.

Walter Brennan is a standout among the adult players.

ROMULUS presents **HUMPHREY BOGART KATHARINE HEPBURN** "**THE AFRICAN QUEEN**" Colour by TECHNICOLOR with **ROBERT MORLEY** in JOHN HUSTON'S from the novel by C. S. FORESTER

A ROMULUS - HORIZON PRODUCTION · INDEPENDENT FILM DISTRIBUTORS Certificate "U"

He is the village drunkard, Muff Potter, accused of the graveyard murder.

May Robson loses no opportunities as Aunt Polly, whose life by turn is celestial and hellish depending upon the vagaries of Tom's vivid imagination.

Injun Joe is played by Victor Jory with all the fiendish villainy in the part.

THE AFRICAN QUEEN

1951, 104 mins, ◇ Ⓥ *Dir* John Huston   UK

★ *Stars* Humphrey Bogart, Katharine Hepburn, Robert Morley, Peter Bull, Theodore Bikel, Walter Gotell

This story of adventure and romance, experienced by an unlikely couple in Africa just as World War I got underway, is an engrossing motion picture. Just offbeat enough in story, with the locale and star teaming of Humphrey Bogart and Katharine Hepburn to stimulate the imagination, it is a picture with an unassuming warmth and naturalness.

The independent production unit took stars and cameras to East Africa to film C.S. Forester's well-known novel,

Adventure and romance on a river boat in **The African Queen,** *with Humphrey Bogart and Katharine Hepburn.*

African Queen, against its actual background.

Performance-wise, Bogart has never been seen to better advantage than in this movie. Nor has he ever had a more knowing and talented film partner than co-star Hepburn.

The plot concerns a man and woman, completely incongruous as to coupling, who are thrown together when the war news comes to German East Africa in 1914. The man, a sloven gin-swilling, ne'er-do-well pilot of a steam-driven river launch, teams with the angular, old-maid sister of a dead English missionary to contribute a little to the cause of the Empire.

The impossible deed they plan is to take Bogart's small and decrepit 30-foot launch known as *African Queen* down uncharted rivers to a large Central Africa lake and then use the small boat as a torpedo to sink a German gunboat that is patrolling the waters, and preventing invasion by British forces.

John Huston's scripting and direction, and the playing, leaven the story telling with a lot of good humor. Unfoldment has a leisureness that goes with the characters and situations.

AFRICA — TEXAS STYLE

1967, 110 mins, ◇ ⓥ   *Dir* Andrew Marton   US

★ *Stars* Hugh O'Brian, John Mills, Nigel Green, Tom Nardini, Adrienne Corri

Africa – Texas Style is a slick and exceptionally well-turned-out piece of adventure picture-making, its title the only weight of heaviness about it.

Shot entirely in Kenya, director Andrew Marton, scripter Andy White and cameraman Paul Beeson have thoroughly caught feeling of Africa. They make effective use of the terrain as an atmospheric setting and thousands of animals of all descriptions to lend authenticity.

Story twirls about the subject of game ranching, the domestication and breeding of wild animal life as a potentially huge source of meat and as a means of preserving many of Africa's rapidly vanishing species of wild beasts.

Premise is given punch via its human story of rancher John Mills importing Texas cowboys Hugh O'Brian and his Navajo pal Tom Nardini to rope and corral as many animals as they can ride down.

AIR AMERICA

1990, 112 mins, ◇ ⓥ   *Dir* Roger Spottiswoode   US

★ *Stars* Mel Gibson, Robert Downey Jr, Nancy Travis, Ken Jenkins, David Marshall Grant, Lane Smith

Spectacular action sequences and engaging perfs by Mel Gibson and Robert Downey Jr make this big-budgeter entertaining and provocative.

It's probably news to most even at this late date that the CIA, through its proprietary Air America, was using drug money to finance the war in Southeast Asia and condoning the refining and exportation of heroin both to GIs in that part of the world and to the American public. Air America became known as 'a dope airline', as Christopher Robbins'

Mel Gibson finds himself surrounded in Air America, pic about the CIA-run airline during the Vietnam War.

Give this plane full throttle — if you don't then I will

Burt Lancaster and George Kennedy check the status of a snowbound plane blocking the runway in Airport.

1979 source book puts it, and the filmmakers don't shrink from showing Gibson knowingly flying opium and cynically justifying it as essential to the US war effort.

Starting off as a reckless radio station helicopter pilot in a wild stunt sequence on an LA freeway in 1969, Downey is recruited by the CIA to perform his hair-raising flying feats for Uncle Sam in Laos, where oxymoronic military intelligence officer Marshall Grant insists, 'We're not actually here.'

With his reported $35 million budget and a vast army of tech assistants to help carry out the stunt flying and crashes on the atmospheric Thailand locations, director Roger Spottiswoode does an efficient job in marshaling his forces and walking the thin line required to keep a black comedy from becoming gruesome or flippant.

AIRPORT

1970, 137 mins ◇ ⓥ   *Dir* George Seaton   US

★ *Stars* Burt Lancaster, Dean Martin, Jean Seberg, Jacqueline Bisset, George Kennedy, Helen Hayes

Academy Award 1970: Best Picture (Nomination)

Based on the novel by Arthur Hailey overproduced by Ross Hunter with a cast of stars as long as a jet runway, and adapted and directed by George Seaton in a glossy, slick style, *Airport* is a handsome, often dramatically involving $10 million epitaph to a bygone brand of filmmaking.

However, the ultimate dramatic situation of a passenger-loaded jet liner with a psychopathic bomber aboard that has to be brought into a blizzard-swept airport with runways blocked by a snow-stalled plane actually does not create suspense because the audience knows how it's going to end.

As the cigar chomping, bull boss of the maintenance men, George Kennedy gives a strong portrayal. But here again there's not a moment of plot doubt that he is going to get that stuck plane cleared off the runway in time for the emergency landing.

A

Richard Chamberlain as Quartermain in the Indiana Jones-style **Allan Quartermain and the Lost City of Gold.**

ALLAN QUATERMAIN AND THE LOST CITY OF GOLD

1987, 99 mins, ◇ Ⓥ *Dir* Gary Nelsen   US

★ *Stars* Richard Chamberlain, Sharon Stone, James Earl Jones, Henry Silva, Robert Donner

Pic is a remake of Harry Alan Towers' 1977 film *King Solomon's Treasure*, which starred John Colicos as H. Rider Haggard's adventure hero Allan Quatermain (from the book by that name).

Embarrassing screenplay jettisons Haggard's enduring fantasy and myth-making in favor of a back-of-the-envelope plotline and anachronistic jokes about Cleveland. Quatermain (Richard Chamberlain) receives a gold piece from a dying man that inspires him to trek to East Africa in search of his brother Robeson (Martin Rabbett). Joining him are his archeologist girlfriend (Sharon Stone) and African warrior (James Earl Jones), a comic relief mystic (Robert Donner camping it up) and five native African expendable bearers.

After considerable filler, they find the lost race of Phoenicians, ruled by bland beauty contest queen Nyleptha (Aileen Marson).

A poor followup to the same producers' 1985 *King Solomon's Mines*, film relies frequently on a very phony gimmick of a spear-proof tunic and story completely runs out of gas once the heroes arrive at their destination.

ALL THE BROTHERS WERE VALIANT

1953, 94 mins, ◇ *Dir* Richard Thorpe   US

★ *Stars* Robert Taylor, Stewart Granger, Ann Blyth, Betta St John, Keenan Wynn, James Whitmore

Special effects are used to advantage to spotlight the high romance of adventuring on the bounding main. Film's big moments include the excitement stirred up by the dangers of 19th century whaling and the climactic mass battle with mutineers aboard a sailing vessel.

Directorial vigor of Richard Thorpe helps picture through its faltering spots. The latter come from shallow character development in the script [from a novel by Ben Ames Williams] and a rambling story line. Stars Robert Taylor, Stewart Granger and Ann Blyth are competent but the people they portray haven't enough depth or reality to come robustly alive.

Taylor and Granger are brothers in a seafaring family. When Granger, the elder, disappears on a whaling voyage, Taylor takes over his ship and, with his bride (Blyth) sails off

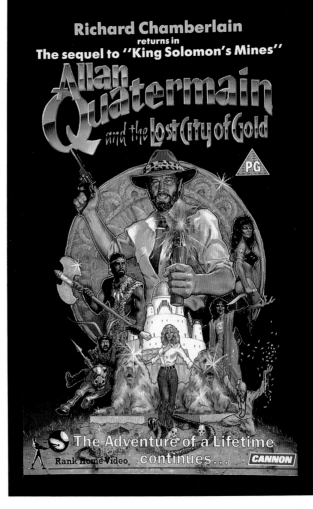

to find him. At a South Seas stopover he finds Granger who goes for his brother's bride and incites a mutiny aboard ship, which he wants to use to recover a fortune in pearls he had found during his disappearance.

ASHANTI

1979, 117 mins, ◇ Ⓥ *Dir* Richard Fleischer   SWITZERLAND

★ *Stars* Michael Caine, Peter Ustinov, Beverly Johnson, Omar Sharif, Rex Harrison, Willliam Holden

A polished but lackluster adventure entertainment. Michael Caine and Beverly Johnson are World Health Organization medics on a visit to an African tribe when the lady becomes a prize catch of Arabian slave trader Peter Ustinov. Caine's retrieval odyssey thereafter is variously aided by Rex Harrison as an ambiguous go-between, William Holden as a mercenary pilot, and Kabir Bedi as a Bedouin with his own score to settle with Ustinov. All acquit themselves with professional grace but unremarkable impact.

No help to the film's grip on interest is director Richard Fleischer's minuet pacing. He seems to have come under the spell of those Saharan sand dunes lavishly dwelled upon, as Caine and Bedi pick up Ustinov's trail.

Michael Caine (right), with the help of William Holden, fights of the attentions of Arab slave traders in **Ashanti.**

ASSAULT ON A QUEEN

1966, 106 mins, ◇ *Dir* Jack Donohue   US

★ **Stars** Frank Sinatra, Virna Lisi, Anthony Franciosa, Richard Conte, Alf Kjellin, Errol John

Producer William Goetz has supervised a remarkable job of making plausible the admittedly wild-eyed adventures of an odd assortment of moral derelicts who salvage a submarine with the intent of robbing the *Queen Mary* (hence the title) [based on the novel by Jack Finney].

Virna Lisi, Anthony Franciosa and Alf Kjellin, on the hunt for a sunken treasure ship off the Bahamas, hire Frank Sinatra and his partner, Errol John, who run a fishing boat business, to help them find the treasure. Sinatra, instead, finds a small sunken German submarine. Kjellin, a former German U-boat commander, talks the group into salvaging it and holding up the *Queen Mary.*

Only Kjellin is able to create a well-rounded character and is outstanding as the apparently bland German, holding in control his diabolic intent. Sinatra and Lisi are very good in roles that make few demands on their acting ability. John, while efficient in the tenser moments, seems inhibited in scenes where he must wax sentimental over his rehabilitation by Sinatra.

ATLANTIS, THE LOST CONTINENT

1961, 91 mins, ◇ *Dir* George Pal   US

★ **Stars** Anthony Hall, Joyce Taylor, Frank De Kova, John Dall

After establishing legendary significance via an arresting prolog in which the basis for age-old suspicion of the existence of a lost continental cultural link in the middle of the Atlantic is discussed, scenarist Daniel Mainwaring promptly proceeds to ignore the more compelling possibilities of the hypothesis in favor of erecting a tired, shopworn melodrama out of Gerald Hargreaves' play.

There is an astonishing similarity to the stevereevesian spectacles. An 'ordeal by fire and water' ritual conducted in a great, crowded stadium seems almost a replica of gladiatorial combat in the Colosseum. When Atlantis is burning to a cinder at the climax, one can almost hear Nero fiddling. Even Russ Garcia's score has that pompous, martial Roman air about it. And at least several of the mob spectacle scenes have been lifted from Roman screen spectacles of the past (the 1951 version of *Quo Vadis* looks like the source). The acting is routine.

AVALANCHE

1978, 91 mins, ◇ ⓥ *Dir* Corey Allen   US

★ **Stars** Rock Hudson, Mia Farrow, Robert Forster, Jeanette Nolan, Rick Moses, Steve Franken

Rock Hudson and Mia Farrow head the cast of characters gathered at a ski lodge beneath an uneasy cornice of snow. They warned Hudson not to build the lodge on this particular spot, but he went ahead with the same stubbornness that cost him the wife he still loves.

Farrow, that's the ex-wife, is on hand for the grand opening and quickly beds down with Robert Forster, the naturalist photographer who keeps complaining about the trees Hudson is cutting down. Hudson, in turn, is having a steamroom fling with his secretary.

Eventually, the whole mountain top comes down on the crowd of skaters, skiers and sledders. Using a lot of archive footage of an actual massive avalanche, director Corey Allen and crew have done a very good job of creating realistic scenes. Unfortunately, much of the archive footage is badly scratched so some of the big boulders look like they're sliding down on wires.

Overall, the performances are fine.

BACKDRAFT

1991, 135 mins, ◇ ⓥ *Dir* Ron Howard   US

★ **Stars** Kurt Russell, William Baldwin, Robert De Niro, Donald Sutherland, Jennifer Jason Leigh, Scott Glenn

Director Ron Howard torches off more thrilling scenes in *Backdraft* than any Saturday matinee serial ever dared. Visually, pic often is exhilarating, but it's shapeless and dragged down by corny, melodramatic characters and situations.

Ex-fireman Gregory Widen's script about Chicago

smokeaters begins with a scene of the two central characters as boys in 1971. This provides shorthand for later formulaic conflicts between fire-fighting brothers Kurt Russell and William Baldwin.

Baldwin is ambivalent about fire-fighting as a result of a childhood experience. His older brother, the charismatic Russell, is a hardboiled sort, even more recklessly heroic than the father.

Widen uncertainly blends these tiresome family quarrels with a suspense plot involving fire department investigator Robert De Niro's search for a mysterious arsonist. His intense obsessive characterization is a major plus for the film but isn't given enough screen time.

Though De Niro is portrayed as the Sherlock Holmes of arson investigators, script has him and Baldwin led to the truth by the airheaded assistant (Jennifer Jason Leigh) of a corrupt local alderman (J.T. Walsh) and by an institutionalized pyromaniac played by Donald Sutherland with his customary glee.

The spectacular fire scenes are done with terrifying believability (usually with the actors in the same shot as the fire effects) and a kind of sci-fi grandeur.

THE BANDIT OF SHERWOOD FOREST

1946, 85 mins, ◇ *Dir* George Sherman, Henry Levin   US

★ *Stars* Cornel Wilde, Anita Louise, Henry Daniell, George Macready, Jill Esmond

Technicolor spectacle of high adventure in Sherwood Forest. It's a costume western, in effect, offering the fictional escapades of the son of Robin Hood, a hard-riding, hard-loving hombre who uses his trusty bow and arrow to right injustice and tyranny back in the days of feudal England.

There is considerable ineptness in writing, production and direction but it still stands up as okay escapist film fare for the not-too-critical.

There is a concentration of chases and 'they-went-thata-way' flavor about the doings that hints at the western feature training of producers and directors.

Plot has the son of Robin Hood coming back to Sherwood Forest to save England's Magna Carta and young king from the cruel plotting of a wicked regent. With his long bow, sword and trusty horse, Wilde proves himself more than a match for the villain, saves the young king's life, the Magna Carta and wins true love and knighthood. Concocting the script, full of dialog cliches and ten-twent-thirt dramatics, were Wilfrid H. Pettitt and Melvin Levy, working from a story by Paul A. Castleton and Pettitt, based on the novel *Son of Robin Hood* by Castleton.

Wilde is properly swashbuckling as the hero, and probably had himself a time enacting the dare-and-do.

BEAU GESTE

1926, 129 mins, ⊗ *Dir* Herbert Brenon   US

★ *Stars* Ronald Colman, Neil Hamilton, Ralph Forbes, Alice Joyce, Mary Brian, Noah Beery

Beau Geste is a 'man's' picture. The story revolves around three brothers and their love for each other. And a great looking trio – Ronald Colman, Neil Hamilton and Ralph Forbes. Beyond that the love interest is strictly secondary, practically nil.

The picture is all story. In fact, only one cast member seems to get above the scenario. This is Noah Beery as the

Beau Geste, Foreign Legion classic with Robert Preston, Ray Milland and Gary Cooper as the brothers Geste.

bestial sergeant-major. A part that only comes along every so often, and Beery gives it the same prominence in which P.C. Wren, the author, conceived it. It's undoubtedly one of his best portrayals.

When all is said and done, Colman, in the title role, hasn't so very much to do. Hamilton equals him for footage and Forbes exceeds him. Forbes, in his first picture, impresses all the way. Hamilton also gives a sincere performance. But there can be no question that Beery is the outstanding figure of the picture.

BEAU GESTE

1939, 114 mins, ⊗ *Dir* William A. Wellman   US

★ **Stars** Gary Cooper, Ray Milland, Robert Preston, Brian Donlevy, Susan Hayward, Broderick Crawford

Beau Geste has been produced with vigorous realism and spectacular sweep. Director William Wellman has focused attention on the melodramatic and vividly gruesome aspects of the story, and skimmed lightly over the episodes and motivation which highlighted Percival Christopher Wren's original novel.

Beau employs the flashback method in unfolding the adventures of three Geste brothers in the Foreign Legion. Audience interest is gained at the start with presentation of the mystery of the desert fort with relief patrol finding the entire garrison dead and dead soldiers propped up for battle in the parapets. Confused by the weirdness of the situation, the head of the patrol pitches camp in the nearby oasis. Suddenly the fort is enveloped in flames and destroyed.

Gary Cooper is okay in the title spot. Ray Milland and Robert Preston work hard and competently to get over their respective characterizations. Trio are overshadowed, however, by the vivid Brian Donlevy as the savagely brutal sergeant of the Legion.

BEAU GESTE

1966, 105 mins, ◇ ⊗ *Dir* Douglas Heyes   US

★ **Stars** Guy Stockwell, Doug McClure, Leslie Nielsen, Telly Savalas, David Mauro, Robert Wolders

Third time out for one of the most memorable silent films still packs hardy entertainment. The production is an expertly-made translation of Percival Christopher Wren's novel of the French Foreign Legion in a lonely Sahara outpost, and is distinguished by good acting, fine photographic values and fast direction. Guy Stockwell delineates the title role.

Plot has been slightly changed. Beau and his brother, John, are now Americans instead of English, and the third brother, Digby, has been eliminated. While still a story of brother love under fire, this facet has been somewhat subordinated for a script focusing on the savagery of the sergeant, a dominant point previously but accentuated even more in

this version. Basic storyline has been little altered, Beau having joined the Legion after shouldering the blame for a crime he did not commit to save another from disgrace. Topnotch performances are contributed right down the line. Stockwell handles himself creditably and convincingly.

THE BEDFORD INCIDENT

1965, 102 mins, ⊘ *Dir* James B. Harris   US

★ **Stars** Richard Widmark, Sidney Poitier, James MacArthur, Martin Balsam, Wally Cox, Eric Portman

The Bedford Incident is an excellent contemporary sea drama based on a little-known but day-to-day reality of the Cold War, the monitoring of Russian submarine activity by US Navy destroyers. The production, made at England's Shepperton Studios, has salty scripting and solid performances, including one of the finest in Richard Widmark's career.

James Poe's adaptation of the Mark Rascovich novel depicts the 'hunt-to-exhaustion' tactic in anti-submarine warfare, whereby a sub contact is pursued until one side or the other either gives up or eludes.

Widmark stars as the skipper of the USS *Bedford*, a modern destroyer, equipped with tactical nuclear weapons, on patrol in the North Atlantic. Widmark's skipper is that rare breed whom the crew not only follows, but worships. The character of this sea dog is drawn out by the helicopter arrival of Sidney Poitier, as a wise-guy magazine writer, and Martin Balsam, a Reserve medic back on active duty.

Poitier does an excellent job in both the light and serious aspects of his role, and manages to leave a personal stamp on his scenes.

BEHOLD A PALE HORSE

1964, 119 mins, ⊗ *Dir* Fred Zinnemann   US

★ **Stars** Gregory Peck, Anthony Quinn, Omar Sharif, Raymond Pellegrin, Paola Stoppa, Mildred Dunnock

Pale Horse [from the novel *Killing a Mouse on Sunday* by Emeric Pressburger] is rooted in the Spanish Civil War, using introductory newsreel footage and the fighting to set the background for a story that happens 20 years later and essentially concerns a Spanish guerrilla (Gregory Peck) who continues to live the war alone. He is thrown again into the fray in a personal attack against a vain and arrogant police captain (Anthony Quinn) who has vowed his death.

The one-man fight against a corrupt and powerful adversary is an obvious losing battle, but the guerrilla's last stand, he knows, can be his most effective.

Peck is a worn-out, untidy broken man who once again surges with force and energy in a characterization that ranks among the better in his long career. There also is an excellent performance from Quinn, who is coarse, crude and worldly as the arrogant police chief but shows his own insecurity beneath a physically courageous false front. Omar Sharif shows a warm, sensitive side in this film, playing the role of a young priest torn between obligations of personal morality and the official laws of government.

BENEATH THE 12-MILE REEF

1953, 102 mins, ◇ ⑨ *Dir* Robert D. Webb   US

★ *Stars* Robert Wagner, Terry Moore, Gilbert Roland, J. Carrol Naish, Richard Boone, Peter Graves

Set among the sponge-diving Greek colony at Tarpon Springs, Fla, the squeeze-lensing gives punch in the display of underwater wonders, the seascapes and the brilliant, beautiful sunrises and sunsets of the Florida Gulf coast.

In handling the young cast, Robert D. Webb's direction is less effective, particularly in the case of Robert Wagner and Terry Moore. Both are likable, so the shallowness of their performances is no serious handicap to the entertainment. Thesping quality is maintained by the more experienced casters. Scoring resoundingly is Gilbert Roland, colorful Greek diver and father of Wagner. Angela Clarke also clicks as the wife and mother.

The plot takes on two lines of conflict – the age-old battle between man and the sea, the more personal rivalry between the diving Greeks of Tarpon Springs and the hook-spongers of the shallow Key West waters.

Romance gets in its licks when the daring Gilbert ventures into Key West waters controlled by Boone and the young Wagner meets conch-girl Moore. It's an instant attraction between the pair and their romance builds to a runaway marriage after Gilbert is killed diving at the dangerous 12-mile reef. Wagner then becomes the man of the family, proving his right to the title by diving where his father met death, fighting off an octopus and beating Graves in an underwater battle.

BEN-HUR

1959, 212 mins, ◇ ⑨ *Dir* William Wyler   US

★ *Stars* Charlton Heston, Jack Hawkins, Stephen Boyd, Haya Harareet, Hugh Griffith, Sam Jaffe

Academy Award 1959: Best Picture

The $15 million *Ben-Hur* is a majestic achievement, representing a superb blending of the motion picture arts by master craftsmen.

The big difference between *Ben-Hur* and other spectacles, biblical or otherwise, is its sincere concern for human beings. They're not just pawns reciting flowery dialog to fill gaps between the action. This has been accomplished without sacrificing the impact of the spectacle elements.

The famous chariot race between Ben-Hur, the Prince of Judea, and Messala, the Roman tribune – directed by Andrew Marton and Yakima Canutt – represents some 40

J. Carroll Naish (left), Robert Wagner and Gilbert Roland as Greek sponge divers in **Beneath the 12-Mile Reef.**

minutes of the most hair-raising excitement ever witnessed.

Wisely, however, the film does not depend wholly on sheer spectacle. The family relationship between Ben-Hur and his mother Miriam and his sister Tirzah; his touching romance with Esther, the former slave; his admiration of the Roman consul, Quintus Arrius, whom he rescues after a sea battle; his association with the Arab horseowner, Sheik Ilderim; and his struggle with Messala, the boyhood friend who becomes his mortal enemy, make moving scenes. And overshadowing these personal conflicts is the deeply religious theme involving the birth and crucifixion of Christ.

Karl Tunberg receives sole screen credit, although such heavyweight writers as Maxwell Anderson, S.N. Behrman, Gore Vidal and Christopher Fry also worked on the film. Fry, a respected British poet-playwright, was present on the set throughout the production in Rome.

Charlton Heston is excellent as the brawny yet kindly Ben-Hur who survives the life of a galley slave to seek revenge of his enemy Messala. Haya Harareet, an Israeli actress making her first appearance in an American film is sensitive and revealing as Esther. Jack Hawkins, as Quintus Arrius, the Roman consul who adopts Ben-Hur, adds another fine depiction to his career. Stephen Boyd, as Ben-Hur's enemy Messala, is not the standard villain, but succeeds in giving understanding to this position in his dedication to the Roman Empire.

The film took 10 months to complete at Rome's Cinecitta Studios. The 300 sets are one of the highlights of the film, particularly the massive arena for the chariot sequence. The musical score by Miklos Rozsa also contributes to the overall excellence of the giant project.

Ben-Hur is a fitting climax to Zimbalist's career as a producer. He died of a heart attack in Rome when the film was near completion.

BEYOND THE POSEIDON ADVENTURE

B

1979, 122 mins, ◇ Ⓥ *Dir* Irwin Allen   US

★ *Stars* Michael Caine, Sally Field, Telly Savalas, Peter Boyle, Jack Warden, Karl Malden

Beyond the Poseidon Adventure comes off as a virtual remake of the 1972 original, without that film's mounting suspense and excitement. Recap of original premise, a luxury liner turned upside down by gigantic tidal wave, is accomplished in a few seconds.

New plot turns pits salvage tug operators Michael Caine, Karl Malden and Sally Field against evildoer Telly Savalas for looting rights to the big boat. Caine and company are after hard cash, while Savalas, posing as a medico, is searching out a cargo of valuable plutonium.

The only change in this group's struggle to reach the top (really, the bottom) of the boat is a set of different faces.

Because the outcome is so predictable, the defects in the script take on greater magnitude.

BIG TROUBLE IN LITTLE CHINA

1986, 99 mins, ◇ Ⓥ *Dir* John Carpenter   US

★ *Stars* Kurt Russell, Kim Cattrall, Dennis Dun, James Hong, Victor Wong, Kate Burton

Story is promising, involving an ancient Chinese magician Lo Pan (James Hong) who controls an evil empire beneath San Francisco's Chinatown while he searches for a green-eyed Chinese beauty to mate with and make him mortal.

Director John Carpenter seems to be trying to make an action-adventure along the lines of *Indiana Jones and the Temple of Doom.* The effect goes horribly awry.

Leading the cast is Kurt Russell who looks embarrassed, and indeed should be, playing his CB philosophizing truck driver character as a cross between a swaggering John Wayne, an adventurous Harrison Ford and a wacky Bill Murray.

He's caught in Hong's supposedly ghostly underworld with restaurateur friend Wang Chi (Dennis Dun) while trying to rescue Wang's green-eyed Chinese fiancee, Miao Yin (Suzee Pai), from Hong's lascivious clutches.

THE BLACK ARROW

1948, 76 mins, Ⓥ *Dir* Gordon M. Douglas   US

★ *Stars* Louis Hayward, Janet Blair, George Macready, Edgar Buchanan

Using Robert Louis Stevenson's *The Black Arrow* for the takeoff, Columbia has made an action-filled cloak-and-dagger romance. The picture is virtually a western of lethal combat, hard riding, intrigue and deep-dyed villainy – all in when-knighthood-was-in-flower terms. Maybe it isn't exactly art, but it is good entertainment.

The romantic angle has been accented heavily in the translation from Stevenson's dispassionate narrative. The red-blooded hero returns from the 30 Years War to learn that his uncle has murdered his father to seize the House of York and has had the neighboring Lord of the House of Lancaster

Kurt Russell and Kim Cattrall find **Big Trouble in Little China** *in this actioner set in San Francisco's Chinatown.*

executed for the crime. And he understandably tumbles hard for the nifty Lancaster daughter.

BLACKBEARD THE PIRATE

1952, 98 mins, ◇ ⓥ *Dir* Raoul Walsh   US

★ *Stars* Robert Newton, Linda Darnell, William Bendix, Keith Andes, Torin Thatcher

Blackbeard the Pirate is a rollicking swashbuckler stacked with high adventure, extensive swordplay and all the things big pirate pictures are made of. Alan Le May's scripting of the DeVallon Scott story gives a neat blending to the tongue-in-cheek and on-the-level ingredients.

It's the 17th century on the Spanish Main again. Torin Thatcher, a 'reformed' pirate, has been commissioned by the King of England to rid the seas of Robert ('Blackbeard') Newton. Keith Andes, a young sailor of fortune out to collect some reward money, allows himself to be shanghaied. Also going aboard, is Thatcher's adopted daughter, (Linda Darnell). Once on board, the pair discover the captain has been murdered and 'Blackbeard' has taken over. Newton turns in a memorable performance.

THE BLACK ROSE

1950, 120 mins, ◇ ⓥ *Dir* Henry Hathaway   US

★ *Stars* Tyrone Power, Orson Welles, Cecile Aubry, Jack Hawkins, Michael Rennie, Herbert Lom

Produced in England and North Africa with frozen currency, and with a supporting British cast, *Rose* is an adaptation of the Thomas Costain bestseller. It is 13th-century drama that seems hardly to have ignored a thing in its plotting.

Black Rose is the story of Saxon revolt against Norman domination, 200 years after the conquest. The central figure in the Saxon fight is Walter of Gurnie (Tyrone Power), the illegitimate son of a Saxon peer.

In a picture of warring, there is only the suggestion of battle. Perhaps one good scene, with some honest-to-goodness cinematic blood-letting, might have done something to increase the tempo of the picture.

Power is credible in the lead role, while Welles underplays effectively the part of Bayan.

THE BLACK WATCH

1929, 91 mins, *Dir* John Ford   US

★ *Stars* Victor McLaglen, Myrna Loy, David Rollins, Roy D'Arcy, Walter Long, Mitchell Lewis

Story is loose-jointed and far from well-knit, the audience being asked to take plenty for granted. Talbot Mundy's tale is that of the Scottish Captain King (Victor McLaglen), who is ordered to India to prevent a native uprising on the eve his regiment is leaving for France. He gets into a drunken brawl, during which he supposedly kills a fellow service man, the ruse being an escape among the pack of fanatics planning to overthrow British rule.

The natives worship a woman (Myrna Loy) as their goddess, who, in turn, succumbs to the brawn of King. Just how King manages to get about a dozen British soldiers among the hordes, who, at a signal, throw off their robes to reveal khaki, is not explained.

Director John Ford's best work is the opening of a Scottish officers' dinner on the eve of war, with bagpipes wailing. Joseph August's camerawork is superb. McLaglen's performance is just normal. Loy sheds an attractive appearance under, at times, outstanding lighting, aided by long robes.

BLIND FURY

1989, 85 mins, ◇ ⓥ *Dir* Phillip Noyce   US

★ *Stars* Rutger Hauer, Brandon Call, Terrance O'Quinn, Lisa Blount, Meg Foster, Sho Kosugi

Blind Fury is an action film with an amusing gimmick, toplining Rutger Hauer as the pic's hero, an apparently invincible blind Vietnam vet who wields a samurai sword with consummate skill.

Nick Parker (Hauer) is actually based on Zatoichi, the heroic blind samurai who starred in a couple of dozen popular actions films for Japanese company Daiei in the 1960s and early 1970s.

First problem for writer Charles Robert Carner [adapting a screen play by Ryozo Kasahara] is to find a way to Americanize such a character. This is solved by having Parker blinded and lost in action in Vietnam and then trained by friendly Vietnamese to use his other senses to survive.

Twenty years later, Parker is back in Miami to look up an old army buddy, Frank Deveraux (Terrance O'Quinn) who's in trouble with the mob in Reno. Parker's in time to prevent the kidnapping of Billy (Brandon Call), Frank's son, but not to stop the murder of Frank's ex-wife, Lynn (Meg Foster, in for only one scene) by the vicious Slag, played by Randall 'Tex' Cobb.

The remainder of the film is simply a series of fights and chases as Parker heads for Reno to reunite Billy with his father.

BLOOD AND SAND

1941, 123 mins, ◇ ⓥ *Dir* Rouben Mamoulian   US

★ *Stars* Tyrone Power, Linda Darnell, Rita Hayworth, Nazimova, Anthony Quinn, John Carradine

Blood and Sand [from the novel by Blasco Vicente Ibanez] is associated in the memories of theatre-goers as a hot and

Tyrone Power as a dashing matador finding himself torn between two women in **Blood and Sand.**

BORDERLINE

1980, 97 mins, ◇ Ⓥ   *Dir* Gerrold Freedman   US

★ *Stars* Charles Bronson, Bruno Kirby, Ed Harris, Karmin Murcelo, Michael Lerner

Directed by Gerrold Freedman, this Charles Bronson vehicle tackles a serious subject – the profiteering in illicit Mexican immigration – with workmanlike dramatic skill and a notable preference for realism over hokum.

The film's big name is self-effacing almost to the point of elusiveness. As a long-serving compassionate border patrolman, Bronson is hunched and hated virtually throughout; his face is mostly masked by heavy shadow.

The professionally-honed, conventional plot pits him against a younger, ruthless racketeer who runs wetbacks across the border at an exploitative price on behalf of a US business corporation.

Newcomer Ed Harris is memorable as the frontline

Chuck Bronson as a US border guard trying to stem the flow of Mexicans across the border in **Borderline.**

decidedly sexy piece of merchandise, chiefly because of Valentino's silent version two decades ago. The revival follows the original as a straight drama of the bullfight ring.

Especially effective are the bullfight arena sequences, which disclose exceptional camera angles and intercutting of shots of crowds at arena in Mexico City with studio shots.

Tyrone Power is a peon kid in Seville, son of a bull-fighter killed in the ring, decidedly illiterate, and with a passion for bullfighting. He has an adolescent love for Linda Darnell and finally runs off to Madrid with a bunch of his pals. Ten years later, as a minor league matador, he returns to Seville, marries Darnell and goes on to become the most famous and widely acclaimed matador of the time. Surrounded by leeches, Power is continually in debt, but happy with his wife until fascinated by sexy Rita Hayworth, socialite flame.

Power delivers a persuasive performance as Ibanez's hero while Darnell is pretty and naive as the young wife. Hayworth is excellent as the vamp and catches major attention on a par with Nazimova, who gives a corking performance as Power's mother.

villain displaying screen presence to match the star's and thus injecting a powerful sense of danger.

THE BOUNTY

1984, 130 mins, ◇ ⓥ *Dir* Roger Donaldson   US

★ *Stars* Mel Gibson, Anthony Hopkins, Laurence Olivier, Edward Fox, Daniel Day-Lewis, Bernard Hill

The Bounty is an intelligent, first-rate, revisionist telling of the famous tale of Fletcher Christian's mutiny against Captain Bligh. The $20 million-plus film is particularly distinguished by a sensational, and startlingly human, performance by Anthony Hopkins as Bligh, heretofore one of history's most one-dimensional villains.

Present third version of the yarn was initiated by director David Lean, who brought Robert Bolt aboard to write the entire *Bounty* saga. Lean eventually moved on, and Dino De Laurentiis, paid for the construction of a replica ship.

This is a remake with a reason, that being the exoneration and rehabilitation of the reputation of William Bligh. A British Naval court-martial, which serves to frame Bolt's dramatization, ultimately absolved Bligh of blame for the mutiny, and he went on to enjoy a distinguished career.

The mutiny itself is here presented as a chaotic mess, with Christian nearly delirious. Bligh's subsequent 4,000-mile voyage to safety in an open boat is depicted as the amazing, arduous achievement that it was.

Tailor-made physically to fit the mold of old-style heroes, Mel Gibson gets across Christian's melancholy and torn motivations in excellent fashion.

THE BUCCANEER

1958, 121 mins, ◇ ⓥ *Dir* Anthony Quinn   US

★ *Stars* Yul Brynner, Charlton Heston, Claire Bloom, Charles Boyer, Inger Stevens, E.G. Marshall

Romance is effectively brought in the Cecil B. DeMille-supervised production that focuses on the colorful historical character of Jean Lafitte. On the deficit side is a wordy script that lacks any large degree of excitement.

It's a first-time-out for Henry Wilcoxon as producer, after several credits as associate to DeMille, with the latter in the role of 'supervisor'. It marks the debut for Anthony Quinn as director.

DeMille appears in a prologue to cite chapter and verse about the role Lafitte played in American history.

Continuity-wise, *Buccaneer* is a scrambled affair in the early reels. Open to question, also, are the story angles in the screenplay which derives from a previous *Buccaneer* scenario put out by DeMille in 1938 which, in turn, came from an adaptation of the original book, *Lafitte the Pirate*, by Lyle Saxon.

It's the War of 1812 against Britain and the battle area is New Orleans. The action takes place on land with the ex-

Set during the US war against the Brits, **The Buccaneer** *showcased Yul Brynner, Claire Bloom and Charles Boyer.*

ception of the sinking of one ship, which is curiously underplayed, by a renegade buccaneer. Highpoint is the land battle between Andrew Jackson's forces and the British, with Jackson aided by Lafitte's personnel and ammunition. The British, like so many toy soldiers, go down in defeat as Lafitte rules the mast.

Yul Brynner is masterly as the pirate. Charlton Heston is a hard, firm Andrew Jackson, who, while mounted on horse, sees the wisdom of making a deal with the pirate Lafitte. Claire Bloom is a fiery creation who alternately hates and loves Lafitte; Charles Boyer is light as Lafitte's aide (a role basically inconsequential), and Inger Stevens is properly attractive as Lafitte's true love and daughter of the governor.

BWANA DEVIL

1952, 79 mins, ◇ *Dir* Arch Oboler   US

★ *Stars* Robert Stack, Barbara Britton, Nigel Bruce, Ramsay Hill, Paul McVey

This novelty feature boasts of being the first full-length film in Natural Vision 3-D. Although adding backsides to usually flat actors and depth to landscapes, the 3-D technique still needs further technical advances.

Without the paper-framed, polaroid glasses Natural Vision looks like a ghosty television picture. While watching 3-D, viewers are constantly being forced to refocus their vision as the focus of the film changes, resulting in a tiring eye workout.

The Oboler production is full of tricks devised to show off the process, rather than to tell the screen story effectively. The much-ballyhooed point of a lion seemingly leaping out of the screen into the auditorium comes off very mildly. The single gasper is the throwing of a spear by a native, which has the illusion of coming right into the audience.

With banal dialog, stilted sequences and impossibly-directed players, Oboler tells a story, based on fact, of how two lions halt the building of a railroad in British East Africa.

CALL OF THE WILD

1935, 89 mins, *Dir* William Wellman   US

★ *Stars* Clark Gable, Loretta Young, Jack Oakie, Frank
Conroy, Reginald Owen, Sidney Toler

The lion-hearted dog that was Jack London's creation as the
leading character of *Call of the Wild* emerges now as a
stooge for a rather conventional pair of human love birds.
Changes have made the canine classic hardly recognizable,
but they have not done any damage.

The big and exceptionally wild St Bernard, known as
Buck, is not entirely submerged, since such of his feats as
the haul of a 1,000-pound load over the snow and his mat-
ing with a femme wolf are included, but he has been decidedly picture-house broken in this version.

Clark Gable strong-and-silents himself expertly and
Loretta Young, in the opposite corner of the revised love af-

*Clark Gable and Loretta Young star in Hollywood's
adaptation of Jack London's classic book Call of the Wild.*

fair, is lovely and competent. But Jack Oakie has the laughs,
and they land him on top.

It's a story of treachery, hardship, violence and unre-
quited love in Alaska, so anything that does away with sadness for a momentary giggle is highly welcome. Gable and
Oakie's rescue of Young, whose husband has apparently lost
his way and perished; their finding of the gold mine; their
encounter with the villainous Reginald Owen; the return of
Young's husband, lending a bitter-sweet finish to the romance, are the highlights of the story's human element.

This is the second trip for the London novel to the
screen. Pathe made it silent in 1923.

CALL OF THE WILD

1973, 100 mins, ◇ Ⓥ *Dir* Ken Annakin
W. GERMANY, SPAIN, ITALY

★ *Stars* Charlton Heston, Raimund Harmsdorf, Michele
Mercier, George Eastman, Sancho Garcia, Rik Battaglia

Jack London's thrilling, often-filmed tail trails a couple of
roughnecks, John and Pete, on their gold-digging, mail-
hopping, and booze-deal fortune hunts in Alaska's snowbound wilderness. Time and again, they are outsmarted and
outroughed by an assorted pack of rivals.

Director Ken Annakin picked a few good actors
(Charlton Heston and Italo-western hero George Eastman)
and some others capable of no more than looking their parts

(Raimund Harmsdorf, Michele Mercier). But everybody appears to play merely along action line on his own and creates a vacuum around him.

Thus lacking the density of London's original *Call of the Wild*, the picture falls to pieces with all that frozen gore, dog fights, sled chases, saloon brawls and other knock-down melodramatics.

CAMPBELL'S KINGDOM

1957, 100 mins, ◇ *Dir* Ralph Thomas   UK

★ *Stars* Dirk Bogarde, Stanley Baker, Michael Craig, Barbara Murray, James Robertson Justice, Athene Seyler

Campbell's Kingdom is virtually a British western. It is a straightforward, virile, action-packed yarn with ample excitement and mounting drama.

Story is a simple clash between a stiff-lipped hero and a glowering villain. When Dirk Bogarde, with only six months to live, arrives in the township of Come Lucky in the Rockies to take up his grandfather's inheritance, a whole train of skulduggery is unleashed. Said inheritance is Campbell's Kingdom, a valley which has been a problem child for some years. The old man obstinately insisted that it held oil. The local inhabitants invested their money in his idea. Meanwhile ruthless contractor Stanley Baker wants to flood the valley as part of a new hydro-electric scheme involving building of a new dam with inferior cement.

The plot unfolds slowly but gathers tremendous momentum, with the dam crashing a great thrill.

The alleged Rockies were lensed brilliantly in Cortina by Ernest Steward. Director Ralph Thomas wisely resists the temptation to allow his characters to indulge in personal rough stuff. Film keeps fairly close to the novel [by Hammond Innes].

CANNONBALL

1976, 93 mins, ◇ ⊛ *Dir* Paul Bartel   US, HONG KONG

★ *Stars* David Carradine, Bill McKinney, Veronica Hamel, Gerrit Graham, Robert Carradine, Martin Scorsese

Cannonball will please those who won't rest until they see every car in creation destroyed and aflame.

The sophisticated story line puts David Carradine, Bill McKinney and various other drivers and characters in autos in Los Angeles and promises $100,000 to the first to arrive in New York. Surely, goodness, mercy and high octane will triumph over villainy with lead in their guns, if not in their gas.

That's not to say *Cannonball* has no appeal beyond the crash crowd. It's full of handy highway hints, like what to do when someone steals your jack and then blasts your back tire apart with a pistol.

Best of all, though, is Carradine's inspirational automotive fortitude. When frustrated, he spins in circles, kicks his wheels, mutters oaths – just like the average weekend driver.

THE CANNONBALL RUN

1981, 93 mins, ◇ *Dir* Hal Needham   US

★ *Stars* Burt Reynolds, Roger Moore, Farrah Fawcett, Dom DeLuise, Dean Martin, Sammy Davis Jr

Full of inside showbiz jokes and populated by what could be called Burt and Hal's Rat Pack, film takes place in that redneck never-never land where most of the guys are beer-guzzling good ole boys and all the gals well built tootsies.

Cross-country race of the title comes off as almost entirely incidental to the star turns. Overall effect is akin to watching the troupe take a vacation.

Reynolds doesn't even lay a finger on Farrah Fawcett, settling instead for a nice chat in the back of his speedy ambulance. Tuxedoed Roger Moore drives around in his Aston-Martin and tries to convince everyone he's really Roger Moore and not one Seymour Goldfarb. Oriental driver Jackie Chan distracts (and almost kills) himself by putting on a videotape of *Behind the Green Door*, one way to stay awake on a coast-to-coast trip. Partner Michael Hui plays it straight.

CANNON FOR CORDOBA

1970, 104 mins, ◇ *Dir* Paul Wendkos   US

★ *Stars* George Peppard, Giovanna Ralli, Raf Vallone, Pete Duel, Don Gordon, Francine York

The story is about Mex outlaws who are a source of agony to the American military. Brig-Gen John J. Pershing (John Russell) dispatches his intelligence captain (George Peppard) to quell the disturbances. Peppard and friends conquer the army led by adversary Cordoba (Raf Vallone).

Interspersed are the episodes with a couple of girls, Giovanna Ralli and Francine York, whose effects are not special. Ralli, the double-dealing one, is pretty and treacherous and the observer gets to wonder about her costume changes in the heat of battle.

Director Paul Wendkos, cued by writer Stephen Kandel, might have put together a fairly arresting actioner. But they show an unsteady composite hand, for the script (if it has been adhered to) is an unorganized thing.

CAPTAIN BLOOD

1935, 119 mins, ⊛ *Dir* Michael Curtiz   US

★ *Stars* Errol Flynn, Olivia de Havilland, Basil Rathbone, Lionel Atwill, Ross Alexander, Guy Kibbee

Academy Award 1935: Best Picture (Nomination)

Captain Blood, from the Rafael Sabatini novel, is a big picture. It's a spectacle which establishes both Errol Flynn

Errol Flynn and Basil Rathbone team up in **Captain Blood,** *a lavish swashbuckling saga of pirates in the Spanish Main.*

and Olivia de Havilland. Director Michael Curtiz hasn't spared the horses. It's a lavish, swashbuckling saga of the Spanish main.

The engaging Flynn is the titular Peter Blood, erstwhile physician, later sold into West Indian slavery. He emerges thereafter as a peer among Caribbean pirates, Captain Blood, only later to be pardoned, his crew of runaway slaves likewise granted their freedom, and sworn into the King's navy.

Flynn impresses favorably from the start. One lives with him in the unfairness of a tyrannical King Charles which causes him and his fellow Englishmen to be sold into slavery overseas. One suffers with their travail; the audience roots with them in their ultimately fruitless plot for escape from the island. And then he is catapulted into leadership of a pirate ship.

De Havilland, who came to attention in Warner's *A Midsummer Night's Dream,* is romantically beauteous as the unsympathetic plantation owner's (later governor's) niece. This supplies a modicum of romantic interest, although all too paltry. It's one of the prime shortcomings of the production. Lionel Atwill is sufficiently hateful as the uncle. Basil Rathbone is an effective co-pirate captain (French brigands, this time), he and Flynn engaging in an arresting duel in the course of events.

CAPTAIN FROM CASTILE

1947, 140 mins, ◇ *Dir* Henry King   US

★ **Stars** Tyrone Power, Jean Peters, Cesar Romero, Lee J. Cobb, Antonio Moreno

Based on Samuel Shellaberger's 1945 best-selling historical novel, the cinema adaptation hews closely to the structure of the book, capturing the vast sweep of its story and adding to it an eye-stunning Technicolor dimension. The coin poured into this production, reported to be around $4.5 million, is visible in every inch of the footage.

For this plume-and-sabre epic of 16th-century Spanish imperial conquerors, producer and production chief have assembled a group of thespers who are cleanly tailored for the various parts. Led by Tyrone Power, who's rarely been shown to better advantage, the roster is buttressed by Cesar Romero, in a stirringly virile protrait of Cortez; Lee J Cobb, as a fortune hunter; John Sutton, as a velvety villain, and newcomer Jean Peters, a buxom, appealing wench for the romantic byplay.

From one viewpoint, this picture is constructed like a self-contained double feature. In the first half, the locale is Spain during the Inquisition, with Power and his family unjustly persecuted for heresy. Escaping from Spain, Power finds himself during the second half in Mexico as a recruit in Cortez's expedition of plunder against the Aztec empire ruled by Montezuma.

There are, however, several soft spots in the storyline that interfere with credibility. There is, for instance, the fact that Power narrowly escapes death no less than three times under the most extreme circumstances. Sutton, likewise, fantastically cheats death two times despite his being stabbed through the heart with a foot of steel one time and near-strangled the next.

CAPTAIN HORATIO HORNBLOWER, R.N.

1951, 116 mins, ◇ *Dir* Raoul Walsh   UK

★ **Stars** Gregory Peck, Virginia Mayo, Robert Beatty, James Kenney, James Robertson Justice, Stanley Baker

The exploits of one of Britain's greatest fictional naval adventurers have been filmed by Warner with spectacular success. *Captain Horatio Hornblower, R.N.* has been brought to the screen as effervescent entertainment with action the whole of the way.

Three C.S. Forester stories provide the basis for the pic, and the author, in preparing his own adaptation, has selected the best material from these. It is an incisive study of a man who is dispassionate, aloof and remote, yet often capable of finer feelings.

In his interpretation of the title role, Gregory Peck stands out as a skilled artist, capturing the spirit of the character and atmosphere of the period. Whether as the ruthless captain ordering a flogging as a face-saving act for a junior officer or tenderly nursing Virginia Mayo through yellow fever, he never fails to reflect the Forester character.

The film is divided into two halves. In the opening, Hornblower (Peck) is commanding the frigate Lydia through Pacific waters to fulfill a British mission to provide arms to enemies of Spain. On his return to England, he participates in an exciting adventure against Napoleon's fleet, eventually becoming a national hero. The major action sequences have been lensed with great skill.

CAPTAIN KIDD

1945, 89 mins, ⊕   *Dir* Rowland V. Lee   US

★ **Stars** Charles Laughton, Randolph Scott, Barbara Britton, John Carradine, Gilbert Roland, John Qualen

Captain Kidd is a swashbuckler which will please generally, despite its minimum of feminine appeal. Barbara Britton, who is co-starred with Charles Laughton and Randolph Scott, could phone her stuff into the celluloid for all its impact, coming on past midsection of the footage, but it's sufficiently adequate to inject a modicum of romance.

Story [from an original by Robert N. Lee] in the main focuses around the piratical rogues of the late 17th century when Captain Kidd (Laughton) freebooted the Spanish Main on the route of ships from England to fabulously rich India. When the king enlists Kidd as a loyal subject of the empire to give safe escort to treasury-laden vessels belonging to the crown, Kidd's doublecrossing leads him to the gallows. The footage inbetween is replete with piratical skullduggery. Laughton is capital as the ruthless brigand of the seas, ruling his equally villainous rogues with stern cruelty.

CARAVANS

1978, 127 mins, ◇ ⊕   *Dir* James Fargo   US, IRAN

★ **Stars** Anthony Quinn, Michael Sarrazin, Jennifer O'Neill, Christopher Lee, Joseph Cotten, Behrooz Vosoughi

The main trouble with this tale of 1948 Persia isn't the Iranians, it's Hollywood. Almost every fake moment in the film, and there are lots of them, has the touch of Hollywood laid on with a heavy coating. Fortunately for the average viewer, the scenic scope of the film, based on James Michener's epic story, and shot entirely on locations in Iran, is so sweeping that the tale that is told is almost palatable. But barely.

Briefly, the film deals with the search of a minor American consular employee (Michael Sarrazin) for an American woman (Jennifer O'Neill) who has married an Iranian colonel (Behrooz Vosoughi) but deserted him for a Kochi chieftain (Anthony Quinn) and has disappeared. Sarrazin finds her in short order. That's when the real trouble begins. She won't go back and he won't go back without her and off everyone goes into the desert.

Sarrazin, Quinn and O'Neill carry most of the story. The other non-Persians – Christopher Lee, Barry Sullivan, Jeremy Kemp and Joseph Cotten – are seen so briefly they may have done their roles over a long weekend. Histrionically, only Quinn is believable, followed closely by Vosoughi.

CARAVAN TO VACCARES

1974, 98 mins, ◇ ⊕   *Dir* Geoffrey Reeve   UK, FRANCE

★ **Stars** Charlotte Rampling, David Birney, Michel Lonsdale, Marcel Bozuffi, Michael Bryant, Manitas de Plata

There's good, reliable stuff in this Alistair MacLean action-adventure item, colorfully location-set in Southern France's Camargue area and well-acted by a carefully chosen Franco-British cast.

Plot basics involve the attempt to smuggle an East European scientist out of France and into the US, attempt which is hampered by repeated harassment and kidnappings by a scruple-less rival gang bent on gleaning the fugitive's secrets for resale to the highest bidder.

Principally involved are a footloose young American (David Birney), hired by a French Duke (Michel Lonsdale) to whisk the scientist onto a US-bound plane, and a pretty young British photographer (Charlotte Rampling) who gets involved when she hitches a ride with Birney.

THE CASSANDRA CROSSING

1977, 126 mins, ◇ ⊕   *Dir* George P. Cosmatos   US

★ **Stars** Sophia Loren, Richard Harris, Ava Gardner, Burt Lancaster, Martin Sheen, Ingrid Thulin

The Cassandra Crossing is a tired, hokey and sometimes unintentionally funny disaster film in which a trainload of disease-exposed passengers lurch to their fate.

One is asked to accept the premise that a terrorist bomber, accidentally exposed to some awesome plague, spreads the disease aboard a European express train. Mismatched leading players, all play directly to the camera, for themselves only, without betraying a hint of belief in their script.

While Richard Harris, a brilliant doctor, is active among those posturing leads on the train, Burt Lancaster and Ingrid Thulin hold down a command post where desperate efforts are made to isolate the train from the rest of civilization.

THE CHARGE OF THE LIGHT BRIGADE

1936, 115 mins, ⊕   *Dir* Michael Curtiz   US

★ **Stars** Errol Flynn, Oliva de Havilland, Patric Knowles, Henry Stephenson, Donald Crisp, David Niven

Warner has turned out a magnificent production in this story based on Tennyson's immortal poem and historical facts. Foreword explains that history was consulted for background, but characters and development are fictionized.

Before the climactic sweeping drive of the cavalry there is the dramatic defense of the Chukoti garrison and the

ruthless massacre of soldiers, wives and children after they have surrendered. The major who witnessed the slaughter is depicted as switching an order of the British high command. This results in the 600 cavalrymen riding into 'the valley of death' in the face of cannon fire and a force four or five times their number.

The tremendous sweep of this surging charge constitutes the pic's highlight. It has been skillfully done by means of close-ups, a traveling camera shot depicting the changing pace of the horses as column after column races towards the enemy, and via some truly extraordinary process shots.

The dual love affair, two brothers seeking the hand of the colonel's daughter, is nicely intertwined with the more adventurous moments of the story.

Errol Flynn lives up to the promise of previous film efforts as the youthful major who sacrifices all to avenge the slaughter of his comrades. Donald Crisp is strong in the character portrayal of the colonel.

THE CHARGE OF THE LIGHT BRIGADE

1968, 145 mins, ◇ *Dir* Tony Richardson   UK

★ **Stars** Trevor Howard, Vanessa Redgrave, John Gielgud, Harry Andrews, Jill Bennett, David Hemmings

Thanks mainly to Lord Tennyson's piece of durable doggerel millions of people have at least a sketchy idea of

Trevor Howard as Lord Cardigan in Tony Richardson's compelling version of **The Charge of the Light Brigade.**

the historical incident, though director Tony Richardson's treatment is almost disdainfully indifferent to the actual physical charge.

He is more concerned with analyzing the reasons behind one of the most notorious blunders in military history. He's also intent on attacking by ridicule the class war and bigotry of the British mid-19th-century regime, and the futility of the Crimean War as a whole.

Those fascinated by the class distinction, crass stupidity, muddled thinking and old school tie snobbishness prevailing at that time, will find richness in the earthy screenplay.

Film starts leisurely, carefully building up to the atmosphere of the times. In fact, despite Richardson's frequently lively direction and the brisk, electric editing, the pace of the film is remarkably easygoing, building up in a vague story line to the crass Charge as a finale which comes almost as an anti-climax.

Apart from some masterly directorial touches Richardson has made clever use of animated sequences wittily drawn by Richard Williams, living caricatures based on broadsides and cartoons of the mid-Victorian period.

They are not only consistently amusing but also deftly link the action, explain the historical background and compress what would be unwieldy scenes into quick, understandable comment.

CHINA SEAS

1935, 87 mins, ⓥ *Dir* Tay Garnett   US

★ *Stars* Clark Gable, Jean Harlow, Wallace Beery, Rosalind Russell, Lewis Stone, Dudley Digges

This is a story of love – sordid and otherwise – of piracy and violence and heroism on a passenger boat run from Shanghai to Singapore [from a novel by Crosbie Garstin]. Clark Gable is a valiant sea captain, Wallace Beery a villainous pirate boss, and Jean Harlow a blond trollop who motivates the romance and most of the action. All do their jobs expertly.

Harlow is crossed in love when Gable, who has been her sweetheart in a sort of sparring partner but true-love affair, is tempted to return to English aristocracy. Temptation arrives in the form of the refined Rosalind Russell, a home town acquaintance. The social gap between Harlow and Rosalind touches off the fireworks.

Spurned by Gable, Harlow seeks to get hunk by slipping Beery the key to the ship's arsenal which makes it a cinch for the raiding pirates. But the raid fails, for Gable refuses to reveal the hiding place of a cargo of gold.

The pirate raid and its unsuccessful termination (for the pirates) is full of shooting, suspense and action. Add a running atmosphere of suspense through the picture, and there's plenty of excitement.

CITY BENEATH THE SEA

1953, 87 mins, ◇ *Dir* Budd Boetticher   US

★ *Stars* Robert Ryan, Mala Powers, Anthony Quinn, Suzan Ball, George Mathews, Karel Stepanek

High romance of the pulp-fiction variety is niftily shaped in *City Beneath the Sea*. The film stages a thrilling undersea 'earthquake' as a capper to the derring-do yarn laid in the West Indies.

A couple of lusty, adventurous deep-sea divers, a sunken treasure, comely femmes and the earthquake are expertly mixed to provide chimerical film entertainment. The direction by Budd Boetticher is slanted to take the most advantage of the action, amatory and thrill situations in the story based on Harry E. Reiseberg's *Port Royal – Ghost City Beneath the Sea*. Picture is not necessarily logical, but it tells its tale with a robust sense of humor.

The earthquake sequence is a real thriller. Scene is the historic sunken city of Port Royal, Jamaica, which went to the bottom of the Caribbean during a 1692 earthquake. Robert Ryan and Anthony Quinn team excellently as the daring divers, ever ready for the adventures offered by sunken treasure or shapely femmes. They come to Kingston, Jamaica, to dive for $1 million in gold bullion that went down with a freighter, without knowing their employer (Karel Stepanek) doesn't want the treasure found just yet.

Plot tangents boil along while Ryan woos Mala Powers, owner of a small, coastwise ship, and Quinn makes time with Suzan Ball, singer in a waterfront nitery.

COMA

1978, 113 mins, ◇ ⓥ *Dir* Michael Crichton   US

★ *Stars* Genevieve Bujold, Michael Douglas, Elizabeth Ashley, Rip Torn, Richard Widmark, Lois Chiles

Coma is an extremely entertaining suspense drama in the Hitchcock tradition. Director-adapter Michael Crichton neatly builds mystery and empathy around star Genevieve Bujold, a doctor who grows to suspect her superiors of deliberate surgical error. Michael Douglas also stars as her disbelieving lover.

Robin Cook's novel is adapted by Crichton into a smartly-paced tale which combines traditional Hitchcock elements with contemporary personal relationships. Thus Bujold and Douglas wrestle in sub-plot with separate identity and mutual romantic problems while she becomes the innocent enmeshed in suspicious medical wrongdoing. When lifelong friend Lois Chiles goes into permanent coma during an otherwise routine operation, Bujold begins probing a series of similar incidents.

Arrayed against her are hospital superiors Richard Widmark and Rip Torn, and even Douglas himself. Lance Le Gault is a hired killer whom Bujold outwits to the relief of the entire audience.

Elizabeth Ashley is notable as the head of a dubious medical experimental centre where the comatose victims vegetate pending ghoulish, but all-too-plausible disposition.

COMMANDO

1985, 88 mins, ◇ ⓥ *Dir* Mark L. Lester   US

★ *Stars* Arnold Schwarzenegger, Rae Dawn Chong, Dan Hedaya, Vernon Wells, David Patrick Kelly, Alyssa Milano

In *Commando*, the fetching surprise is the glancing humor between the quixotic and larky Rae Dawn Chong and the straight-faced killing machine of Arnold Schwarzenegger. Chong lights up the film like a firefly, Schwarzenegger delivers a certain light touch of his own, the result is palatable action comics.

Director Mark L. Lester, compelled to deal with an absurd plot [by Joseph Loeb III, Matthew Weisman and Steven de Souza], is blessed by the decision to cast Chong, who enjoys an offbeat sexuality and an insouciance that is irresistible.

Credit Lester with chiseling the quick, subtly romantic byplay between the two stars – unlikely mates thrown together in pursuit of a deadly Latin neo-dictator – and pulling off a terrific series of tracking shots during a riotous chase in a crowded galleria complex.

Heavies are vividly drawn in the cases of the obsessed Vernon Wells, the punk David Patrick Kelly, and sullen, ice-cold Bill Duke.

*Arnold Schwarzenegger is muscle-man **Conan the Barbarian** in this tale of swords and sorcerers.*

CONAN THE BARBARIAN

1982, 129 mins, ◇ Ⓥ *Dir* John Milius   US

★ *Stars* Arnold Schwarzenegger, James Earl Jones, Max Von Sydow, Sandahl Bergman, Mako, Gerry Lopez

The opening is promising enough as child Conan witnesses the brutal deaths of his father and mother at the whim of the evil Thulsa Doom (James Earl Jones). Conan Jr grows up as a slave who eventually has the good fortune of turning into Arnold Schwarzenegger.

It's the baddies' fatal flaw that they shove Conan into an arena to fight chosen competitors to the death. The guy naturally realizes he's pretty strong and decides to strike out on his own to see how far his muscles can take him.

In those days it was pretty far. On the road he meets up with a fellow drifter (Gerry Lopez), beautiful cohort and eventual lover Sandahl Bergman, needy king Max Von Sydow and goofy wizard Mako.

Director John Milius does a nice job of setting up the initial story. There is a real anticipation as Schwarzenegger is unveiled as the barbarian and sets off on the road to independence. But for whatever reasons, the actor has a minimum of dialog and fails to convey much about the character through his actions.

This is compounded by the script by Milius and Oliver Stone, which is nothing more than a series of meaningless adventures and ambiguous references until the final expected confrontation with Jones.

CONAN THE DESTROYER

1984, 103 mins, ◇ Ⓥ *Dir* Richard Fleischer   US

★ *Stars* Arnold Schwarzenegger, Grace Jones, Wilt Chamberlain, Mako, Tracey Walter, Sarah Douglas

Conan the Destroyer is the ideal sword and sorcery picture. Plot is appropriately elemental. Conan is recruited by sexy queen Sarah Douglas to accompany teenage princess Olivia D'Abo to a distant castle, wherein lies a gem that will supposedly unleash many secret powers.

Unbeknownst to Conan, Douglas has instructed her henchman Chamberlain to kill the muscleman once the mission is accomplished, and to deliver D'Abo back home with her virginity intact so that she can be properly sacrificed.

Along the way, group also picks up fiery warrioress Grace Jones.

As Conan, Arnold Schwarzenegger seems more animated and much funnier under Fleischer's direction than he did under John Milius' in the original – he even has an amusing drunk scene. Jones just about runs off with the picture. Coming on like a full-fledged star from her very first scene,

singer throws herself into her wild woman role with complete abandon.

THE CONCORDE – AIRPORT '79

1979, 123 mins, ◇ Ⓥ *Dir* David Lowell Rich   US

★ *Stars* Alain Delon, Susan Blakely, Robert Wagner, Sylvia Kristel, George Kennedy, Eddie Albert

Unintentional comedy still seems the *Airport* series' forte, although excellent special effects work, and some decent dramatics help *Concorde* take off.

This time out, the title entity is pursued by a dogged

electronic missile, avoids an attack by a French fighter jet, barely makes a runway landing with no brakes, suffers a lost cargo door that rips open the bottom of the plane, manages a crash landing in an Alpine snow bank, and explodes just as its chic passengers disembark. That's all just part of a couple of days' work for pilots George Kennedy, Alain Delon and flight engineer David Warner.

Concorde does feature some better-than-average thesping from Delon, who survives the transition to American pix surprisingly well.

THE CONQUEROR

1956, 111 mins, ◇ ⊛ *Dir* Dick Powell   US

★ *Stars* John Wayne, Susan Hayward, Pedro Armendariz, Agnes Moorehead, Thomas Gomez, William Conrad

Just so there will be no misunderstanding about *The Conqueror*, a foreword baldly states that it is fiction, although with some basis in fact. With that warning out of the way, the viewer can sit back and thoroughly enjoy a huge, brawling, sex-and-sand actioner purporting to show how a 12th-Century Mongol leader became known as Genghis Khan.

The marquee value of the John Wayne–Susan Hayward teaming more than offsets any incongruity of the

Richard Chamberlain stars as the hero in Alexander Dumas' classic tale **The Count of Monte Cristo.**

casting, which has him as the Mongol leader and she as the Tartar princess he captures and forcibly takes as mate.

Co-starring is the excellent Pedro Armendariz, who makes believable his role of Wayne's blood-brother and is an important essential in the entertainment.

The s.a. pitch is in a harem dance choreographed by Robert Sidney, in which a covey of lookers give the appearance of being almost completely bare while gyrating to the Oriental strains of Victor Young's first-rate music.

CONVOY

1978, 110 mins, ◇ ⊛ *Dir* Sam Peckinpah   US

★ *Stars* Kris Kristofferson, Ali MacGraw, Ernest Borgnine, Burt Young, Madge Sinclair, Franklyn Ajaye

Sam Peckinpah's *Convoy* starts out as *Smokey and the Bandit*, segues into either *Moby Dick* or *Les Miserables*, and ends in the usual script confusion and disarray, the whole stew peppered with the vulgar excess of random truck crashes and miscellaneous destruction. Kris Kristofferson stars as a likeable roustabout who accidentally becomes a folk hero, while Ali MacGraw recycles about three formula reactions throughout her nothing part.

B.W.L. Norton gets writing credit using C.W. McCall's c&w poptune lyric as a basis. No matter. Peckinpah's films display common elements and clumsy analogies, overwhelmed with logistical fireworks and drunken changes of dramatic emphasis.

This time around, Kristofferson (who, miraculously, seems to survive these banalities) is a trucker whose longtime nemesis, speed-trap-blackmailer cop Ernest Borgnine, pursues him with a vengeance through what appears to be three states. Every few minutes there's some new roadblock to run, alternating with pithy comments on The Meaning Of It All. There's a whole lot of nothing going on here.

THE CORSICAN BROTHERS

1941, 111 mins, ⊛ *Dir* Gregory Ratoff   US

★ *Stars* Douglas Fairbanks Jr, Ruth Warrick, Akim Tamiroff, J. Carrol Naish, H.B. Warner, Henry Wilcoxon

Dumas' story of the *Corsican Brothers* is widely known. Born Siamese twins of Corsican aristocracy, the babies are separated at birth by a miraculous operation, and saved from a vendetta attack that kills their immediate family. One child goes to Paris for upbringing and education, while the other remains to be reared by a former family servant.

Twenty-one years later the twins (both portrayed by Douglas Fairbanks Jr) are reunited, introduced, and informed of the enemy of their forebears. Swearing to avenge the family murders, the two boys separate to confuse their enemy with widely separated attacks on his henchmen. Title foreword warns audiences that this is an incredible tale – and then the picture proceeds on that basis.

Script [from a free adaptation] by George Bruce and Howard Estabrook is well set up to display the action qualities, but rather studious on the dialog and story motivation. Gregory Ratoff's direction is okay.

THE COUNT OF MONTE CRISTO

1934, 113 mins, *Dir* Rowland V. Lee   US

★ **Stars** Robert Donat, Elissa Landi, Louis Calhern, Sidney Blackmer, Raymond Walburn, O. P. Heggie

Monte Cristo is a near-perfect blend of thrilling action and grand dialog, both of which elements are inherent in Alexandre Dumas' original story.

Robert Donat is a fortunate selection for the lead. His intelligent handling of the many-sided top role hallmarks a sparkling piece of acting. Louis Calhern (De Villefort), Sidney Blackmer (Mondego) and Raymond Walburn (Danglars) are the three principal male supports in the extra large cast, and as the trio upon whom Cristo wreaks his vengeance they fill the order. Elissa Landi as Mercedes looks and acts the part, but the acting in this case isn't as important as the looks, and Landi has had tougher assignments.

THE COUNT OF MONTE CRISTO

1976, 103 mins, ◇ ⓥ *Dir* David Greene   UK

★ **Stars** Richard Chamberlain, Tony Curtis, Trevor Howard, Louis Jourdan, Donald Pleasence, Kate Nelligan

Richard Chamberlain is Edmond Dantes, the romantic young sailor railroaded to prison for 15 years. After his escape, aided by an old fellow prisoner, the story gets down to his obsessive revenge against the four money and/or power-hungry men who conspired against him.

All this is retailed in a most workmanlike fashion. Script and moral values appear respectful of the Dumas original. The saga is performed with ample conviction and polish, but is developed with more sincerity than interest or dramatic originality, and with no style of its own.

Chamberlain is appealing and reasonably persuasive as the hero robbed of both his best years and his betrothed, the latter played touchingly in a promising feature bow by British-based Canadian Kate Nelligan.

THE CRIMSON PIRATE

1952, 104 mins, ◇ ⓥ *Dir* Robert Siodmak   UK, US

★ **Stars** Burt Lancaster, Eva Bartok, Nick Cravat, Torin Thatcher, James Hayter, Margot Grahame

Swashbucking sea fables get a good-natured spoofing in *The Crimson Pirate*, with Burt Lancaster providing the muscles and dash for the takeoff.

The screen story is cloaked with a sense of humor as it pictures Lancaster, the famed Crimson Pirate, plying his trade on the high seas. Opening finds the pirates capturing a 30-gun galleon by trickery and then scheming to sell its cargo of cannon to rebels trying to shake off the shackles of the King of Spain. The buccaneers also plan to then reveal the rebel group's whereabouts to the crown for more gold, but there are a girl and such complications as an awakening to right and wrong.

Lancaster and his deaf-mute pal (Nick Cravat) sock the acrobatics required of hero and partner to a fare-thee-well under Robert Siodmak's direction.

THE DAY OF THE JACKAL

1973, 141 mins, ◇ ⓥ *Dir* Fred Zinnemann   UK, FRANCE

★ **Stars** Edward Fox, Alan Badel, Tony Britton, Cyril Cusack, Michel Lonsdale, Delphine Seyrig

Fred Zinnemann's film of *The Day of the Jackal* is a patient, studied and quasi-documentary translation of Frederick Forsyth's big-selling political suspense novel. Film appeals more to the intellect than the brute senses as it traces the detection of an assassin hired to kill French President Charles de Gaulle.

The recruitment of Edward Fox as the assassin and his planning of the murder is a sort of carrier frequency for the story. Around this is the mobilization of French and other national law enforcement agencies to discover and foil the plot. The final confluence of the plot lines is somewhat brief and anti-climactic.

The major asset of the film is that it succeeds in maintaining interest and suspense despite obvious viewer fore-knowledge of the outcome.

Fox does very well as the innocent-looking youth who plans his stalk with meticulous care.

DAYS OF THUNDER

1990, 107 mins, ◇ ⓥ *Dir* Tony Scott   US

★ **Stars** Tom Cruise, Robert Duvall, Nicole Kidman, Randy Quaid, Michael Rooker, Cary Elwes

This expensive genre film about stock car racing has many of the elements that made the same team's *Top Gun* a blockbuster, but the producers recruited scripter Robert Towne to make more out of the story than junk food.

There's the cocky but insecure young challenger (Tom Cruise) breaking into the big time, the hardened champion

Stock car action from Days of Thunder, *starring Tom Cruise as the rookie driver breaking into the big time.*

he's trying to unseat (Michael Rooker), the grizzled manager who dispenses fatherly wisdom (Robert Duvall), the crass promoter (Randy Quaid), and the sexy lady from outside (Nicole Kidman) who questions the point of it all.

Director Tony Scott plunges the viewer into the maelstrom of stock car racing. A highly effective blending of car-mounted camerawork and long lenses imparts documentary credibility and impact.

Days of Thunder zigzags between exploiting Cruise's likable grin and charming vulnerability and portraying him as an emotional loser. It's an uncertain and unsatisfying mix.

The film's real glory is Duvall. His duplicitous, ruthless streak hovers just below the surface, giving a sense of inner danger to the racing scenes in which he coaches the untrusting Cruise by radio from trackside.

THE DECKS RAN RED

1958, 97 mins, *Dir* Andrew Stone   US

★ *Stars* James Mason, Dorothy Dandridge, Broderick Crawford, Stuart Whitman, Katharine Bard

The Decks Ran Red is a descriptive title for this story, presented as fact, of an attempted mutiny at sea. Before the mutineers have been beaten down, they have spilled enough blood to make the decks sticky, if not actually running, with gore.

The plot is a plan by Broderick Crawford and Stuart

Whitman, crew members of a chartered freighter, to kill off other members of the crew, rig the ship to make it look like an abandoned derelict, and then bring it in as salvage. According to maritime law, it's said, they will get half the ship's value – $1 million – as prize money.

James Mason, who has been first officer on a trim Matson liner, is flown to Australia to take charge of this dingy vessel when its captain mysteriously dies. He quickly discovers he is in for trouble from a lacklustre and sullen crew, trouble that is compounded by taking aboard a native Maori cook and his wife, latter being Dorothy Dandridge.

The story is faintly incredible at times and there is a tendency to impose dialog on a scene when the action has already spoken for itself. But the picture moves swiftly and absorbingly.

THE DEEP

1977, 124 mins, ◇ Ⓥ *Dir* Peter Yates   US

★ *Stars* Robert Shaw, Jacqueline Bisset, Nick Nolte, Louis Gossett, Eli Wallach, Robert Tessier

The Deep is an efficient but rather colorless film based on the Peter Benchley novel about a perilous search for treasure in the waters off Bermuda.

Fully 40% of the film takes place underwater, and the actors and crew learned how to dive, playing long scenes without dialog on the ocean floor. Director Peter Yates keeps up the tension in a low-key way – with a few shocker moments thrown in from time to time – and these scenes are more involving than the ones above the surface.

It's possible that inside this slick piece of engineering

there is a genuinely mordant satire of human greed struggling to get out, but it never quite gets to the surface.

Ned Beatty, Jon Voight, Ronny Cox, Bill McKinney and Burt Reynolds on an ill-fated hunting trip in **Deliverance.**

DELIVERANCE

1972, 109 mins, ◇   *Dir* John Boorman   US

★ *Stars* Jon Voight, Burt Reynolds, Ned Beatty, Ronny Cox, Bill McKinney, James Dickey

Academy Award 1972: Best Picture (Nomination)

Deliverance can be considered a stark, uncompromising showdown between basic survival instincts against the character pretensions of a mannered and material society. Unfortunately for John Boorman's heavy film of James Dickey's first novel, it can just as easily be argued as a virile, mountain country transposition of nihilistic, specious philosophising which exploits rather than explores its moments of violent drama.

Against the majestic setting of a river being dammed, Dickey's story takes four city men out for a last weekend trip down the river. Unexpected malevolence forces each to test his personal values in order to survive.

It is, however, in the fleshing out that the script fumbles, and with it the direction and acting. The unofficial group leader of the sailing trip is Burt Reynolds, a volatile, calculating, aggressive and offensive tempter of fate.

Why the best friend Jon Voight would maintain an apparent longstanding relationship with Reynolds' character is an early plot chuck-hole.

What makes for a pervading uneasiness is the implication of the story: the strongest shall survive. The values of Reynolds' character are repulsive; Ronny Cox is a cardboard-cutout as an intellectual type; Ned Beatty is the easy-going, middle-class figurehead patronized by both the 'doers' and the 'thinkers' of the world; leaving Voight apparently as the one to lead them out of travail.

In the depiction of sudden, violent death, there is the rhapsodic wallowing in the deadly beauty of it all: protruding arrows, agonizing expiration, etc. It's the stuff of which slapdash oaters and crime programmers are made but the obvious ambitions of *Deliverance* are supposed to be on a higher plane.

THE DELTA FORCE

1986, 129 mins, ◇ Ⓥ   *Dir* Menahem Golan   US

★ *Stars* Chuck Norris, Lee Marvin, Martin Balsam, Joey Bishop, Robert Forster, Lainie Kazan

Directed with the throttle wide open, pic roots itself firmly in very fresh history, then proceeds to brashly rewrite it, thereby turning itself into an exercise in wish fulfilment for those who favor using force instead of diplomacy.

First hour is mostly devoted to what seems to be a quite accurate rendition of the 1985 TWA Athens hijacking.

From here, film is purest fantasy pitting the noble Yankees against the dirty, low-down Palestinians. In an attempt at 'make my day' immortality, Chuck Norris growls at one of them, 'Sleep tight, sucker,' before blowing him away, and gets a chance to make ample use of his martial arts skills.

DELTA FORCE 2 THE COLOMBIAN CONNECTION

1990, 105 mins, ◇ Ⓥ *Dir* Aaron Norris   US

★ **Stars** Chuck Norris, Billy Drago, Bobby Chavez, John R. Ryan, Richard Jaeckel

Chuck Norris fans have all they could ask for with *Delta Force 2*. Norris and a dozen US marines fly into the South American drug capital San Carlos, destroy half the country's cocaine production, and rub out the land's untouchable drug czar, in a carthartic blaze of exploding missiles and flying fists.

(During the filming, five people were killed in a 15 May 1989, helicopter crash in the Philippines: pilot Jo Jo Imperial, stuntmen Geoffrey Brewer, Mike Graham and Gadi Danzig, and gaffer Don Marshall. Three others were injured.)

Production values are high with an endless stream of ammunition and extras. Lensing is pro, and score has a tropical flavor that stays pleasantly in the background.

Norris is a minimalist actor, rightly concentrating on the action. As the sadistic Coda, Billy Drago has a Medusa-like presence that produces shivers just from looking at him.

THE DEVIL AT 4 O'CLOCK

1961, 125 mins, ◇ Ⓥ *Dir* Mervyn LeRoy   US

★ **Stars** Spencer Tracy, Frank Sinatra, Kerwin Mathews, Jean-Pierre Aumont, Gregoire Aslan, Barbara Luna

A small volcanic South Seas isle makes a colorful setting for this tale of heroism and sacrifice, but vying with interest in characterizations are the exceptional special effects of an island being blown to pieces.

Based on a novel by Max Catto, plot is off the beaten path for an adventure yarn. Story is of a priest (Spencer Tracy) who with three convicts (Frank Sinatra, Gregoire Aslan, Bernie Hamilton) saves the lives of the children in a mountain-top leper hospital by leading them through fire and lava flow to the coast and a waiting schooner after the volcano erupts and island is doomed to certain destruction.

Tracy delivers one of his more colorful portrayals in his hard-drinking cleric who has lost faith in his God, walloping over a character which sparks entire action of film. Sinatra's role, first-class but minor in comparison, is overshadowed in interest by Aslan, one of the convicts in a steal-

Bruce Willis and Bonnie Bedelia in the tough, high tech action thriller **Die Hard.**

ing part who lightens some of the more dramatic action. Third con, Hamilton, also delivers solidly as the strong man who holds up a tottering wooden bridge over a deep gorge while the children and others from hospital cross to safety.

Special effects of Larry Butler and Willis Cook highlight the picture, filmed impressively by Joseph Biroc on the vivid island of Maui in the Hawaiian group.

DIE HARD

1988, 131 mins, ◇ Ⓥ *Dir* John McTiernan   US

★ **Stars** Bruce Willis, Alan Rickman, Bonnie Bedelia, Alexander Godunov, Reginald Veljohnson

Die Hard is as high tech, rock hard and souped up as an action film can be, a suspenser [based on the novel *Nothing Lasts Forever* by Roderick Thorpe] pitting a lone wolf cop against a group of terrorists that has taken over a highrise office tower.

Bruce Willis plays John McClane, an overworked New York policeman who flies into Los Angeles at Christmas to visit his two daughters and estranged wife Holly (Bonnie Bedelia).

Planning a rather different holiday agenda are the terrorists led by Hans Gruber (Alan Rickman). The dastardly dozen invade the plush 30th floor offices of Nakatomi Corp during its Christmas party, and hold the employees hostage while a computer whiz cracks a code that will put the mainly German bad boys in possession of $600 million in negotiable bonds.

Slipping out of the party in the nick of time with nothing but his handgun, Willis is the fly in the ointment of the criminals' plans, picking off one, then two more of the scouts sent on pest control missions.

Beefed up considerably for his role, Willis is amiable enough in the opening stretch, but overdoes the grimacing and heavy emoting later on. The cooler and more humorous he is the better. Rickman has a giddy good time but sometimes goes over the top as the henchman.

DIE HARD 2

1990, 124 mins, ◇ ⓥ *Dir* Renny Harlin   US

★ *Stars* Bruce Willis, Bonnie Bedelia, William Atherton, Franco Nero, William Sadler

Die Hard 2 lacks the inventiveness of the original but compensates with relentless action. The film [based on the novel *58 Minutes* by Walter Wager] works for the most part as sheer entertainment, a full-color comic book with shootouts, brutal fistfights and bloodletting aplenty.

Minding his own business, John McClane (Bruce Willis) is in DCs Dulles Airport to pick up wife Holly (Bonnie Bedelia) to spend Christmas with her folks. They've reconciled since the events in *Die Hard* and the Gotham cop has joined the LAPD. Unlike most domestic flights, the story takes off immediately, as terrorists seize control of the airport to free a Manuel Noriegaesque foreign dictator (Franco Nero) being transported to the US.

Director Renny Harlin does a creditable job with such a daunting large-scale assignment. But Harlin lacks *Die Hard* director John McTiernan's vicelike grip on action and strays into areas that derail certain scenes, using slow-motion in early sequences and sapping their energy.

THE DOGS OF WAR

1980, 122 mins, ◇ ⓥ *Dir* John Irvin   UK

★ *Stars* Christopher Walken, Tom Berenger, Colin Blakely, Hugh Millais, Paul Freeman, JoBeth Williams

The Dogs of War [from Frederick Forsyth's novel] is an intelligent and occasionally forceful treatment of a

provocative but little-examined theme, that of mercenary warrior involvement in the overthrow of a corrupt black African dictatorship.

Script focuses almost exclusively on Christopher Walken, an 'irresponsible' American who is drawn to the mercenary's loner, adventurous life.

Film fails to really get at the heart of the whys and hows of mercenary life, and also rejects the idea of generating any sense of camaraderie among the men.

Details of life in a contempo African dictatorship country, from the bribery and censorship to the military strong-arming and oppressive economic conditions, are effectively sketched. Pic displays the political realities without editorializing.

DON JUAN

1926, 100 mins, *Dir* Alan Crosland   US

★ *Stars* John Barrymore, Mary Astor, Estelle Taylor, Warner Oland, Montagu Love, Myrna Loy

Several outstanders in this splendidly written, directed and produced feature. Not alone does John Barrymore's superb playing become one of them, but his athletics, as well. A chase scene is a bear. It's of Don Juan carrying his Adriana away, followed by about a dozen swordsmen on horses, with Barrymore placing his charge in a tree, to return and knock off all of the riders, one by one or in twos.

The complete surprise is the performance of Estelle Taylor as Lucretia Borgia. Her Lucretia is a fine piece of work. She makes it sardonic in treatment, conveying precisely the woman Lucretia is presumed to have been. The other outstanding performance is that of Mary Astor's Adriana. Astor has but comparatively little action, but fills the part so thoroughly that she is a dominating figure. Warner Oland is Cesare, the savage brother, and he looks the role.

DR. NO

1962, 110 mins, ◇ ⓥ *Dir* Terence Young   UK

★ *Stars* Sean Connery, Ursula Andress, Joseph Wiseman, Jack Lord, Bernard Lee, Zena Marshall

First screen adventure of Ian Fleming's hardhitting, fearless, imperturbable, girl-loving Secret Service Agent 007, James Bond, is an entertaining piece of tongue-in-cheek action hokum. Sean Connery excellently puts over a cool, fearless, on-the-ball fictional Secret Service guy. Terence Young directs with a pace which only occasionally lags.

The hero is exposed to pretty (and sometimes treacherous) gals, a poison tarantula spider, a sinister crook, flame throwers, gunshot, bloodhounds, beating up, near drowning

Ursula Andress and Sean Connery in Dr. No, the first film outing for British Secret Service agent James Bond.

Douglas Fairbanks stars as **Don Q, Son of Zorro,** *the adventures of sword-fighting bandit Zorro.*

and plenty of other mayhem and malarkey, and comes through it all with good humour, resourcefulness and what have you.

Connery is sent to Jamaica to investigate the murder of a British confidential agent and his secretary. Since both murders happen within three or four minutes of the credit titles the pic gets away to an exhilarating start. He becomes involved with the activities of Dr. No, a sinister Chinese scientist (Joseph Wiseman) who from an island called Crab Key is using a nuclear laboratory to divert off course the rockets being propelled from Cape Canaveral .

Among the dames with whom Connery becomes involved are easy-on-the-eye Ursula Andress, who shares his perilous adventures on Crab Key, and spends most of her time in a bikini, Zena Marshall as an Oriental charmer who nearly decoys him to doom in her boudoir and Eunice Gayson, whom he picks up in a gambling club in London and who promises to be the biggest menace of the lot .

DON Q, SON OF ZORRO

1925, 110 mins, ◇ ⊘ ⊕ *Dir* Donald Crisp   US

★ *Stars* Douglas Fairbanks, Mary Astor, Jack McDonald, Donald Crisp, Warner Oland, Jean Hersholt

Don Q gives Fairbanks a chance to play a double role, as the youthful Don Q and as Zorro, the father of the dashing young Californian who is completing his education in Spain.

His adventures there form the basis of the picture. He becomes involved with royalty, is accused of the murder of a visiting archduke, feigns suicide, almost loses the girl, but in the end emerges triumphant.

Mary Astor plays opposite the star. She appears to beautiful advantage in the little that she has to do, while Donald Crisp as the heavy scores, although the supporting cast honors of the picture must be divided between Jean Hersholt and Warner Oland. Hersholt gets rather the better of it. His role isn't as strong as the one he had in *Greed*, but it shows him capable of intense characterization that registers heavily.

DOWN TO THE SEA IN SHIPS

1949, 120 mins, *Dir* Henry Hathaway   US

★ *Stars* Richard Widmark, Lionel Barrymore, Dean Stockwell, Gene Lockhart

Down to the Sea in Ships is a lengthy saga of early whaling ships and the men who commanded them. It is told with emphasis on character study rather than action. The first half is becalmed in a rather thorough development of the characters. In the last hour, picture really shakes out its sails and goes wing-and-winging before the wind.

The taking of a whale and the rendering of blubber to oil, the dangers of fog and the menace of a wreck on an iceberg is sturdy excitement that serves as a fitting climax to the story of an old whaler captain, his young grandson and of a young first mate. Richard Widmark has a chance at a sympathetic role and proves himself versatile. Lionel Barrymore carries off the fat part of whaling captain with fewer of the usual Barrymore tricks. Despite his youth, Dean Stockwell is a skilled thespian who more than holds his own in scenes with the adults.

THE DRUM

1938, 101 mins, ◇ ⊚ *Dir* Zoltan Korda   US

★ *Stars* Sabu, Raymond Massey, Roger Livesey, Valerie Hobson, David Tree, Francis L. Sullivan

Film is based on a story written specially for the screen by A.E.W. Mason. He supplies an excellent machine-made suspensive tale laid in India, with fine dialog.

Entire action is laid in the tribal territory of the northwest frontier of India. An elderly khan is anxious for British protection to ensure his throne for his son, Prince Axim (Sabu). Ruler's brother, Prince Ghul, is fanatically anti-British, kills the old man, and the plot involves the attempt to do away with the young prince.

Sabu, the 14-year-old Indian youth who came to attention in *Elephant Boy* (1937), lives up to the promise given in that film and conducts himself with requisite dignity. He now speaks very good English. Raymond Massey is sufficiently sinister as the throne usurper; Roger Livesey is excellent as the military commander.

THE DUELLISTS

1977, 95 mins, ◇ ⊚ *Dir* Ridley Scott   UK

★ *Stars* Keith Carradine, Harvey Keitel, Cristina Raines, Edward Fox, Robert Stephens, Albert Finney

The Napoleonic Wars are behind this stubborn sword slashing and then pistols of two men whose personalities are caught up in their own personal vendetta within the epic European battles of the times. Narrative : Harvey Keitel is an almost obsessed dueller who is asked to appear before the general due to his duels, by Keith Carradine who practically volunteers for the job.

Keitel is jaunty and menacing and Carradine more determined and a bit troubled but also caught up in this strange need of one to prove honor and the other slaking a twisted nature.

It does not quite achieve a more lusty visual feel for the times and the strange relations of these two men to themselves and to the women in and out of their lives.

Fine thesps in smaller roles help with even Albert Finney in as the Napoleonic head of the Paris police.

THE EAGLE AND THE HAWK

1933, 74 mins, *Dir* Stuart Walker, Mitchell Leisen   US

★ *Stars* Fredric March, Cary Grant, Jack Oakie, Carole Lombard, Guy Standing, Forrester Harvey

Strictly a formula story of the Royal Flying Corps by the man who wrote *Wings* [John Monk Saunders] with a laboriously dragged in romantic bit. Nothing much new in the matter of plot, the same old yarn of the man who gets fed up on the uselessness of war.

Basic idea is the hero who is broken by the strain. He has lost observer after observer without serious injury to

Scene from disaster epic Earthquake, *which combined brilliant special effects and an above average plot line.*

himself, and it breaks his morale. His last observer is a rather tough-fibered chap and there is bad blood between them. Fredric March is sent back home to regain his poise, there is a brief two-scene interlude with Carole Lombard, and he comes back to the lines still shaken.

Yarn is adroitly told in both dialog and action, Jack Oakie contributing some sorely-needed comedy touches here and there. It is the only relief save for a delightfully played bit between Oakie and Adrienne D'Ambicourt, who makes the most of her single scene. Lombard contributes little in spite of sincere playing. March offers a finely sensitive study, acting with force, but entirely without bombast. Cary Grant is more along usual lines, but he supplies the complementary action effectively, and Guy Standing as the commander gets a brief chance now and then.

EARTHQUAKE

1974, 122 mins, ◇ ⓥ   Dir Mark Robson   US

★ **Stars** Charlton Heston, Ava Gardner, George Kennedy, Lorne Greene, Genevieve Bujold, Richard Roundtree

Mark Robson's *Earthquake* is an excellent dramatic exploitation extravaganza, combining brilliant special effects with a multi-character plot line which is surprisingly above average for this type film. Large cast is headed by Charlton Heston, who comes off better than usual because he is not Superman, instead just one of the gang.

Ava Gardner, ravishingly beautiful, plays Heston's jealous wife, who also is the daughter of Lorne Greene, Heston's architect boss. Gardner's fits of jealous pique concern Genevieve Bujold.

The film spends its first 53 minutes establishing most of the key plot situations, but regularly teases with some foreshocks to the big quake. When that occurs, the first big special effects sequence provides an excellent, unstinting panorama of destruction.

THE EGYPTIAN

1954, 140 mins, ◇ ⓥ   Dir Michael Curtiz   US

★ **Stars** Jean Simmons, Victor Mature, Gene Tierney, Michael Wilding, Bella Darvi, Peter Ustinov

The decision to bring Mika Waltari's masterly scholarly-detailed [novel] *The Egyptian* to the screen must have taken a lot of courage, for this is a long way off the standard spectacle beat. The book tells a strange and unusual story laid against the exotic and yet harshly realistic background of the Egypt of 33 centuries ago, when there was a Pharaoh who believed in one god, and a physician who glimpsed a great truth and tried to live it.

Big coin – around $4.2 million – was splurged on bringing ancient Egypt to life again and the results justify the expense.

A big cast with good marquee appeal goes through its

Clint Eastwood starred in and directed The Eiger Sanction, a spy story that involves spectacular climbing sequences.

paces with obvious enjoyment. In the title part, Edmund Purdom etches a strong handsome profile. As the truth-seeking doctor who grows from weakness to the maturity of a new conviction, Purdom brings *The Egyptian* to life and makes him a man with whom the audience can easily identify and sympathize. Jean Simmons is lovely and warm as the tavern maid. Victor Mature as the robust Horemheb, the soldier who is to become ruler, is a strong asset to the cast.

THE EIGER SANCTION

1975, 125 mins, ◇   Dir Clint Eastwood   US

★ **Stars** Clint Eastwood, George Kennedy, Vonetta McGee, Jack Cassidy, Herdi Bruhl, Thayer David

The Eiger Sanction, based on the novel by Trevanian, focuses on Clint Eastwood, a retired mountain climber and hired assassin, being recalled from retirement by head of a secret intelligence organization for another lethal assignment.

Pic takes its title from the leader's euphemism for

E

assassination, to be carried out on Switzerland's Eiger Mountain during an international team's climb.

To condition himself for the ascent Eastwood flies to the Arizona ranch of George Kennedy, an old climbing friend, who puts him through his paces in the magnificent reaches of Monument Valley.

Eastwood, who also directs and according to studio did his own mountain climbing without doubles, manages fine suspense. His direction displays a knowledge that permits rugged action.

EL CID

1961, 180 mins, ◇ Ⓥ *Dir* Anthony Mann   US, SPAIN, ITALY

★ *Stars* Charlton Heston, Sophia Loren, Raf Vallone, Gary Raymond, John Fraser, Genevieve Page

El Cid is a fast-action, color-rich, corpse-strewn, battle picture. The Spanish scenery is magnificent with a kind of gaunt beauty. The medieval costumes are vivid, and the chain mail and Toledo steel gear impressive. Perhaps the 11th century of art directors Veniero Colasanti and John Moore exceeds reality, but only scholars will complain of

Charlton Heston as El Cid, *the legendary Spanish leader who fought to expel the Moors from Spain.*

that. Action rather than acting characterizes this film.

Yet the film creates respect for its sheer picturemaking skills. Director Anthony Mann, with assists from associate producer Michael Waszynski who worked closely with him, battle manager Yakima Canutt, and a vast number of technicians, have labored to create stunning panoramic images.

Of acting there is less to say after acknowledging that Charlton Heston's masculine personality ideally suits the title role. His powerful performance is the central arch of the narrative. Sophia Loren, as first his sweetheart and later his wife, has a relatively passive role, in the Spanish preference. While Heston is out doing the picture's business – fighting, fighting, fighting – the glamorous Italian has little to do in the last half but keep the lamp in the window.

Two actors in *King of Kings* who remained over in Spain to appear in *El Cid* ended up as bit actors. Hurd Hatfield is the court herald in a couple of scenes, Frank Thring is a most unconvincing Moorish emir with a shaved noggin who lolls about in a harem registering a kind of sulky impatience.

Italy's Raf Vallone is the other man who never has a chance with Chimene. After betraying El Cid he is spared and, at a later period, becomes a follower only to die, tortured, by the invading North African monster, Britain's Herbert Lom. Lom has the curious experience of doing almost all his acting with his face covered to the eyes by a black mask.

Most provocative performance among the supporting players is that of Genevieve Page, as the self-willed princess who protects the weakling brother who becomes king after she, sweet sibling, has the older brother slain. As the sniveling prince, John Fraser starts slowly but ends up creating some conviction.

THE EMERALD FOREST

1985, 113 mins, ◇ ⓥ *Dir* John Boorman   US

★ *Stars* Powers Boothe, Meg Foster, Charley Boorman, Dira Pass, Rui Polonah, Claudio Moreno

Based on an uncredited true story about a Peruvian whose son disappeared in the jungles of Brazil, screenplay trades on numerous enduring myths and legends about the return to nature and growing up in the wild.

Powers Boothe, an American engineer and designer assigned to build an enormous dam in Brazil, loses his young son in the wilderness and, against seemingly hopeless odds, sets out to find him.

Ten years later, the two finally meet up under perilous circumstances. By this time, the son, played by the director's own sprog, Charley Boorman, has become well integrated into the ways of a friendly Indian tribe and has little desire to return to the outside world.

Once he has been exposed to the simple virtues of 'uncivilized' life, Boothe begins to have serious doubts about the nature of his work in the area.

Despite some lumps in the narrative and characterization and some occasionally awkward tension between the documentary realism enforced by the subject and the heavy stylization of the director's approach, film proves engrossing and visually fascinating.

ESCAPE FROM ALCATRAZ

1979, 112 mins, ◇ ⓥ *Dir* Don Siegel   US

★ *Stars* Clint Eastwood, Patrick McGoohan, Fred Ward, Roberts Blossom, Bruce M. Fischer, Paul Benjamin

Considering that the escape itself from rock-bound Alcatraz prison consumes only the film's final half-hour, screenwriter Richard Tuggle [adapting the book by J. Campbell Bruce] and director Don Siegel provide a model of super-efficient filmmaking. From the moment Clint Eastwood walks onto The Rock, until the final title card explaining the three

Clint Eastwood in Escape from Alcatraz, *the story of the 1962 break-out from the 'impregnable' rock-bound prison.*

escapees were never heard from again, *Escape from Alcatraz* is relentless in establishing a mood and pace of unrelieved tension.

Pic's only fault may be an ambiguous ending, tied, of course, to the historical reality of the 1962 escape, only successful one in Alcatraz' 29-year history as America's most repressive penal institution.

Key counterpoint to Eastwood's character comes from Patrick McGoohan as the megalomaniacal warden.

EUREKA STOCKADE

1949, 103 mins, *Dir* Harry Watt   UK, AUSTRALIA

★ *Stars* Chips Rafferty, Gordon Jackson, Peter Finch, Jane Barrett, Jack Lambert, Peter Illing

Eureka Stockade is staged in the middle of the 19th century when the first gold strike in Australia leads to economic chaos in the colony. There are no men to till the land or sail the ships as they have all gone in search of gold. And there is also a large influx of foreigners, all of whom hope to find their fortune.

In an endeavor to save the nation's finances, vicious taxes are imposed on the diggers, and the men themselves are hounded by the police. The gold seekers seek to impose their will by mob law, but a leader arises.

If action alone could make a picture, this one would very nearly take full marks, for the entire emphasis is on movement, and the pitched battle comes as a climax to a series of big-scale scenes. The main weakness of the production, which contributes in large measure to its failure to grip, is the low standard of acting.

EXCALIBUR

1981, 140 mins, ◇ *Dir* John Boorman   US

★ *Stars* Nigel Terry, Nicol Williamson, Nicholas Clay, Helen Mirren, Cheri Lunghi, Corin Redgrave

Excalibur is exquisite, a near-perfect blend of action, romance, fantasy and philosophy, finely acted and beautifully filmed by director John Boorman and cinematographer Alex Thomson.

It is essentially the legend of King Arthur, embellished a bit by Boorman and co-scripter Rospo Pallenberg, working from the Malory classic, *Morte d'Arthur*.

Filmed in timeless Irish locales, the film rests solidly on a feeling that this, indeed, must have been what life was like in the feudal ages, even as it resists being pinned to any historical point and accepts magic and sorcery on faith.

Nicol Williamson stands out early as the wizard Merlin, at times a magician, flim-flam artist and philosopher, always interesting. The tangle of lust and betrayal that leads to Arthur's conception, the planting of Excalibur in the stone and Arthur's rise to Camelot after extracting it, is followed by restlessness and more dark deeds.

If *Excalibur* has a major fault, it's a somewhat extended sequence of the Knights of the Round Table in search of the Grail, seemingly ill-established and overdrawn.

EXODUS

1960, 212 mins, ◇ Ⓥ *Dir* Otto Preminger   US

★ *Stars* Paul Newman, Eva Maria Saint, Ralph Richardson, Peter Lawford, Lee J. Cobb, Sal Mineo

Transposing Leon Uris' hefty novel to the screen was not an easy task. It is to the credit of director Otto Preminger and scenarist Dalton Trumbo that they have done as well as they have. One can, however, wish that they had been blessed with more dramatic incisiveness. (Estimated cost of pic was $3.5–4 million.)

The picture wanders frequently in attempting to bring into focus various political and personal aspirations that existed within the Jewish nationalist movement itself as well as in regards to Arab opposition to the partitioning of Palestine and the unhappy role that Great Britain played as custodian of the status quo while a young United Nations pondered the fate of a new nation.

One of the overwhelming moments is played aboard a rusty old freighter in which 611 Jews of all ages, from all over the face of Europe and spirited out of an internment camp on Cyprus under the nose of the British, attempt to sail to Palestine. The whole spirit that brought Israel into being is reflected in this particular sequence toward the end of the first part of the film. It's a real dramatic gem.

The romance that develops slowly between young, dedicated Hagana leader Paul Newman and Eva Marie Saint, as a widowed American who contributes her nursing abilities to Jewish refugees on Cyprus and later in Palestine, as Arabs attack the new settlers, is conventional. Techincally Newman gives a sound performance, but he fails to give the role warmth. Saint has several good scenes and makes the most of them, as does Ralph Richardson, a sympathetic British general.

Lee J. Cobb gives his customary dependable, thoroughly professionl performance as a conservative elder Hagana community leader, father of Newman and brother of the fanatical violence advocate played by David Opatoshu. The brothers' silent meeting after years of separation through a barred slot in a prison door is great pictorial drama.

Sal Mineo as a loyal Irgun youngster, who has been brutalized by the Nazis, is excellent and John Derek stands out too as an Arab whose friendship for Newman and his family goes back to boyhood.

THE EXTERMINATOR

1980, 101 mins, ◇ Ⓥ *Dir* James Glickenhaus   US

★ *Stars* Christopher George, Samantha Eggar, Robert Ginty, Steve James

For his second pic, writer-director James Glickenhaus commits the major sin of shooting an action film with little action. Contrived script instead opts for grotesque violence in a series of glum, distasteful scenes.

The Exterminator returns to New York City for a listlessly paced tale of Robert Ginty suddenly deciding to avenge his war buddy, paralyzed from an encounter with a youth gang. Absence of proper transition scenes and script's frequent reliance upon coincidence loses credibility for Ginty's actions early on.

Christopher George's walkthrough as a policeman is regrettable, while Samantha Eggar as both the buddy's doctor and George's girlfriend must have calculated that this travesty would never be released.

EYE OF THE TIGER

1986, 90 mins, ◇ Ⓥ *Dir* Richard Sarafian   US

★ *Stars* Gary Busey, Yaphet Kotto, Seymour Cassel, Bert Remsen, William Smith

Gary Busey is yet another lone vigilante out to avenge his wife's brutal murder in *Eye of the Tiger*. The pic opens with Buck Matthews' (Busey) release from prison. Matthews' hometown is being terrorized by a gang of motorcycle-riding drug peddlers, all of whom wear black with black helmets and ride in packs.

The motorcycle gang visits Matthews' house, killing his wife, beating him up and sending their daughter into a catatonic state. The rest of the film is about Matthews' one-man quest for vengeance, most of which is set to the pounding beat of rock music. The best character in the film has to be J.B. Deveraux (Yaphet Kotto), one of the sheriff's lackeys.

Nigel Havers and Nick Nolte set off on a raid with Nolte's tribe in Farewell to the King, set in war-torn Borneo.

FAREWELL TO THE KING

1989, 117 mins ◇ ⊘ *Dir* John Milius   US

★ *Stars* Nick Nolte, Nigel Havers, James Fox, Marilyn Tokuda, Frank McRae, Gerry Lopez

The cliches are as thick as the foliage in *Farewell to the King*, John Milius' adaptation of a novel by French author-filmmaker Pierre Schoendoerffer. Pic recycles familiar situations and stock characters in an overlong actioner that never builds to a spiritual climax.

Two British army officers (Nigel Havers and Frank McRae) are parachuted into the Borneo jungle to rally the tribes against imminent Japanese invasion in the latter days of World War II. They come across a virile and fulfilled Nick Nolte, playing a freedom-loving white man who's anxious to protect his natives from the barbarities of civilization.

Nolte, however, needs no further prompting to fight when the Japanese slaughter his own family. Hitting the Rambo warpath, the ex-Yank sergeant (who deserted after General MacArthur's defeat at Corregidor) performs a ruthless clean-up operation.

Nolte, in a purely exterior performance, never rises to the nobility and tragic majesty the at-first sceptical British officers finally see in him. Havers is a sympathetic presence in

an equally empty role. Other performers, including James Fox as Havers' commanding officer, are treated as trite thumbnail portraits.

FATHOM

1967, 100 mins, ◇ *Dir* Leslie Martinson   US

★ *Stars* Raquel Welch, Anthony Franciosa, Ronald Fraser, Greta Chi, Richard Briers, Tom Adams

Fathom, lensed on location in Spain to take full advantage of scenic backdrops, is a melange of melodramatic ingredients personalized by the lush presence of Raquel Welsh. Actress stars with Tony Franciosa in this production, highlighted by some exciting parachute scenes.

Script, based on the Larry Forrester novel, was obviously triggered by the real-life incident of an American H-bomb accidentally lost off the coast of Spain.

Welch's services, as a parachute jumper, are enlised to help recover what is described as an electronic device which will fire the bomb, now in the possession of certain evil forces, and which was not retrieved at the time the bomb itself was salvaged.

FEAR IS THE KEY

1973, 105 mins, ◇ *Dir* Michael Tuchner   UK

★ *Stars* Barry Newman, Suzy Kendall, John Vernon, Dolph Sweet, Ben Kingsley, Ray McAnally

Sustained interest and suspense mark *Fear Is the Key*, well-made action stuff [from the novel by Alistair MacLean]

including the obligatory auto chase routine around the highways and byways of Louisiana where pic was shot.

Barry Newman and Suzy Kendall are top-featured, he as a deepsea salvage expert, she as an oil heiress and kidnap victim. When Newman's wife, brother and child are shot out of the sky while fetching a salvage cargo of priceless gems, he goes undercover in cahoots with the law to avenge the killings. An elaborate charade ensues wherein he feigns the murder of a cop and kidnap of Kendall from a courtroom, all designed to land him in the lair of the villains who are contriving to retrieve the gems from the aircraft on the floor of the Gulf of Mexico.

Michael Tuchner's direction, abetted by tight editing, unravels the yarn at a crisp clip. The auto pursuit sequence is superbly staged by stunt coordinator Carey Loftin and crew.

55 DAYS AT PEKING

1963, 150 mins, ◇ ⊘ *Dir* Nicholas Ray   US

★ *Stars* Charlton Heston, Ava Gardner, David Niven, Flora Robson, John Ireland, Leo Genn

Producer Samuel Bronston shows characteristic lavishness in the pictorial scope, the vivid and realistic sets and extras by the thousands in his reproduction of the capital of Imperial China in 1900. The lensing was in Spain where the company built an entire city.

The screenplay presumably adheres to the historical basics in its description of the violent rebellion of the 'Boxers' against the major powers of the period – Great Britain, Russia, France, Germany, Italy, Japan, and the United States – because of their commercial exploitation of tradition-bound and unmodern (backward) China. These market-seeking nations have in their Peking outpost gallant fighting men who, although only a few hundred in number, withstand the merciless 55-day siege. *55 Days at Peking* takes sides with imperialism.

While Ray is identified as director, some of the battle scenes were actually directed by Andrew Marton. This came to be in a period when Ray was ill.

David Niven plays the part of the British embassy head who stubbornly refuses to surrender, risking the safety of all about him, including his wife and two children. Both he and Charlton Heston perform with conviction, Heston as the American Marine major who commands the defense. Ava Gardner's role is not too well conceived however. Hers is the part of the widow of a Russian bigshot who killed himself upon learning of his wife's infidelity with a Chinese official.

Lynne Sue Moon gives a poignant performance as an Oriental 12-year-old whose American father, an army captain, is killed in battle. Flora Robson appears strikingly authentic as the Dowager Empress Tzu Hsi whose sympathies lie with the outlaws.

Jack Hildyard's photography is excellent, particularly in getting on the big screen the savage attack scenes which take up the ma jor part of the picture. Dimitri Tiomkin provides engaging music.

FIRE BIRDS

1990, 85 mins, ◇ ⊘ *Dir* David Green   US

★ *Stars* Nicolas Cage, Tommy Lee Jones, Sean Young, Bert Rhine

Originally titled *Wings of the Apache* for the Apache assault helicopters prominently featured, *Fire Birds* is a paean to Yankee air power, showing the US Army as a take-charge outfit able to kick the butt of those South American drug cartel jerks.

Not surprisingly, given changing times and politics, *Fire Birds* has a tongue-in-cheek aspect. Camaraderie and rat-a-tat-tat dialog may have started out as fun but emerges at times as a satire of the genre.

Formula script, which inevitably recalls *Top Gun*, has Nicolas Cage training to use the army's Apache aircraft while vainly trying to rekindle a romance with old flame Sean Young. Tommy Lee Jones is dead-on as the taskmaster instructor who cornily singles out Cage for rough treatment. Film's main novelty is having Young also sent into combat instead of being the woman sitting on the sidelines.

FIREFOX

1982, 137 mins, ◇ ⊘ *Dir* Clint Eastwood   US

★ *Stars* Clint Eastwood, Freddie Jones, David Huffman, Warren Clarke, Ronald Lacey, Kenneth Colley

Firefox is lethargic, characterless and at least a half-hour too long, a Cold War espionage saga [from the novel by Craig Thomas] about an American pilot smuggled into the USSR to steal an advanced fighter jet.

It all sounded good on paper – Clint Eastwood, as a retired ace flyer, infiltrating the Russian Air Force to spirit away the supposedly top-secret Firefox, a plane capable of Mach 5 speed and equipped with a thought-controlled weapons system.

But Eastwood, who generally displays astuteness when controlling his own projects has inexplicably dropped the ball here. Despite the tense mission being depicted, there's no suspense, excitement or thrills to be had, and laxidaisical pacing gives viewers plenty of time to ponder the gaping implausibilities.

FIRST BLOOD

1982, 94 mins, ◇ ⊘ *Dir* Ted Kotcheff   US

★ *Stars* Sylvester Stallone, Richard Crenna, Brian Dennehy, David Caruso, Jack Starrett, Michael Talbot

Sylvester Stallone plays a former Green Beret, a 'killing machine' who's so tough if there had been one more of him, the Viet Cong wouldn't have had a chance.

Arriving unshaven at the quiet community of Hope, Stallone is greeted by sheriff Brian Dennehy, who does not invite him to join the local Lion's club. In fact, Dennehy won't even let him linger for a sandwich. This naturally upsets the taciturn Stallone and he winds up at the town's slammer. Beating up the whole station house, he escapes into the woods.

Richard Crenna shows up, a Green Beret colonel who trained Stallone. They trap Stallone in a mine and blast the dickens out of it with a rocket. But our boy commandeers an army truck and machine gun and goes back to level Dennehy's quiet little town.

Director Ted Kotcheff has all sorts of trouble with this mess, aside from credibility. Supposedly, the real villain here is society itself, which invented a debacle like Vietnam and must now deal with its lingering tragedies. But *First Blood* cops out completely on that one, not even trying to find a solution to Stallone's problems.

THE FLAME AND THE ARROW

1950, 89 mins, ◇ ⑰   *Dir* Jacques Tourneur   US

★ *Stars* Burt Lancaster, Virginia Mayo, Robert Douglas, Nick Cravat, Aline MacMahon, Frank Allenby

The Flame and the Arrow is a romantic costume drama geared to attract action audiences. Setting is medieval Italy with a Robin Hood plot of how injustice is put down under the daring leadership of a heroic mountaineer.

Burt Lancaster does the latter, portraying the Arrow of the title with just the right amount of dash.

Virginia Mayo is the niece of the hated ruler. She figures romantically with Lancaster in the byplay and also gives an assist to the rebellion of the mountain people against Hessian cruelty.

Jacques Tourneur does not overlook the development of any number of interesting characters. Best of these is Cravat, partner of Lancaster during latter's circus-vaude tumbling days before entering films.

FLESH + BLOOD

1985, 126 mins, ◇ ⑰   *Dir* Paul Verhoeven   US

★ *Stars* Rutger Hauer, Jennifer Jason Leigh, Tom Burlinson, Jack Thompson, Susan Tyrrell, Ron Lacey

Flesh + Blood is a vivid and muscular, if less than fully startling, account of lust, savagery, revenge, betrayal and assorted other dark doings in the Middle Ages, toplining Rutger Hauer.

Drama opens with a successful siege on a castle by Lord Arnolfini (Fernando Hillbeck), who has recently been ousted from the premises. After promising them loot, Hillbeck goes back on his word and banishes the mercenaries who have helped him in his conquest.

Before long, warrior leader Martin (Hauer) and his rag-tag band gets theirs back by nearly killing Hillbeck in an ambush and capturing lovely young Agnes (Jennifer Jason Leigh), the intended bride of Hillbeck's studious son Steven (Tom Burlinson).

Director Paul Verhoeven has told his tale in visceral, involving fashion and, for the amount of carnage that piles up, explicit gore is kept to a minimum.

Fine use is made of Belmonte Castle (on view in *El Cid*) and other Spanish locales.

THE FLIGHT OF THE PHOENIX

1965, 149 mins, ◇ ⑰   *Dir* Robert Aldrich   US

★ *Stars* James Stewart, Richard Attenborough, Peter Finch, Hardy Kruger, Ernest Borgnine, Ian Bannen

The Flight of the Phoenix is a grim, tenseful, realistic tale of a small group of men forced down on the North African desert and their desperate efforts to build a single-engine plane out of the wreckage of the twin job in which they crashed during a sandstorm. Robert Aldrich's filmic translation of the Elleston Trevor book is an often-fascinating and superlative piece of filmmaking highlighted by standout performances and touches that show producer-director at his best.

James Stewart, as the pilot of a desert oil company cargo-passenger plane who flies by the seat of his pants, is strongly cast in role and is strongly backed by entire cast. Each, seemingly hand-picked for the individual parts, are everyday persons who might either be employees of an oil company or business visitors.

A young aircraft designer, who had been visiting his brother at the oil camp, comes up with the extraordinary idea that a make-shift plane might be fashioned to fly the survivors to safety. So work starts, and it is this endeavor in its various phases that makes the story.

FOUR FEATHERS

1929, 80 mins, ⊗   *Dir* Merian C. Cooper, Ernest B. Schoedsack
US

★ *Stars* Richard Arlen, Fay Wray, Clive Brook, William Powell, Theodore von Eltz, Noah Beery

Four Feathers is a good picture. Merian C. Cooper and Ernest B. Schoedsack were the producers. They made *Chang*. It is no secret that *Feathers'* treatment was primarily photographic. The dramatics followed. Cooper and Schoedsack must also have been the directors of the story part, for no one else is credited. Nor is a photographer named.

Have you ever seen a herd of hippo slide down a steep bank of a jungle watering place? Have you seen a large family of baboons hop from limb to limb to escape a forest fire? Or a huge army of black savages dashing to battle on

British Lion Film Corporation Ltd. re-presents · AN ALEXANDER KORDA PRODUCTION · A. E. W. MASON'S "THE FOUR FEATHERS" with John Clements, Ralph Richardson, C. Aubrey Smith, June Duprez · Directed by ZOLTAN KORDA · Colour by TECHNICOLOR

John Clements leads disgraced British Army officer Ralph Richardson through the desert in The Four Feathers.

white camels? These three items are *Four Feathers*.

The white feather is the symbol of cowardice in the British army. The principal character and subsequent hero of A.W. Mason's novel receives four white feathers.

Tale is set late in the last century and is highly reminiscent of *Beau Geste*. Pictorially they are much the same.

Richard Arlen's performance is good most of the while, excellent at times. William Powell is next with the most to do and does it like Powell. Clive Brook is not handed his usual weighty part and isn't impressive because of that, while Theodore von Eltz, as the lesser of the four chums, has no opportunity to be more than satisfactory. Fay Wray only has to look good.

his pals and his fiancee hand him white feathers, indicative of cowardice. The next day he disappears. Alone and unaided in Egypt, he goes through harrowing ordeals to gain his reinstatement in their eyes.

June Duprez, the fiancee, is the only woman in the cast. She postulates prettily, with little else to do. Rest of the cast is excellent, with C. Aubrey Smith, enacting a lovable, elderly bore. John Clements, the hero, is excellent.

Photography is excellent along with the direction.

THE FOUR FEATHERS

1939, 130 mins, ◇ Ⓥ *Dir* Zoltan Korda   UK

★ **Stars** John Clements, Ralph Richardson, C. Aubrey Smith, June Duprez

The Four Feathers has been filmed before, with the book [by A.E.W. Mason] from which it was adapted having enjoyed big world sale.

A young British officer resigns from his regiment the night before it embarks for an Egyptian campaign. Three of

FOUR FRIGHTENED PEOPLE

1934, 95 mins, *Dir* Cecil B. DeMille   US

★ **Stars** Claudette Colbert, Herbert Marshall, Mary Boland, William Gargan, Leo Carrillo, Tetsu Komai

The adventures of the quartet who are lost in the Malayan jungle are episodic and disjointed, running the gamut from stark tragedy to unbelievable farce. The pic is based on a novel by E. Arnot-Robertson.

The four frightened people are thrown together by a

bubonic plague outbreak on the Dutch coastal steamer which was carrying them from their respective ports of departure back to civilization. In self-preservation they shanghai a lifeboat and meet a half-caste guide who thinks he can safely trek them through the jungle to the sea.

The bombastic newspaper correspondent (William Gargan) talks like something out of Richard Harding Davis and never coincides with the post-*Front Page* conceptions of newspaperdom. Herbert Marshall is a chemist interested in Dutch plantation rubber, licked by life and a wife, who finds romance with the begoggled geography teacher from Chicago (Claudette Colbert) who likewise asserts herself in the jungle. Mary Boland is the wife of a British official which accounts for her presence. The DeMilleian bathtub penchant evidences itself even in the jungle when Colbert, sans cheaters and very Eve (when a playful chimpanzee steals her clothes) emerges with plenty of s.a. for both men.

An introductory title heralds that the film was actually shot in South Pacific locations.

THE FOUR MUSKETEERS

1975, 108 mins, ◇   *Dir* Richard Lester   PANAMA

★ *Stars* Oliver Reed, Raquel Welch, Richard Chamberlain, Michael York, Frank Finlay, Christopher Lee

The Four Musketeers continues the story of Oliver Reed, Richard Chamberlain, Frank Finlay and Michael York as they joust with evil plotter Charlton Heston and evil seductress Faye Dunaway, defend fair lady queen Geraldine Chaplin, bypass imbecile King Jean Pierre Cassel, and eventually triumph over arch fiend Christopher Lee.

The same mixture of teenybopper naughtiness, acne spiciness, contrived tastelessness and derring-don't as found in the earlier film (*The Three Musketeers*) are laid on with the same deft trowel herein. Perhaps the film is a triumph of controlled and deliberate mediocrity, but it still closer resembles a clumsy carbon of a bad satire on the original.

THE FRENCH CONNECTION

1971, 104 mins, ◇ ⓥ   *Dir* William Friedkin   US

★ *Stars* Gene Hackman, Fernando Rey, Roy Scheider, Tony LoBianco, Marcel Bozzuffi, Frederic De Pasquale

Academy Award 1971: Best Picture

So many changes have been made in Robin Moore's taut, factual reprise of one of the biggest narcotics hauls in New York police history that only the skeleton remains, but producer and screenwriter have added enough fictional flesh to provide director William Friedkin and his overall topnotch cast with plenty of material, and they make the most of it.

Gene Hackman stops French drug runner Marcel Bozzuffi after a hair-raising car chase in **The French Connection.**

Gene Hackman and Roy Scheider are very believable as two hard-nosed narcotics officers who stumble onto what turned out to be the biggest narcotics haul to date. As suave and cool as the two cops are overworked, tired and mean, Fernando Rey is the French mastermind of the almost-perfect criminal plan.

Friedkin includes a great elevated train-automobile chase sequence that becomes almost too tense to be enjoyable, especially for New Yorkers who are familiar with such activities.

Shot almost entirely in and around New York, Owen Roizman's fluid color camera explores most of Manhattan and much of Brooklyn without prettifying the backgrounds .

FRENCH CONNECTION II

1975, 119 mins, ◇ *Dir* John Frankenheimer   US

★ **Stars** Gene Hackman, Fernando Rey, Bernard Fresson, Jean-Pierre Castaldi, Charles Millot, Cathleen Nesbitt

John Frankenheimer's *French Connection II* is both complementary to, yet distinctly different from, William Friedkin's *The French Connection.*

Gene Hackman as Popeye Doyle goes to Marseilles in search of heroin czar Fernando Rey (also encoring from the first pic). The assignment in reality is a setup (thereby implying that high-level law enforcement corruption still exists), and Hackman is duly kidnapped, drugged and left for dead by criminal Rey.

Hackman's addiction and withdrawal sequences are terrifyingly real and make uncompromisingly clear the personal and social horror of drug abuse.

This plot turn is both intelligent and clever. Bernard Fresson is excellent as the French narc who must cope not only with his country's dope problem, but also Hackman's unruly presence.

Hackman's performance is another career highlight, ranging from cocky narc, Ugly American, helpless addict, humbled ego and relentless avenger.

FRISCO KID

1935, 80 mins, *Dir* Lloyd Bacon   US

★ **Stars** James Cagney, Margaret Lindsay, Ricardo Cortez, Lili Damita, Donald Woods, Barton MacLane

So similar to *Barbary Coast* as to be almost its twin *Frisco Kid* is, nevertheless, good entertainment. Since an identical locale and period are used in both, outstanding characters have been twice fictionized and resemblances are great.

Vigilantes, meetings, hangings, burning of the Coast, crusading newspaper and other details are used once again. For its principal character *Frisco Kid* has James Cagney as against *Barbary's* Miriam Hopkins. That is the only point in which the two films differ to any real extent.

Through Cagney this picture has the benefit of a more vigorous central character. Romantic phase is secondary and, with Cagney to handle the punches, *Frisco* takes in more territory and contains more action.

Story traces the career of Cagney from his arrival as a poor sailor through his rise to power and riches by right of might, his almost hopeless romance with a girl from the other and nicer side of the tracks, and finally his reformation.

GATOR

1976, 115 mins, ◇ ⊛ *Dir* Burt Reynolds   US

★ **Stars** Burt Reynolds, Jack Weston, Lauren Hutton, Jerry Reed, Alice Ghostley, Dub Taylor

This followup to *White Lightning* never takes itself seriously, veering as it does through many incompatible dramatic and violent moods for nearly two hours.

William Norton's coloring books script picks up Burt Reynolds' Gator McKlusky character, now on parole from moonshining time. State governor Mike Douglas can't realize political ambitions until a notorious back-water county, run by crime czar Jerry Reed, gets cleaned up.

Enter Jack Weston as Dept of Justice undercover agent, who (somewhat unclearly) blackmails Reynolds into working against old pal Reed.

Reynolds clearly was shot down as a director by the story structure which also works to defeat much of the time even his screen charisma and credibility.

THE GENERAL DIED AT DAWN

1936, 98 mins, ⊛ *Dir* Lewis Milestone   US

★ **Stars** Gary Cooper, Madeleine Carroll, Akim Tamiroff, Dudley Digges, Porter Hall, William Frawley

In Clifford Odets' first film attempt his hand is distinctly visible throughout. But without stars Gary Cooper and Madeleine Carroll to top an A-1 cast, all the splendid trouping, all the splendid imagery of direction, the photography, music and general production might well have jelled into an artistic flop.

Story supplied by Charles G. Booth's novel is an old-fashioned piece of claptrap. It has to do with intrigue in the Far East, gun-runners, smugglers, and spies. Odets has left all that alone but has underlined Gary Cooper as the agent for the ammunition runners by making him engaged in the dangerous work not because of the adventure or money, but because he's trying to help the downtrodden Chinese rid themselves of a money-grubbing, rapacious Chinese war lord, General Yang (Akim Tamiroff).

Cooper, as the daredevil American, is at top form throughout; Madeleine Carroll as his vis-a-vis in a difficult assignment, impresses. Comparatively unknown, Tamiroff and Hall turn in exceptionally strong performances. Hall, as a sniveling, broken-down villain, handles an unusual job beautifully; John O'Hara, the novelist, does a bit as a newspaperman, looking the part. Allegedly Odets, director Milestone and Sidney Skolsky, Hollywood columnist, are also in for a shot or two, but if so it's their secret which scene it is.

GENGHIS KHAN

1965, 124 mins, ◇ *Dir* Henry Levin   US

★ **Stars** Stephen Boyd, Omar Sharif, James Mason, Eli Wallach, Francoise Dorleac, Telly Savalas

Genghis Khan is an introspective biopic about the Mongol chief Temujin who unified Asia's warring tribes in the Dark Ages. An international cast delivers okay performances in occasionally trite script which emphasizes personal motivation rather than sweeping pageantry.

The screenplay, from story by Berkely Mather, hinges on continuing vendetta between tribal chieftain Stephen Boyd and Omar Sharif, once enslaved by Boyd but escaping to forge an empire that threatened western and eastern civilization some eight centuries back.

Sharif does a near-excellent job in projecting with ease the zeal which propelled Temujin from bondage to a political education in China, and finally to realizing at death his dream of Mongol unity. Boyd is less successful as the brutish thorn in Sharif's side, being overall too restrained for sustained characterization despite flashes of earthiness.

Most unusual characterization is essayed by James Mason, playing the neatly-contrasting urbane imperial counsellor who mentors political savvy.

GLEAMING THE CUBE

1988, 105 mins, ◇ Ⓥ *Dir* Graeme Clifford   US

★ **Stars** Christian Slater, Steven Bauer, Min Luong, Art Chudabala, Le Tuan

A skateboarding-obsessed suburban kid (Christian Slater) goes about solving – exploitation style – the death of his adopted Vietnamese brother (Art Chudabala), who Slater knows in his heart was too smart to commit suicide.

Slater skateboards all over Little Saigon, skilfully enough to elude Vietnamese hoods on his trail while conducting some Chuck Norris-inspired sleuthing.

Slater, who sounds as if he is trying to imitate Jack Nicholson, is the only character who has a shading of personality. His skateboarding buddies are funny, considering one needs a glossary to translate their dialog, while the Vietnamese are mostly sleazy cardboard figures. The police are inept and the mastermind villain (Richard Herd) seems to be right out of the Method acting school.

Omar Sharif (on horse), Woody Strode, Stephen Boyd and Telly Savalas in Genghis Khan, *biopic of the Mongol chief.*

GOLD

1974, 118 mins, ◇ Ⓥ *Dir* Peter Hunt   UK

★ **Stars** Roger Moore, Susannah York, Ray Milland, Bradford Dillman, John Gielgud, Simon Sabela

Power of a major physical disaster as theme for an exciting motion picture [based on Wilbur Smith's novel *Goldmine*] is evidenced in this British item, lensed entirely in the South Africa locale of its well-developed narrative. Punishing action is tempered by a modern love story.

Moore is a tough mine foreman unwittingly manipulated by an unscrupulous gang of financiers who want to flood the mine to raise the price of gold on the world market.

Particular attention has been given to the terrifying underground sequences, and tremendous realism is accomplished in an opening tragedy of men caught in the grip of a sudden flood and later in the climactic flooding.

Moore delivers in pat fashion and Susannah York is a love as the wife of the mine operator who is used by her husband in the web of deceit woven by an international syndicate whom he represents.

GOLDEN RENDEZVOUS

1977, 103 mins, ◇ Ⓥ *Dir* Ashley Lazarus   US

★ **Stars** Richard Harris, Ann Turkel, David Janssen, Burgess Meredith, John Vernon, Gordon Jackson

Despite an overabundance of plot, deaths, and explosions, there's virtually nothing in this puddle of a mid-ocean thriller that wouldn't make a 12-year-old cringe in embarrassment.

Pic [adapted from an Alistair MacLean novel] tells the

tale of the Caribbean Star, a combination cargo ship and floating casino, hijacked by mercenary John Vernon. Following the orders of an unknown mastermind, he and his men, with the aid of an atomic device, plan to exchange the captured passengers and bomb for the golden contents of a US Treasury ship.

And so it goes, albeit not as simply, until First Officer Richard Harris, accompanied by Ann Turkel and Gordon Jackson, step in to save the day.

GOLDFINGER

1964, 112 mins, ◇ Ⓥ *Dir* Guy Hamilton   UK

★ *Stars* Sean Connery, Honor Blackman, Gert Frobe, Shirley Eaton, Tania Mallet, Harold Sakata

There's not the least sign of staleness in this third sample of the Bond 007 formula. Some liberties have been taken with Ian Fleming's original novel but without diluting its flavor. The mood is set before the credits show up, with Sean Connery making an arrogant pass at a chick and spying a thug creeping up from behind; he's reflected in the femme's eyeballs. So he heaves the heavy into bathful of water and connects it deftly to a handy supply of electricity.

Thereafter the plot gets its teeth into the real business, which is the duel between Bond and Goldfinger. The latter plans to plant an atomic bomb in Fort Knox and thus contaminate the US hoard of the yellow stuff so that it can't be touched, and thus increase tenfold the value of his own gold, earned by hard international smuggling.

Connery repeats his suave portrayal of the punch-packing Bond, who can find his way around the wine-list as easily as he can negotiate a dame. But, if backroom boys got

Sean Connery as James Bond with the 'golden girl', Shirley Eaton, in Goldfinger.

star billing, it's deserved by Ken Adam, who has designed the production with a wealth of enticing invention. There's a ray-gun that cuts through any metal, and threatens to carve Bond down the middle. There's Goldfinger's automobile - cast in solid gold. And his farm is stocked with furniture that moves at the press of a button.

Honor Blackman makes a fine, sexy partner for Bond. As Pussy Galore, Goldfinger's pilot for his private plane, she does not take things lying down - she's a judo expert who throws Bond until the final k.o. when she's tumbled herself.

Gert Frobe, too, is near-perfect casting as the resourceful Goldfinger, an amoral tycoon who treats gold-cornering as a business like any other.

GRAND PRIX

1966, 179 mins, ◇ Ⓥ *Dir* John Frankenheimer   US

★ *Stars* James Garner, Eva Marie Saint, Yves Montand, Toshiro Mifune, Brian Bedford, Jessica Walter

The roar and whine of engines sending men and machines hurtling over the 10 top road and track courses of Europe, the US and Mexico – the Grand Prix circuits – are the prime motivating forces of this action-crammed adventure that director John Frankenheimer and producer Edward Lewis

Yves Montand is rescued by marshals in Grand Prix, a look at the world of Formula 1 racing, on and off the track.

have interlarded with personal drama that is sometimes introspectively revealing, occasionally mundane, but generally a most serviceable framework.

Frankenheimer has shrewdly varied the length and the importance of the races that figure in the film and the overplay of running commentary on the various events, not always distinct above the roar of motors, imparts a documentary vitality. The director, moreover, frequently divides his outsized screen into sectional panels for a sort of montage interplay of reactions of the principals – a stream of consciousness commentary – that adroitly prevents the road running from overwhelming the personal drama.

There is a curious thing, however, about the exposition of the characters in this screenplay. Under cold examination they are stock characters. James Garner, American competitor in a field of Europeans, is somewhat taciturn, unencumbered by marital involvement. Yves Montand has a wife in name and forms a genuine attachment for American fashion writer Eva Marie Saint, a divorcee. Brian Bedford is the emotionally confused Britisher competing against the memory of his champion-driver brother and whose compulsion to be a champion almost wrecks his marriage to whilom American actress-model Jessica Walter.

GRAND THEFT AUTO

1977, 89 mins, ◇ ⓥ *Dir* Ron Howard   US

★ **Stars** Ron Howard, Nancy Morgan, Marion Ross, Pete Isacksen, Barry Cahill, Hoke Howell

Grand Theft Auto is a non-stop orgy of comic destructiveness.

Ron Howard has directed with a broad but amiable and well-disciplined touch in this screwball comedy about his elopement with heiress Nancy Morgan from LA to Las Vegas, with her father Barry Cahill and dozens of others in pursuit. Howard never tries to hog the screen and lets his co-stars have plenty of funny moments. Morgan is pretty and charming as his spunky partner, and it's a nice touch that Howard lets her drive the getaway car, a gleaming black-and-tan Rolls-Royce.

Aiso along for the chase are Marion Ross as the angry mother of Morgan's oafish fiance, played amusingly straight by Paul Linke, and d.j. Don Steele, who broadcasts a cynical running commentary from a helicopter.

GRAY LADY DOWN

1978, 111 mins, ◇ ⓥ *Dir* David Greene   US

★ **Stars** Charlton Heston, David Carradine, Stacy Keach, Ned Beatty, Stephen McHattie, Ronny Cox

Charlton Heston is back in jeopardy. He's 60 miles off the coast of Connecticut stuck with 41 other sailors on the edge of an ocean canyon in a nuclear submarine, waiting for Stacy Keach to organize a rescue mission. If Keach doesn't hurry one of three disasters will soon happen: water pressure will crush the sub's hull, oxygen will run out, or the boat will slip off the ledge.

David Carradine and Ned Beatty enter the scene after Heston and crew suffer a pair of double setbacks. First their surfacing vessel is rammed by a Norwegian freighter and plunges straight down. Then an earth tremor covers the sub's escape hatch.

Up to this point things are fairly routine [in a story based on the novel *Event 1000* by David Lavallee]. Heston looks courageous; Ronny Cox, the second in command, freaks out; some crew members get sick, and a handful die; Heston's on-shore wife is informed of her husband's condition and adopts a visage of sadness; Keach, a very formal officer, promises Heston and his crew that everything will be all right.

But the second disaster – the escape hatch burial – calls for special action. Enter Carradine, a subdued Navy captain and inventor of an experimental diving vessel known as the Snark, and his assistant, Beatty. They resemble a disaster movie's Laurel and Hardy. They're a nice twist.

THE GREATEST SHOW ON EARTH

1952, 151 mins, ◇ ⓥ *Dir* Cecil B. DeMille   US

★ **Stars** Betty Hutton, Cornel Wilde, Charlton Heston, Dorothy Lamour, Gloria Grahame, James Stewart

Academy Award 1952: Best Picture

The Greatest Show on Earth is as apt a handle for Cecil B. DeMille's Technicolored version of the Ringling Bros.-Barnum & Bailey circus as it is for the sawdust extravaganza itself. This is the circus with more entertainment, more thrills, more spangles and as much Big Top atmosphere as RB-B&B itself can offer.

As has come to be expected from DeMille, the story line is not what could be termed subtle. Betty Hutton is pic-

Charlton Heston in this slice of life under the big top - **The Greatest Show on Earth.**

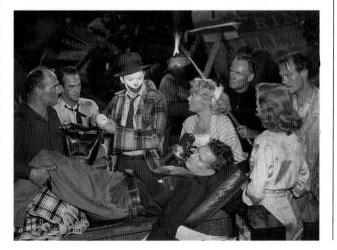

tured as the 'queen flyer' who has a yen for Charlton Heston, the circus manager. Lad has sawdust for blood, however. To strengthen the show and thus enable it to play out a full season, he imports another aerialist, the flamboyant and debonair Sebastian (Cornel Wilde). Latter promptly falls for her and she rifts with Heston. That's quickly exploited by elephant girl Gloria Grahame, who also finds Heston a pretty attractive guy.

James Stewart is woven into the pic as an extraneous but appealing plot element. He's pictured as a police-sought medico who never removes his clown makeup.

THE GREAT RACE

1965, 157 mins, ◇ ⓥ *Dir* Blake Edwards   US

★ **Stars** Jack Lemmon, Tony Curtis, Natalie Wood, Peter Falk, Keenan Wynn, Arthur O'Connell

The Great Race is a big, expensive, whopping, comedy extravaganza, long on slapstick and near-inspired tomfoolery whose tongue-in-cheek treatment liberally sprinkled with corn frequently garners belly laughs.

A certain nostalgic flavor is achieved, both in the 1908 period of an automobile race from New York to Paris and Blake Edwards' broad borrowing from *The Prisoner of Zenda* tale and an earlier Laurel and Hardy comedy for some of his heartiest action.

Characters carry an old-fashioned zest when it was the fashion to hiss the villain and cheer the hero. Slotting into this category, never has there been a villain so dastardly as Jack Lemmon nor a hero so whitely pure as Tony Curtis, rivals in the great race staged by an auto manufacturer to prove his car's worth.

Strongly abetting the two male principals is Natalie Wood as a militant suffragette who wants to be a reporter and sells a NY newspaper publisher on allowing her to enter the race and covering it for his sheet.

To carry on the overall spirit, Curtis always is garbed in snowy white, Lemmon in black, a gent whose every tone is a snarl, and whose laugh would put Woody Woodpecker to shame.

Lemmon plays it dirty throughout and for huge effect. Curtis underplays for equally comic effect. Wood comes through on a par with the two male stars.

THE GREAT TEXAS DYNAMITE CHASE

1976, 90 mins, ◇ ⓥ *Dir* Michael Pressman   US

★ **Stars** Claudia Jennings, Jocelyn Jones, Johnny Crawford, Chris Pennock, Tara Strohmeier, Miles Watkins

The Great Texas Dynamite Chase is a well-made exploitation film which works on two levels, providing kicks for the ozoner crowd and tongue-in-cheek humor for the more sophisticated. The film had some initial playdates under the title *Dynamite Women*.

Claudia Jennings and Jocelyn Jones are stylish and attractive as a pair of brazen Texas bankrobbers. They stay firmly in character throughout as a loyal but very divergent criminal pair.

Jennings is a hardened prison escapee, while Jones goes on the road to avoid the boredom of being a smalltown bank teller. They use lots of dynamite along the way, but there's little bloodshed until the last part of the film, when the film's dominant spoof tone turns uncomfortably and unsuccessfully close to reality.

THE GREAT WALDO PEPPER

1975, 108 mins, ◇ *Dir* George Roy Hill   US

★ **Stars** Robert Redford, Bo Svenson, Bo Brundin, Susan Sarandon, Geoffrey Lewis, Edward Herrman

The Great Waldo Pepper is an uneven and unsatisfying story of anachronistic, pitiable, but misplaced heroism. Robert Redford stars as an aerial ace, unable to cope with the segue from pioneer barnstorming to bigtime aviation.

George Roy Hill's original story was scripted by William Goldman into yet another stab at dramatizing the effect of inexorable social change on pioneers. In this case, Redford and Bo Svenson, two World War I airmen, scratch out a living, and feed their egos, via daring stunts in midwest fields. But Geoffrey Lewis has made the transition from cocky pilot to aviation official, and inventor Edward Herrmann unwittingly complements the shift through his technological advances.

The film stumbles towards its fuzzy climax.

GREEN FIRE

1954, 99 mins, ◇ *Dir* Andrew Marton   US

★ **Stars** Stewart Granger, Grace Kelly, Paul Douglas, John Ericson, Murvyn Vye, Jose Torvay

A good brand of action escapism is offered in *Green Fire*. Its story of emerald mining and romantic adventuring in South America is decorated with the names of Stewart Granger, Grace Kelly and Paul Douglas.

The location filming in Colombia ensured fresh scenic backgrounds against which to play the screen story. *Green Fire's* script supplies believable dialog and reasonably credible situations, of which Andrew Marton's good direction, takes full advantage, and the picture spins off at a fast 99 minutes.

The adventure end of the plot is served by the efforts of Granger to find emeralds in an old mountain mine; in the face of halfhearted opposition from his partner, Douglas; the more active interference of Murvyn Vye, a bandit, and the danger of the mining trade itself. Romance is served through the presence of Kelly, whose coffee plantation lies at the foot of the mountain on which Granger is mining, and the attraction that springs up between these two.

Christopher Lambert as Tarzan in faithful adaptation,
Greystoke: The Legend of Tarzan, Lord of the Apes.

GREYSTOKE THE LEGEND OF TARZAN LORD OF THE APES

1984, 129 mins, ◇ Ⓥ *Dir* Hugh Hudson   US, UK

★ *Stars* Ralph Richardson, Ian Holm, James Fox, Christopher Lambert, Andie MacDowell, Cheryl Campbell

One of the main points of *Greystoke* is that the $33 million pic adheres much more closely to the original Edgar Rice Burroughs story than have the countless previous screen tellings of Tarzan stories.

While a little obligatory vine swinging is on view, this is principally the tale of the education of the seventh Earl of Greystoke, first by the family of apes which raises a stranded white child and eventually accepts him as its protector and leader, then by a Belgian explorer who teaches him language, and finally by the aristocracy of Britain, which attempts to make him one of their own.

With the exception of the warm, slightly batty Ralph Richardson, nearly all the Englishmen on view are impossible, offensive snobs.

Christopher Lambert is a different sort of Tarzan. Tall,

lean, firm but no muscleman, he moves with great agility and mimics the apes to fine effect.

Ian Holm is helpfully energetic as the enterprising Belgian, James Fox is the personification of stiff propriety, and Andie MacDowell [voiced by actress Glenn Close] smiles her way through as the eternally sympathetic Jane.

On a production level, film is a marvel, as fabulous Cameroon locations have been seamlessly blended with studio recreations of jungle settings.

GUNS AT BATASI

1964, 102 mins, *Dir* John Guillermin   UK

★ *Stars* Richard Attenborough, Jack Hawkins, Flora Robson, John Leyton, Mia Farrow, Cecil Parker

Soldiering and politics don't mix, according to this well-developed screenplay and story by Robert Holles [from his novel] which dissects with a piercing personal touch the strict disciplinary attitudes that govern a true British soldier and makes him retain his own individual pride in the face of political forces unappreciative of his principles.

Producer and director come up with a strong and frequently exciting piece of work, the story of a British battalion caught in the midst of the African struggle for independence.

Performances throughout are excellent. Richard

Attenborough's portrayal of the sergeant is tough, crisp and staunch, playing with as much starch as the character implies. Errol John has intense qualities of fanaticism as the lieutenant who seizes the government, and Jack Hawkins, in essentially a cameo spot, plays like the resigned warhorse he is meant to be.

GUNS OF DARKNESS

1962, 102 mins, *Dir* Anthony Asquith   UK

★ *Stars* Leslie Caron, David Niven, James Robertson Justice, David Opatoshu

Anthony Asquith is slightly off form with this one. An advocate of anti-violence, he pursues a theme that he has explored before, that violence is sometimes necessary to achieve peace. But the film does not stand up satisfactorily as a psychological study. And as a pure 'escape' yarn, its moments of tension are only spasmodic.

John Mortimer's screenplay [from Francis Clifford's novel *Act of Mercy*] is not positive enough to enable Asquith to keep a firm grip on the proceedings. There are times when the film plods as laboriously as do the stars in their escape to the frontier. It opens in Tribulacion, capital of a South American republic, during a revolution. The president is deposed in a swift coup and, wounded, has to take off in a hurry.

Niven, a rather boorish PRO with a British-owned plantation, elects to smuggle him across the border, for reasons which are not even clear to Niven himself. Tagging along is Niven's wife (Leslie Caron) with whom he is having an emotional upheaval.

Niven's charm seeps through his mask of boorishness but he manages skilfully to keep up an illusion of high voltage danger. David Opatoshu gives an excellent performance as the disillusioned, yet philosophical president. Caron, however, seems uncomfortable, with her role coming over as curiously colorless.

THE GYPSY MOTHS

1969, 106 mins, ◇ ⓥ *Dir* John Frankenheimer   US

★ *Stars* Burt Lancaster, Deborah Kerr, Gene Hackman, Scott Wilson, Sheree North, Bonnie Bedelia

The Gypsy Moths is the story of three barnstorming skydivers and subsequent events when they arrive in a small Kansas town to stage their exhibition. Pairing Burt Lancaster and Deborah Kerr, stars sometimes are lost in a narrative [from a novel by James Drought] that strives to be a tale of smouldering inner conflicts and pent-up emotions.

At best, aside from exciting skydiving episodes, picture is a lackluster affair insofar as the character relationships are concerned. The stars do not appear particularly happy with their roles. Lancaster seldom speaking, Kerr not particularly well cast.

Lancaster delivers well enough what the script requires of him, and Kerr is mostly grim. Hackman and Wilson are forceful, both giving excellent accounts of themselves.

HATARI!

1962, 159 mins, ◇ ⓥ *Dir* Howard Hawks   US

★ *Stars* John Wayne, Hardy Kruger, Elsa Martinelli, Gerard Blain, Red Buttons, Michele Girardon

Hatari! is an ambitious undertaking. Its cast is an international one, populated by players of many countries. Its wild animals do not come charging out of dusty stock footage studio libraries but have been photographed while beating around the bush of Tanganyika, East Africa. However, in this instance, the strapping physique of the film unhappily emphasizes the anemic condition of the story streaming within.

Leigh Brackett's screenplay, from an original story by Harry Kurnitz, describes at exhaustive length the methods by which a group of game catchers in Tanganyika go about catching wild animals for the zoo when not occupied at catching each other for the woo. Script lacks momentum. It never really advances toward a story goal.

John Wayne heads the colorful cast assembled for this zoological field trip. The vet star plays with his customary effortless (or so it seems) authority a role with which he is identified; the good-natured, but hard-drinking, hot-tempered, big Irishman who 'thinks women are trouble' in a man's world.

Germany's Hardy Kruger and French actor Gerard Blain manage, resourcefully, to pump what vigor they can muster into a pair of undernourished roles. Red Buttons and Elsa Martinelli emerge the histrionic stickouts, Buttons with a jovial portrayal of an excabbie who 'just pretends it's rush hour in Brooklyn' as he jockeys his vehicle through a pack of frightened giraffe, Martinelli as a sweet but spirited shutterbug and part time pachydermatologist.

HEART LIKE A WHEEL

1983, 113 mins, ◇ ⓥ *Dir* Jonathan Kaplan   US

★ *Stars* Bonnie Bedelia, Beau Bridges, Leo Rossi, Hoyt Axton, Bill McKinney, Anthony Edwards

Heart Like A Wheel is a surprisingly fine biopic of Shirley Muldowney, the first professional female race car driver. What could have been a routine good ol' gal success story has been heightened into an emotionally involving, superbly made drama.

Leo Rossi, Bonnie Bedelia and Byron Thomas in **Heart Like a Wheel,** *biopic of drag racer Shirley Muldowney.*

Winning prolog has pa Hoyt Axton letting his little daughter take the wheel of his speeding sedan, an indelible experience which prefigures Shirley, by the mid-1950s, winning drag races against the hottest rods in town.

Happily married to her mechanic husband Jack and with a young son, Shirley finds her innate ability compelling her, by 1966, to enter her first pro race. Roadblocked at first by astonished, and predictably sexist, officials, Shirley proceeds to set the track record in her qualifying run, and her career is underway.

But her husband ultimately can't take her career-mindedness, and she's forced to set out on her own.

Director Jonathan Kaplan has served a long apprenticeship but nothing he has done before prepares one for his mature, accomplished work here.

HELL AND HIGH WATER

1954, 103 mins, ◇ *Dir* Samuel Fuller   US

★ **Stars** Richard Widmark, Bella Darvi, Victor Francen, Cameron Mitchell, Gene Evans, David Wayne

CinemaScope and rip-roaring adventure go together perfectly in *Hell and High Water*, a highly fanciful, but mighty entertaining action feature directed by Samuel Fuller.

As the male star, Richard Widmark takes easily to the rugged assignment, giving it the wallop needed. It is a further projection of the action-adventure type of hero he does quite often, and good. The picture introduces as a new star Polish-born, French-raised Bella Darvi and she creates an interesting impression in her debut.

Plot has to do with a group of individuals of many nationalities who band together to thwart a scheme to start a new world war with an atomic incident that will be blamed on the United States. These private heroes hire Widmark, a former naval submarine officer, to command an underwater trip to the Arctic, where scientists on the voyage will check reports that a Communist atomic arsenal is being built on an isolated island.

HELL DRIVERS

1957, 108 mins, ⊘ *Dir* Cy Endfield   UK

★ **Stars** Stanley Baker, Herbert Lom, Peggy Cummins, Patrick McGoohan, William Hartnell, Wilfrid Lawson

Hell Drivers is a slab of unabashed melodrama. The story has to do with the rivalries of a gang of haulage truck drivers, operating between gravel pits and a construction site. Stanley Baker is an ex-convict who gets a job as one of these drivers and immediately falls foul of Patrick McGoohan, the firm's ace driver.

Baker discovers that McGoohan and William Hartnell, the manager, are running a racket. The head office pays basic salaries for five more drivers than Hartnell actually hires. By overworking the drivers Hartnell keeps the daily schedule of runs up to par and he and McGoohan split the extra cash.

Cy Endfield's direction is straightforward and conventional, but some of the speed sequences provide some tingling thrills. Acting is adequate.

THE HIGH BRIGHT SUN

1965, 114 mins, ◇ *Dir* Ralph Thomas   UK

★ **Stars** Dirk Bogarde, George Chakiris, Susan Strasberg, Denholm Elliott, Gregoire Aslan, Colin Campbell

Betty E. Box and Ralph Thomas elected to make this film because they regarded it 'as a suspenseful drama which could be played against any background'. They certainly played safe. Though set in Cyprus during the 1957 troubles, this sits firmly on a fence and makes virtually no attempt to analyze the troubles, the causes or the attitudes of the cardboard characters.

Film comes out with the British looking at times rather silly and at others very dogged, the Cypriots clearly detesting the British occupation, the Turks shadowy almost to a point of non-existence and America, represented by Susan Strasberg, merely a bewildered intruder.

Strasberg, a dewy-eyed young American archeology student of Cypriot parentage, is visiting Cypriot friends who, unbeknown to her, are mixed up in the local terrorist racket. Strasberg gets to know more than is good for her and is torn between loyalty to the Cypriots and to the British, as represented by an intelligence major (Dirk Bogarde) whose job it is to keep alive the unhelpful young dame for whom he has fallen.

Strasberg brings intelligence and charm to a sketchy role while Bogarde has no trouble with a part as the major which scarcely strains his thesping ability.

HIGH ROAD TO CHINA

1983, 120 mins, ◇ ⊘   *Dir* Brian G. Hutton   US

★ **Stars** Tom Selleck, Bess Armstrong, Jack Weston, Wilford Brimley, Robert Morley, Brian Blessed

High Road to China is a lot of old-fashioned fun, revived for Tom Selleck after his TV schedule kept him from taking the Harrison Ford role in *Raiders Of The Lost Ark*. Ford clearly got the better deal though because *China* just isn't as tense and exciting.

But it has the same Saturday-matinee spirit, with director Brian G. Hutton nicely mixing a lot of action with a storyline [from a book by Jon Cleary] that never seems as absurd as it is, allowing the two hours to move by very quickly.

Selleck is perfect as a grizzled, boozing biplane pilot whom 1920s flapper Bess Armstrong is forced to hire to help her find her father before he's declared dead and her inheritance is stolen. Selleck and Armstrong make a cute couple, even though their bantering, slowly developing romance is deliberately predictable throughout.

HILLS OF KENTUCKY

1927, 70 mins, ⊘ ⊙   *Dir* Howard Bretherton   US

★ **Stars** Rin-Tin-Tin, Jason Robards, Dorothy Dwan

One of the best action pictures, with Rin-Tin-Tin as the star, that have been turned out in this series. It's a story of Kentucky, as the title indicates [adapted from the *The Untamed Heart* by Dorothy Yost]. A little puppy is turned loose by a little boy because his father commands it. When the story itself starts this pup has grown to be the leader of the pack and is known as the Grey Ghost.

In a part of the hills are two Harley brothers, one inclined to be a bully and other a rather diffident youngster. There comes into the picture at this time a young school teacher with her crippled child brother. Both of the Harley men fall in love with her. There is a moment when there are three suspense sequences being carried on at once: the two brothers fighting over the girl in the woods, the dog swimming down the stream toward the falls for the youngster's crutch and the little fellow himself trying to fight off the dog pack. This carries a wallop.

THE HINDENBURG

1975, 125 mins, ◇   *Dir* Robert Wise   US

★ **Stars** George C. Scott, Anne Bancroft, William Atherton, Roy Thinnes, Gig Young, Burgess Meredith

Michael Mooney's non-fiction compendium of the facts and theories behind the German zeppelin's 1937 air disaster at NAS, Lakehurst, new Jersey, was earlier dramatized for the screen by Richard A. Levinson and William Link, and both receive a screen story credit.

George C. Scott stars as an air ace assigned as special security officer on the fatal Atlantic crossing.

The array of characters is dealt boringly from a well-thumbed deck: Anne Bancroft, eccentric German countess; Roy Thinnes, Scott's nasty partner; Gig Young, mysterious and nervous ad agency exec; Burgess Meredith and Rene Auberjonois, an improbable and dull effort at comedy relief

Tom Selleck as a grizzled biplane pilot in **High Road to China**, *an old-fashioned action and adventure yarn.*

Reconstruction of the famous 1937 zeppelin air disaster at Lakehurst, New Jersey for **Hindenburg.**

as tourist-trapping card cheats; Robert Clary, also bombing in cardboard comedy relief, the list goes on. William Atherton emerges as the good-guy crewman saboteur who plans to blow up the ship. A battle of mental wits ensues between Scott, Thinnes and Atherton; it's almost as exciting as watching butter melt.

HIS MAJESTY O'KEEFE

1953, 89 mins, ◇ *Dir* Byron Haskin   US

★ *Stars* Burt Lancaster, Joan Rice, Andre Morell, Archie Savage, Benson Fong, Tessa Prendergast

This swashbuckling South Seas adventure feature is ideally suited to Burt Lancaster's muscular heroics. The Fiji Islands location lensing is a plus factor for interest.

The island of Viti Levu in the South Pacific is the locale used. Lancaster is seen as a daredevil Yankee sea captain, cast overboard off the island by a mutinous crew. Intrigued by the possibilities of making a fortune off the island's copra, he stays on to battle other traders, native idleness and superstition, becoming His Majesty O'Keefe with a beautiful Polynesian (Joan Rice) as queen.

The action emphasis of the screenplay, suggested by a novel by Lawrence Kingman and Gerald Green, provides

Byron Haskin's direction innumerable opportunities for movement, so the film's pace is quick-tempoed. Rice is a sweet romantic foil for Lancaster's swashbuckling. Tessa Prendergast, as another island beauty, teases the eyes.

H.M.S. DEFIANT

1962, 101 mins, ◇ *Dir* Lewis Gilbert   UK

★ *Stars* Alec Guinness, Dirk Bogarde, Anthony Quayle, Tom Bell, Maurice Denham, Victor Maddern

H.M.S. Defiant is a strong naval drama about the days of the Napoleonic wars, enhanced by the strong appeal of Alec Guinness, Dirk Bogarde and Anthony Quayle.

Based on Frank Tilsley's novel, *Mutiny*, story is of the time of old press gangs. British navy conditions were appalling and it was the mutiny depicted in this pic which did much to give the British naval men a new deal. Guinness plays the skipper of the *Defiant* which, when it sets out to help tackle the Napoleonic fleet, is ruptured by a tussle for power between Guinness and his first lieutenant (Bogarde).

Guinness is a humane man, though a stern disciplinarian. Bogarde is a sadist, anxious to jockey Guinness out of position.

Below deck the crew, led by Quayle and Tom Bell, is plotting mutiny against the bad food, stinking living conditions and constant floggings ordered by Bogarde.

Guinness' role does not give this actor scope for his fullest ability. Bogarde's is the more showy portrayal. Quayle

C. Thomas Howell (right) finds he has given a lift to a psycho in the form of Rutger Hauer in **The Hitcher.**

makes an impressive appearance as the leader of the rebels, determined and tough, but realizing that there is a right and a wrong way to stage a mutiny, like anything else.

THE HITCHER

1986, 97 mins, ◇ Ⓥ *Dir* Robert Harman   US

★ *Stars* Rutger Hauer, C. Thomas Howell, Jennifer Jason Leigh, Jeffrey DeMunn

The Hitcher is a highly unimaginative slasher that keeps the tension going with a massacre every 15 minutes.

Film proves mom's admonition not to pick up hitchhikers, especially if they are anything like John Ryder, a psychotic and diabolical killer played with a serene coldness by Rutger Hauer.

Along comes an innocent young man (C. Thomas Howell), who is falling asleep at the wheel and stops to pick Hauer up in the hopes that having a companion will keep him awake. What ensues for the rest of the film is a cat and mouse game where Hauer eliminates just about everyone Howell comes into contact with.

In addition to working with a script that has many holes, filmmakers didn't allow for one laugh in the entire 97 minutes.

HOOPER

1978, 99 mins, ◇ Ⓥ *Dir* Hal Needham   US

★ *Stars* Burt Reynolds, Jan-Michael Vincent, Sally Field, Brian Keith, John Marley, James Best

Individually, the performances in this story of three generations of Hollywood stuntmen are a delight. And Hal Needham's direction and stunt staging are wonderfully crafted.

But it's the ensemble work of Burt Reynolds, Jan-Michael Vincent, Sally Field and Brian Keith, with an able assist from Robert Klein, which boosts an otherwise pedestrian story with lots of crashes and daredevil antics into a touching and likable piece.

Reynolds, with his brash, off-handed wise guy screen persona, plays the world's greatest stuntman. He took over that position 20 years back from Brian Keith. His status is being challenged by newcomer Jan-Michael Vincent.

To cement a place in the stuntman's record books, Reynolds must perform one last stunt, in this case a 325-foot jump in a jet-powered car over a collapsed bridge. All this is to take place in a film, *The Spy Who Laughed At Danger*, some sort of a disaster James Bond type picture being directed by the deliciously obnoxious Klein.

Besides the final jump over the bridge, Needham and stunt coordinator Bobby Bass have arranged a smorgasbord of stunts – car crashes, bar room brawls, chariot races, helicopter jumps and motorcycle slides.

As one would expect from a film about the world of the stuntman, Hooper featured many spectacular stunts.

THE HORSEMEN

1971, 108 mins, ◇ ⑦ *Dir* John Frankenheimer   US

★ **Stars** Omar Sharif, Leigh Taylor-Young, Jack Palance, David De, Peter Jeffrey, Mohammed Shamsi

The Horsemen is a would-be epic stretched thin across Hollywood's 'profound peasant' tradition. It's a misfire, despite offbeat Afghanistan locations and some bizarre action sequences.

Omar Sharif, son of rural Afghanistan clan leader Jack Palance, is injured and humiliated (as he thinks) in a brutal ritual soccer-type game, played with the headless carcass of a calf. Returning home in the company of his now treacherous servant (David De) and a wandering n'untouchable' who is out for his money (Leigh Taylor-Young), Sharif's leg has to be amputated below the knee in a remote mountain village.

Back with his clan, Sharif forgives De and Taylor-Young for two attempts they made on his life and then trains hard to re-establish his honor and reputation.

Dalton Trumbo's cliche script, based on the novel by Joseph Kessel, opts for the kind of mock-poetic dialog even Hugh Griffith might have trouble mouthing. Sharif, however, maintains his composure.

HUDSON HAWK

1991, 95 mins, ◇ ⑦ *Dir* Michael Lehmann   US

★ **Stars** Bruce Willis, Danny Aiello, Andie MacDowell, James Coburn, Richard E. Grant, Sandra Bernhard

Ever wondered what a Three Stooges short would look like with a $40 million budget? Then meet *Hudson Hawk*, a relentlessly annoying clay duck that crash-lands in a sea of wretched excess and silliness. Those willing to check their brains at the door may find sparse amusement in pic's frenzied pace.

Bruce Willis plays just-released-from-prison cat burglar Hudson Hawk, who's immediately drawn into a plot to steal a bunch of Leonardo Da Vinci artifacts by, among others, a twisted billionaire couple (Richard E. Grant, Sandra Bernhard), a twisted CIA agent (James Coburn) and an agent for the Vatican (Andie MacDowell). Mostly, though, Hawk hangs with his pal Tommy (Danny Aiello), as the two croon old tunes to time their escapades.

Director Michael Lehmann, who made his feature debut with the deliciously subversive *Heathers*, simply seems overwhelmed by the scale and banality of the screenplay [from a story by Willis]. Few of the scenes seem connected.

The film primarily gives Willis a chance to toss off poor man's *Moonlighting* one-liners in the midst of utter chaos. Grant, Bernhard and Coburn do produce a few bursts of scatological humor based on the sheer energy of their over-the-top performances.

Afghani tribesmen employed as extras show off their horsemanship in a scene from **The Horsemen.**

THE HUNTER

1980, 117 mins, ◇ ⓥ *Dir* Buzz Kulik   US

★ **Stars** Steve McQueen, Eli Wallach, Kathryn Harrold, Ben Johnson

Fact that the overlong pic is based on adventures of a modern-day bounty hunter may have hampered filmmakers' imagination, as attempt to render contradictions of real-life Ralph 'Papa' Thorson, who's into classical music and astrology as well as hauling in fugitives from justice, has made for an annoyingly unrealized and childish onscreen character.

Steve McQueen may have felt that the time had come to revise his persona a bit, but what's involved here is desecration. Given star's rep since *Bullitt* as a terrific driver, someone thought it might be cute to make him a lousy one here, but seeing him crash stupidly into car after car runs the gag into the ground. *The Hunter* [based on the book by Christopher Keane] is a western in disguise.

Only sequence which remotely delivers the goods has McQueen chasing a gun-toting maniac in Chicago. The film's finale, which has star fainting when pregnant girlfriend Kathryn Harrold gives birth, merely puts capper on overall misconception.

THE HUNT FOR RED OCTOBER

1990, 137 mins, ◇ ⓥ *Dir* John McTiernan   US

★ **Stars** Sean Connery, Alec Baldwin, Scott Glenn, Sam Neill, James Earl Jones, Joss Ackland

The Hunt for Red October is a terrific adventure yarn. Tom Clancy's 1984 Cold War thriller has been thoughtfully adapted to reflect the mellowing in the US-Soviet relationship.

Sean Connery is splendid as the renegade Soviet nuclear sub captain pursued by CIA analyst Alec Baldwin and the fleets of both superpowers as he heads for the coast of Maine. The filmmakers have wisely opted to keep the story set in 1984 – 'shortly before Gorbachev came to power', as the opening title puts it.

Looking magnificent in his captain's uniform and white beard, Connery scores as the Lithuanian Marko Ramius, a coldblooded killer and a meditator on Hindu scripture.

Baldwin's intelligent and likable performance makes his Walter Mittyish character come alive. He's combating not only the bulk of the Soviet fleet but also the reflexive anti-Communist mentality of most of those pursuing on the US side – not including his wise and avuncular CIA superior James Earl Jones.

The Industrial Light & Magic special visual effects unit does yeoman work in this pic in staging the action with cliffhanger intensity.

Above: *Sean Connery as Ramius, captain of a new Soviet nuclear submarine, in* **The Hunt for Red October.**

Below: *Ernest Borgnine and crew fight to save their boat in the Alistair MacLean actioner* **Ice Station Zebra.**

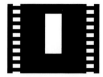

ICE STATION ZEBRA

1968, 152 mins, ◇ Ⓥ *Dir* John Sturges   US

★ *Stars* Rock Hudson, Ernest Borgnine, Patrick McGoohan, Jim Brown, Tony Bill

Action adventure film, in which US and Russian forces race to recover some compromising satellite photography from a remote Polar outpost. Alistair MacLean's novel adapted into a screen story is seeded with elements of intrigue, as Rock Hudson takes aboard a British secret agent, Patrick McGoohan; an expatriate, professional anti-Communist Russian, Ernest Borgnine; and an enigmatic Marine Corps captain, Jim Brown.

Action develops slowly, alternating with some excellent submarine interior footage, and good shots – of diving, surfacing and maneuvering under an ice field.

Film's biggest acting asset is McGoohan, who gives his scenes that elusive 'star' magnetism. He is a most accomplished actor with a three-dimensional presence all his own.

Hudson comes across quite well as a man of muted strength. Borgnine's characterization is a nicely restrained

Harrison Ford and Kate Capshaw surrounded by an adoring crowd in Indiana Jones and the Temple of Doom.

one. Brown, isolated by script to a suspicious personality, makes the most of it.

INDIANA JONES AND THE LAST CRUSADE

1989, 127 mins, ◇ Ⓥ *Dir* Steven Spielberg   US

★ *Stars* Harrison Ford, Sean Connery, Denholm Elliott, Alison Doody, John Rhys-Davies, River Phoenix

More cerebral than the first two Indiana Jones films, and less schmaltzy than the second, this literate adventure should entertain and enlighten kids and adults alike.

The Harrison Ford–Sean Connery father-and-son team gives *Last Crusade* unexpected emotional depth, reminding us that real film magic is not in special effects.

Witty and laconic screenplay, based on a story by George Lucas and Menno Meyjes, takes Ford and Connery on a quest for a prize bigger than the Lost Ark of the Covenant – the Holy Grail.

Connery is a medieval lit prof with strong religious convictions who has spent his life assembling clues to the grail's whereabouts. Father and more intrepid archaeologist son piece them together in an around-the-world adventure, leading to a touching and mystical finale. The love between father and son transcends even the quest for the Grail, which

is guarded by a spectral 700-year-old knight beautifully played by Robert Eddison.

This film minimizes the formulaic love interest, giving newcomer Alison Doody an effectively sinuous but decidedly secondary role.

INDIANA JONES AND THE TEMPLE OF DOOM

1984, 118 mins, ◇ Ⓥ *Dir* Steven Spielberg   US

★ *Stars* Harrison Ford, Kate Capshaw, Ke Huy Quan, Amrish Puri, Roshan Seth, Philip Stone

Steven Spielberg has packed even more thrills and chills into this followup than he did into the earlier pic, but to exhausting and numbing effect.

Prequel finds dapper Harrison Ford as Indiana Jones in a Shanghai nightclub in 1935, and title sequence, which features Kate Capshaw chirping Cole Porter's 'Anything Goes' looks like something out of Spielberg's *1941*.

Ford escapes from an enormous melee with the chanteuse and Oriental moppet Ke Huy Quan and they head by plane to the mountains of Asia where they are forced to jump out in an inflatable raft coming to rest in an impoverished Indian village.

Community's leader implores the ace archaeologist to retrieve a sacred, magical stone which has been stolen by malevolent neighbors.

The remainder of the yarn is set in a labyrinth of horrors lorded over by a prepubescent maharajah, and where untold dangers await the brave heroes.

What with John Williams' incessant score and the library full of sound effects, there isn't a quiet moment in the entire picture.

Ford seems effortlessly to have picked up where he left off when Indiana Jones was last heard from, although Capshaw, who looks fetching in native attire, has unfortunately been asked to react hysterically to everything that happens to her.

THE INN OF THE SIXTH HAPPINESS

1958, 160 mins, ◇ *Dir* Mark Robson   UK

★ *Stars* Ingrid Bergman, Curt Jurgens, Robert Donat, Ronald Squire, Athene Seyler, Peter Chong

Based on Alan Burgess' novel *The Small Woman* which, in turn, was based on the adventures of a real person, the film has Ingrid Bergman as a rejected missionary in China, who gets there determinedly under her own steam. First met with hostility by the natives, she gradually wins their love and esteem. She falls in love with a Eurasian colonel, converts a powerful mandarin to Christianity and becomes involved in the Chino-Japanese war. Finally she guides 100 children to the safety of a northern mission by leading them on an arduous journey across the rugged mountains and through enemy territory.

The inn in the film is run by Bergman and an elderly missionary (Athene Seyler). Here they dispense hospitality and Bible stories to the muleteers in transit. Bergman's early scenes as she strives to get to China and those in which she gradually settles down in her environment and begins the urgent task of winning the confidence of the Chinese are brilliantly done with humor and a sense of urgent dedication.

Curt Jurgens is less happily served as the Eurasian colonel. The slender love theme seems to have been dropped into the main story and Jurgens has less command of the awkward role than usual.

A standout performance comes from Robert Donat as an astute yet benign mandarin. It was Donat's swansong before his untimely death and only rarely can signs of his physical collapse be detected.

The film was shot in Wales and in the Elstree studio, converted expertly into a Chinese village. Mark Robson's direction slickly catches both the sweep of the crowd sequences and the more intimate ones.

THE IRON MASK

1929, 95 mins, ⍉ *Dir* Allan Dwan   US

★ *Stars* Douglas Fairbanks, Nigel de Brulier, Marguerite de la Motte, Leon Barry, Rolfe Sedan, Lon Poff

Typical romantic Fairbanks picture. His direct vocal address is in the form of minute-and-a-half appendages as prologs to the first and second halves, into which the picture was [originally] divided for the premiere. There is no dialog at any time in the direct action.

This is the sequel to Fairbanks' *Three Musketeers* (1921). It's so much of a sequel that, besides Fairbanks, Nigel de Brulier and Lon Poff are again together in this film as Cardinal Richelieu and his aid, Father Joseph; Marguerite de la Motte revives her Constance, and Leon Barry has been recast as Athos.

Current story provides the twist of D'Artagnan going over to the Cardinal's side. It is to protect the young heir apparent who has a twin brother whom Richelieu whisks into hiding at birth to protect the throne.

Allan Dwan, directing, keeps the story moving. Comedy sidelights slip in and out, but Fairbanks and the romantic friendship of the four men hold the picture together.

The brief verbal passages ask the audience to come back to the days of chivalry.

THE ISLAND

1980, 114 mins, ◇ Ⓥ *Dir* Michael Ritchie   US

★ *Stars* Michael Caine, David Warner, Angela Punch McGregor, Frank Middlemass

This latest summertime tale from the water-obsessed pen of Peter Benchley gets off to a bristling start as a charter boatload of boozy business types is ambushed by something or someone that leaves hatchets planted in their skulls and severed limbs scattered aboard.

Cut to British journalist Michael Caine, who persuades his editor that this latest Bermuda Triangle-type ship disappearance justifies his personal research.

But once the mystery is banally resolved – the island is inhabited by a tribe of buccaneers who've been inbreeding for 300 years and prey on pleasure ships – the film degenerates to a violent chase melodrama.

Michael Ritchie's witty direction is abandoned in the violence, and periodic efforts to revive the built-in comedy fall flat.

ISLAND IN THE SKY

1953, 108 mins, *Dir* William A. Wellman   US

★ *Stars* John Wayne, Lloyd Nolan, Walter Abel, James Arness, Andy Devine

An articulate drama of men and planes has been fashioned from Ernest K. Gann's novel. The Wayne-Fellows production was scripted with care by Gann for aviation aficionado William A. Wellman who gives it sock handling to make it a solid piece of drama revolving around an ATC plane crash in Arctic wastes.

The film moves back and forth very smoothly from the tight action at the crash site to the planning and execution of the search. It's a slick job by all concerned.

John Wayne is the ATC pilot downed with his crew,

Jousting scene from **Ivanhoe**, *adapted from Sir Walter Scott's durable tale of knights and maidens in distress.*

James Lydon, Hal Baylor, Sean McClory and Wally Cassell, in an uncharted section of Labrador. How he holds them together during five harrowing days before rescue comes on the sixth is grippingly told. Each of the players has a chance at a big scene and delivers strongly.

The snow-covered Donner Lake area near Truckee, Calif, subbed for the story's Labrador locale and provides a frosty, shivery dressing to the picture. Both the lensing by Archie Stout and the aerial photography by William Clothier are important factors in the drama and thrills. Title derives from the fancy that pilots are men apart, their spirits dwelling on islands in the sky.

IVANHOE

1952, 107 mins, ◇ ⓥ *Dir* Richard Thorpe   UK

★ **Stars** Robert Taylor, Elizabeth Taylor, Joan Fontaine, George Sanders, Emlyn Williams, Robert Douglas

Academy Award 1952: Best Picture (Nomination)

Ivanhoe is a great romantic adventure, mounted extravagantly, crammed with action, and emerges as a spectacular feast.

Both the romance and the action are concentrated around Robert Taylor who, as Ivanhoe, is the courageous Saxon leader fighting for the liberation of King Richard from

an Austrian prison and his restoration to the throne. Two women play an important part in his life. There is Rowena (Joan Fontaine), his father's ward, with whom he is in love; and Rebecca (Elizabeth Taylor), daughter of the Jew who raises the ransom money. She is in love with him.

Taylor sets the pace with a virile contribution which is matched by George Sanders as his principal adversary. Fontaine contributes to all the requisite charm and understanding as Rowena.

JACARE

1942, 65 mins, *Dir* Charles E. Ford   US

★ **Stars** Frank Buck, James M. Dannaldson, Miguel Rojinsky

Produced in Brazil, except for studio scenes introducing Frank Buck, this 'bring-'em-back-alive' jungle thriller stacks up strongly in the Buck string of wild animal screen epics.

This Buck jungler is outstanding for the smooth way in which it unfolds an intelligent story, minus dull spots. Aside from the introductory trimmings, the picture is a series of adventures and struggles to capture denizens of the jungle.

Recital builds suspense as to what the Jacare really is, with climax sharply pointed up as a whole river-bank filled with them is revealed.

Charles E. Ford, former Universal newsreel editor, is credited on the film with directing. Ford died on the Coast after returning from the trip. Production is a credit to his skill at maintaining maximum interest. Buck employs his familiar clipped phrases in narrating the whole picture, and is okay in his brief initial appearance.

JAWS

1975, 124 mins, ◇ *Dir* Steven Spielberg   US

★ **Stars** Roy Scheider, Robert Shaw, Richard Dreyfuss, Lorraine Gary, Murray Hamilton, Carl Gottlieb

Jaws, Peter Benchley's bestseller about a killer shark and a tourist beach town, is an $8 million film of consummate suspense, tension and terror. It stars Roy Scheider as the town's police chief torn between civic duty and the mercantile politics of resort tourism; Robert Shaw, absolutely magnificent as a coarse fisherman finally hired to locate the Great White Shark; and Richard Dreyfuss, in another excellent characterization as a likeable young scientist.

The fast-moving film engenders enormous suspense as the fearsome killer shark attacks a succession of people; the creature is not even seen for about 82 minutes, and a subjective camera technique makes his earlier forays

Richard Dreyfus, shark expert, and Roy Scheider, local police chief, study a great white shark in Spielberg's **Jaws.**

excrutiatingly terrifying all the more for the invisibility.

John Williams' haunting score adds to the mood of impending horror. All other production credits are superior.

JAWS 2

1978, 117 mins, ◇ Ⓥ *Dir* Jeannot Szwarc   US

★ **Stars** Roy Scheider, Lorraine Gary, Murray Hamilton, Joseph Mascolo, Jeffrey Kramer, Collin Wilcox

Despite a notable but effective change in story emphasis, *Jaws 2* is a worthy successor in horror, suspense and terror to its 1975 smash progenitor.

The Peter Benchley characters of offshore island police chief Roy Scheider, loyal spouse Lorraine Gary, temporizing mayor Murray Hamilton and Gee-whiz deputy Jeffrey Kramer are used as the adult pegs for the very good screenplay. The targets of terror, and the principal focus of audience empathy, are scores of happy teenagers.

So strong is the pic's emphasis on adolescent adrenalin that *Jaws 2* might well be described as the most expensive film ($20 million) that American International Pictures never made.

Suffice to say that the story again pits Scheider's concern for public safety against the indifference of the town elders as evidence mounts that there's another great white shark out there in the shallow waters. Ever-more complicated teenage jeopardy leads to the climactic showdown with a buried cable.

J

JAWS 3-D

1983, 97 mins, ◇ Ⓥ *Dir* Joe Alves   US

★ *Stars* Dennis Quaid, Bess Armstrong, Simon MacCorkindale, Louis Gossett Jr, John Putch, Lea Thompson

The *Jaws* cycle has reached its nadir with this surprisingly tepid 3-D version. Gone are Roy Scheider, the summer resort of Amity, and even the ocean. They have been replaced by Florida's Sea World, a lagoon and an Undersea Kingdom that entraps a 35-foot Great White, and a group of young people who run the tourist sea park.

The picture includes two carry-over characters from the first two *Jaws*, Scheider's now-grown sons, who are played by nominal star Dennis Quaid as the older brother turned machine engineer and kid brother John Putch.

Femme cast is headed by Bess Armstrong as an intrepid marine biologist who lives with Quaid.

Director Joe Alves, who was instrumental in the design of the first *Jaws* shark and was the unsung production hero in both the first two pictures, fails to linger long enough on the Great White.

JEOPARDY

1953, 68 mins, *Dir* John Sturges   US

★ *Stars* Barbara Stanwyck, Barry Sullivan, Ralph Meeker, Lee Aaker

The misadventures that befall a family of three vacationing at an isolated coast section of Lower California have been put together in an unpretentious, tightly-drawn suspense melodrama.

There's no waste motion or budget dollars in the presentation. Plot has a tendency to play itself out near the finale, but otherwise is expertly shaped in the screenplay from a story by Maurice Zimm.

Barbara Stanwyck, Barry Sullivan and their small son (Lee Aaker) are vacationing at a deserted Mexican beach. An accident pins Sullivan's leg under a heavy piling that falls from a rotten jetty. Knowing the rising tide will cover him within four hours Stanwyck takes off in the family car to find either help or a rope strong enough to raise the piling. The mission is sidetracked when she comes across Ralph Meeker, a desperate escaped convict. He takes her prisoner and commandeers the car.

The performances by the four-member cast are very good, being expertly fitted to the chance of mood from the happy carefree start to the danger of the accident and the menace of the criminal. Scenes of Sullivan and young Aaker together bravely facing the peril of the tide while Stanwyck frantically seeks help are movingly done.

Barabara Stanwyck and Lee Aaker in Jeopardy, *the story of a family's vacation to Mexico that goes very wrong.*

THE JEWEL OF THE NILE

1985, 104 mins, ◇ Ⓥ *Dir* Lewis Teague   US

★ *Stars* Michael Douglas, Kathleen Turner, Danny DeVito, Spiros Focas, Avner Eisenberg, Paul David Magid

As a sequel to *Romancing the Stone*, the script of *The Jewel of the Nile* is missing the deft touch of the late Diane

Thomas but Lewis Teague's direction matches the energy of the original film.

Michael Douglas and Kathleen Turner again play off each other very well, but the story is much thinner. The main problem is the dialog, which retains some of the old spirit but too often relies on the trite.

Story picks up six months after *Stone's* happy ending and Douglas and Turner have begun to get on each other's nerves. She accepts an invitation from a sinister potentate (Spiros Focas) to accompany him and write a story about his pending ascendency as desert ruler.

Left behind, Douglas runs into the excitable Danny DeVito and they become unwilling allies, again in pursuit of a jewel.

THE JOURNEY OF NATTY GANN

1985, 105 mins, ◇ Ⓥ   *Dir* Jeremy Paul Kagan   US

★ *Stars* Meredith Salenger, John Cusack, Ray Wise, Scatman Crothers, Barry Miller, Lainie Kazan

More a period piece of Americana than a rousing adventure, *The Journey of Natty Gann* is a generally diverting variation on a boy and his dog: this time it's a girl and her wolf.

Set in the Depression in Chicago, story has widower Saul Gann desperate to find employment to support himself and daughter Natty. He's offered a job at the lumber camp out in Washington State and reluctantly takes it, promising to send for Natty as soon as he can. He leaves her under the auspices of a floozie hotel manager.

The girl runs away and remainder of pic is her sojourn across America in search of her dad. Along the way she rescues a wolf from its captors, and he becomes her endearing traveling partner.

Director Jeremy Paul Kagan extracts an engaging performance from Meredith Salenger as the heroine. Rest of the cast is fine, with John Cusack as her begrudging but good buddy and Barry Miller as the witty entrepreneurial leader of a hobo brat pack.

JUDITH

1966, 105 mins, ◇   *Dir* Daniel Mann   US

★ *Stars* Sophia Loren, Peter Finch, Jack Hawkins, Hans Verner, Zharira Charifai, Shraga Friedman

Israel in its birth pains back-drops this frequently-tenseful adventure tale realistically produced in its actual locale. The production combines a moving story with interesting, unfamiliar characters.

The screenplay, based on an original by Lawrence Durrell, is two-pronged: the story of Sophia Loren, as the Jewish ex-wife of a Nazi war criminal who betrayed her and sent her to Dachau, intent upon finding him and wreaking her own brand of vengeance, and the efforts of the Haganah, Israel's underground army, to capture him.

Under Daniel Mann's forceful direction, the two points are fused as femme finds herself obliged to throw in with the Israelis, who use her to track down the man they know is in the Middle East but do not know how to identify.

Loren is excellent. It is a colorful role for her, particularly in her recollections of the young son she thought murdered until the Nazi, finally captured, tells her he is still alive.

Peter Finch, as a kibbutz leader and one of the Haganah, registers effectively and creates an indelible impression of what Israeli leaders accomplished in setting up their own state.

Nicolas Roeg is credited with second unit direction and additional photography.

JUGGERNAUT

1974, 109 mins, ◇ Ⓥ   *Dir* Richard Lester   UK

★ *Stars* Richard Harris, Omar Sharif, David Hemmings, Anthony Hopkins, Shirley Knight, Ian Holm

Juggernaut stars Richard Harris as an explosives demolition expert aboard Omar Sharif's luxury liner where several bombs have been planted.

The action aboard the great ship, to which Harris, David Hemmings and other demolition team members have been flown, alternates with land drama, where shipline executive Ian Holm, detective Anthony Hopkins (whose wife Caroline Mortimer and children are aboard the vessel), and others, attempt to locate the phantom bomber who calls himself Juggernaut in a series of telephone calls demanding a huge ransom.

At sea, Shirley Knight wanders in and out of scenes as a romantic interest for Sharif, while co-star Roy Kinnear comes off best of the whole cast as a compulsively cheerful social director.

KANSAS CITY BOMBER

1972, 99 mins, ◇ Ⓥ   *Dir* Jerrold Freedman   US

★ *Stars* Raquel Welch, Kevin McCarthy, Helena Kallianiotes, Norman Alden, Jeanne Cooper, Jodie Foster

Kansas City Bomber provides a gutsy, sensitive and comprehensive look at the barbaric world of the roller derby. Rugged, brawling action will more than satisfy those who enjoy that type of commercial carnage, while the script explores deftly the cynical manipulation of players and audiences.

Barry Sandler's original story, written for a university thesis, has been scripted into a well-structured screenplay, in which most dialog is appropriate to the environment.

Raquel Welch, who did a lot of her own skating, is most credible as the beauteous but tough star for whom team owner Kevin McCarthy has big plans. A fake grudge fight moves her from KC to Portland, where McCarthy is building his team for a profitable sale. At the same time, Welch is torn between her professional life and her two fatherless children.

KHARTOUM

1966, 134 mins, ◇ ⓥ *Dir* Basil Dearden   UK

★ **Stars** Charlton Heston, Laurence Olivier, Richard Johnson, Ralph Richardson, Alexander Knox, Johnny Sekka

Khartoum is an action-filled entertainment pic which contrasts personal nobility with political expediency. The colorful production builds in spectacular display, enhanced by Cinerama presentation, while Charlton Heston and Laurence Olivier propel towards inevitable tragedy the drama of two sincere opponents.

Filmed in Egypt and finished at England's Pinewood Studios, the historical drama depicts the events leading up to the savage death of General Charles Gordon, famed British soldier, as he sought to mobilize public opinion against the threat of a religious-political leader who would conquer the Arab world.

Heston delivers an accomplished performance as Gordon, looking like the 50-year-old trim soldier that Gordon was when picked to evacuate Khartoum of its Egyptian inhabitants.

Olivier, playing the Mahdi, is excellent in creating audience terror of a zealot who sincerely believes that a mass slaughter is Divine Will, while projecting respect and compassion for his equally-religious adversary.

Basil Dearden directs with a fine hand, while Yakima Canutt, second unit director given prominent screen credit, works simultaneously to create much big-screen razzledazzle action.

KIDNAPPED

1948, 81 mins, *Dir* William Beaudine   US

★ **Stars** Roddy McDowall, Sue England, Dan O'Herlihy, Roland Winters

Robert Louis Stevenson's swashbuckler of feuding Scots and foul play in the 18th century has lost a lot of its punch in the screen adaptation. *Kidnapped* is only mildly entertaining, telling its story with a too leisurely pace that keeps things at a walk for 81 minutes.

The Stevenson classic concerns a young Scot who comes to claim an inheritance from his uncle. Latter has him kidnapped and shipped off to slavery but lad is saved by a political adventurer.

Roddy McDowall portrays the young Scot and does

well enough in the role. (Actor also served as associate producer with Ace Herman on the film.) Dan O'Herlihy is the political adventurer and Sue England the pert young miss who joins the safari across Scotland.

KIDNAPPED

1960, 97 mins, ◇ ⓥ *Dir* Robert Stevenson   US

★ **Stars** Peter Finch, James MacArthur, Bernard Lee, Niall MacGinnis, John Laurie, Peter O'Toole

Walt Disney's live-action feature is a faithful recreation of the Robert Louis Stevenson classic. The film itself is sluggish because its story line is not clear enough and for other reasons does not arouse any great anxiety or excitement in the spectator.

James MacArthur plays the young 18th-century Scottish boy cheated of his inheritance by a conniving uncle. The boy is kidnapped by a cruel shipsmaster for sale as an indentured servant in the Carolinas. He escapes through the aid of a dashing fellow Scotsman (Peter Finch).

From a story point of view, the screenplay is weak. It is never clear what the aim of the principals is, so there is not much for the spectator to pull for. Individual scenes play, but there is no mounting or cumulative effect.

Kidnapped was photographed on location in Scotland and at Pinewood, London. The locations pay off richly, with an authentic flavor. Perhaps too richly, with accents as thick as Scotch oatmeal.

Finch as the swashbuckling follower of the exiled Stuart kings is a tremendous aid to the production. MacArthur gives a sturdy performance, handicapped by little opportunity for flexibility of character.

KIDNAPPED

1972, 100 mins, ◇ ⓥ *Dir* Delbert Mann   UK

★ **Stars** Michael Caine, Trevor Howard, Jack Hawkins, Donald Pleasence, Gordon Jackson, Vivien Heilbron

Combination of Robert Louis Stevenson's *Kidnapped* and its lesser-known sequel *Catriona* results in an intriguing adventure piece set against the period in Scottish history when the English were trying to take over the country.

The dying struggle between a few remaining clans who refuse to relinquish their sovereignty, and English King George who sends his redcoats into the Highlands to stamp out rebellion, is graphically depicted through the personalized story of one of the Stuarts. This overshadows the story of David Balfour, hero of *Kidnapped*, the 18th-century Scottish lad cheated of his inheritance by a conniving uncle, but pic loses nothing in the telling.

Michael Caine plays the swashbuckling character of Alan Breck, who embodies the spirit of the bloody but unbowed Highlanders. Delbert Mann's direction catches the proper flavor of the times.

Lawrence Douglas portrays David Balfour, who becomes a follower of Breck, a man with a price on his head, trying to escape to France after the bloodbath of Culloden in 1746.

KILLER McCOY

1947, 103 mins, *Dir* Roy Rowland   US

★ *Stars* Mickey Rooney, Brian Donlevy, Ann Blyth, James Dunn

Metro has concocted a fast action melodrama in *Killer McCoy* [based on the screenplay for their 1938 film, *The Crowd Roars*], to introduce Mickey Rooney to adult roles. Sentimental hoke is mixed with prize ring action but never gets too far out of hand.

Rooney makes much of his tailormade assignment in the title role. He's a tough kid who comes up to ring prominence after accidentally killing his friend, the ex-champ, who had started him on the road up. There's nothing that's very original with the story but scripting by Frederick Hazlitt Brennan has given it realistic dialog that pays off.

Plot develops from time Rooney and his sot of a father, James Dunn, become a song-and-dance team to pad out vaude tour being made by a lightweight champion. Through this association Rooney moves into the ring.

Highlights are 'Swanee River' soft-shoed by Rooney and Dunn; sentimental courting of Rooney and Ann Blyth; and the fistic finale that features plenty of rugged action.

Brian Donlevy gives strong touch to the gambler role and Blyth gets the most out of every scene. Dunn hokes up assignment as the drunken actor-father with just the right amount of overplaying to stress 'ham' character.

KING OF THE KHYBER RIFLES

1953, 100 mins, ◇   *Dir* Henry King   US

★ *Stars* Tyrone Power, Terry Moore, Michael Rennie, John Justin, Guy Rolfe

Picture is laid in the India of 1857 when British colonial troops were having trouble with Afridi tribesmen. The plot

Guy Rolfe and Tyrone Power at opposite ends of the spectrum in King of the Khyber Rifles.

opens with Tyrone Power, a half-caste English officer, being assigned to the Khyber Rifles, a native troop at a garrison headed by Michael Rennie, English general. For romance in the film, Rennie has a daughter, Terry Moore, who is instantly attracted to Power despite British snobbery over his mixed blood.

From here on, the footage is taken up with developing the romance while the hero protects the heroine from native dangers and kidnap attempts by Guy Rolfe, leader of the Afridis and a foster brother of Power's.

The male heroics are played with a stiff-lipped, stout-fellowish Britishism perfectly appropriate to the characters. Power is a good hero, Moore attractively handles the heroine unabashedly pursuing her man. Rennie is excellent as the commanding general and Rolfe does another of his topnotch evil villains.

A rousing finale climaxes the story, based on the Talbot Mundy novel, and in between CinemaScope adds sweep and spectacle to the India settings, facsimiled by the terrain around California's Lone Pine area.

KING RICHARD AND THE CRUSADERS

1954, 113 mins, ◇ Ⓥ *Dir* David Butler   US

★ **Stars** Rex Harrison, Virginia Mayo, George Sanders, Laurence Harvey, Robert Douglas, Michael Pate

The Talisman, Walter Scott's classic about the third crusade, gets the full spectacle treatment in this entry.

The Scott classic details the efforts of Christian nations from Europe, marshalled under the leadership of England's King Richard, to gain the Holy Grail from the Mohammedans. In addition to the fighting wiles of the crafty Moslems, King Richard must contend with the sinister ambitions of some of his entourage and these rivalries almost doom the crusade.

David Butler's direction manages to keep a long show nearly always moving at a fast clip. Especially attractive to the action-minded will be the jousting sequences, either those showing training or those in deadly seriousness, and the bold battling is mostly concerned with combat between the forces of good and evil among the crusaders themselves. The script is especially good in its dialog, particularly that handed to Rex Harrison.

KING SOLOMON'S MINES

1937, 80 mins, Ⓥ *Dir* Robert Stevenson   UK

★ **Stars** Paul Robeson, Cedric Hardwicke, Roland Young, John Loder, Anna Lee, Makubalo Hlubi

With all the dramatic moments of H. Rider Haggard's adventure yarn, and production values reaching high and spectacular standards, *King Solomon's Mines* is a slab of genuine adventure decked in finely done, realistic African settings and led off by grand acting from Cedric Hardwicke and Paul Robeson, whose rich voice is not neglected.

Entire action is laid in the African interior, and shifts from the veldt and the desert to a native kraal, where the tale is enlivened by spectacular sequences of native war councils, with a pitched battle between two tribes magnificently and thrillingly staged.

Climax carries the action into the long-lost mines, where untold diamond wealth is hoarded, closing with a terrifying eruption of a volcano.

Robeson is a fine, impressive figure as the native carrier who is proved to be a king, and puts on a proud dignity that his frequent lapses into rolling song cannot bring down. Hardwicke is excellent as a tough white hunter, and Roland Young puts in his lively vein of comedy to excellent effect. John Loder and Anna Lee are less effective on the romantic side.

KING SOLOMON'S MINES

1950, 102 mins, Ⓥ *Dir* Compton Bennett, Andrew Marton US

★ **Stars** Stewart Granger, Deborah Kerr, Richard Carlson, Hugo Haas

Academy Award 1950: Best Picture (Nomination)

King Solomon's Mines has been filmed against an authentic African background, lending an extremely realistic air to the H. Rider Haggard classic novel of a dangerous safari and discovery of a legendary mine full of King Solomon's treasure.

The standout sequence is the animal stampede, minutes long, that roars across the screen to the terrifying noise of panic-driven hoofbeats. It's a boff thriller scene.

Cast-wise, the choice of players is perfect. Stewart Granger scores strongly as the African hunter who takes Deborah Kerr and her brother (Richard Carlson) on the dangerous search for her missing husband. Kerr is an excellent personification of an English lady tossed into the raw jungle life, and Carlson gets across as the third white member of the safari.

KING SOLOMON'S MINES

1985, 100 mins, ◇ Ⓥ *Dir* J. Lee Thompson   US

★ **Stars** Richard Chamberlain, Sharon Stone, Herbert Lom, John Rhys-Davies, Ken Gampu, June Buthelezi

Cannon's remake of *King Solomon's Mines* treads very heavily in the footsteps of that other great modern hero, Indiana Jones – too heavily.

Where Jones was deft and graceful in moving from crisis to crisis, *King Solomon's Mines* is often clumsy with logic, making the action hopelessly cartoonish. Once painted into the corner, scenes don't resolve so much as end before they spill into the next cliff-hanger.

It suffers an unrelenting pace with no variation which

Above: *Robert Douglas as Sir Giles Amaury in a scene from* **King Richard and the Crusaders.**

Below: *Richard Chamberlain is Allan Quartermain in the 1985 version of Rider Haggard's* **King Solomon's Mines.**

ultimately becomes tedious. Neither the camp humor or the romance between Richard Chamberlain as the African adventurer Allan Quatermain and heroine-in-distress Sharon Stone breaks the monotony of the action.

Script plays something like a child's maze with numerous deadends and detours on the way to the buried treasure.

KINGS OF THE SUN

1963, 108 mins, ◇   *Dir* J. Lee Thompson   US

★ **Stars** Yul Brynner, George Chakiris, Shirley Anne Field, Richard Basehart, Brad Dexter, Barry Morse

The screenplay from a story by Elliott Arnold is a kind of southern western. It describes, in broad, vague, romantic strokes the flight of the Mayan people from their homeland after crushing military defeat, their establishment of a new home, and their successful defense of it against their former conquerors thanks to the aid of a friendly resident tribe that has been willing to share the region in which the Mayans have chosen to relocate.

In more intimate terms, it is the story of the young Mayan king (George Chakiris), the leader (Yul Brynner) of the not-so-savage tribe that comes to the ultimate defense of the Mayans, and a Mayan maiden (Shirley Anne Field).

Brynner easily steals the show with his sinewy authority, masculinity and cat-like grace. Chakiris is adequate, although he lacks the epic, heroic stature with which the role might have been filled. Field is an attractive pivot for the romantic story. Others of importance include Basehart as a high priest and advisor who gives consistently lousy advice.

Direction by J. Lee Thompson has its lags and lapses, but he has mounted his spectacle handsomely and commandeered the all-important battle sequences with vigor and imagination. The picture was filmed entirely in Mexico: interiors in Mexico City and exteriors in the coastal area of Mazatlan and in Chichen Itza near Yucatan.

KNIGHTS OF THE ROUND TABLE

1953, 115 mins, ◇ ▼   *Dir* Richard Thorpe   US, UK

★ **Stars** Ava Gardner, Mel Ferrer, Anne Crawford, Stanley Baker, Gabriel Woolf

Metro's first-time-out via CinemaScope is a dynamic interpretation of Thomas Malory's classic *Morte d'Arthur*. The action is fierce as the gallant Lancelot fights for his king, and armies of lancers engage in combat to the death. The story has dramatic movement – it could easily have come off stiltedly under less skilful handling – as the knight's love for his queen nearly causes the death of both.

The carefully developed script plus knowing direction by Richard Thorpe give the legendary tale credibility. It's storybook stuff – and must be accepted as such – but the astute staging results in a walloping package of entertainment for all except, perhaps, the blasé.

Robert Taylor as Sir Lancelot in M-G-M's story of King Arthur and Camelot: **Knights of the Round Table.**

Robert Taylor handles the Lancelot part with conviction; apparently he's right at home with derring-do heroics. Not apparently so at home is Ava Gardner. She gets by fair enough but the role of the lovely Guinevere calls for more projected warmth. Mel Ferrer does an excellent job of portraying the sincere and sympathetic King Arthur. Gabriel Woolf, as the knight in search of the Holy Grail, is standout.

KNIGHT WITHOUT ARMOUR

1937, 108 mins, ⓥ   *Dir* Jacques Feyder   UK

★ **Stars** Marlene Dietrich, Robert Donat, Irene Vanbrugh, Herbert Lomas, Austin Trevor, Basil Gill

A labored effort to keep this picture neutral on the subject of the Russian Revolution finally completely overshadows the simple love story intertwining Marlene Dietrich and Robert Donat.

Film is not a standout because Frances Marion's screenplay, for one thing, has lost a great deal of James Hilton's characterization in the original novel and dispensed almost entirely with the economic and physical-privation angles leading up to the revolution. Result is that only those familiar with the pre-1917 Russia will understand what the shootin's all about.

Story reveals Donat as a young British secret service agent who becomes a Red to achieve his purpose. He's sent to Siberia just before the outbreak of the World War and returns after the revolution as an assistant commissar. He rescues Dietrich's countess from execution.

Performances on the whole are good, though Dietrich restricts herself to just looking glamorous in any setting or costume. Donat handles himself with restraint and capability. There's only one other important cast assignment, John Clements as a hyper-sensitive commissar.

THE LAST AMERICAN HERO

1973, 95 mins, ◇ Ⓥ *Dir* Lamont Johnson   US

★ *Stars* Jeff Bridges, Valerie Perrine, Geraldine Fitzgerald, Ned Beatty, Art Lund, Gary Busey

After a fumbling start which looks like bad editing for TV, *The Last American Hero* [based on two articles by Tom Wolfe] settles into some good, gritty, family Americana, with Jeff Bridges excellent as a flamboyant auto racer determined to succeed on his own terms and right a wrong to his father, played expertly by Art Lund.

Bridges and Gary Busey are moonshiner Lund's boys, with Geraldine Fitzgerald a concerned wife and mother. Bridges' backroad hot-rodding outrages a revenuer into busting Lund, who gets time for illegal liquor distilling. Bridges takes to the racing circuit to buy Lund prison privileges.

Between the script, Lamont Johnson's sure direction, and the excellent performances, all but the early choppy scenes add up to a well-told story.

THE LAST DAYS OF POMPEII

1935, 96 mins, Ⓥ *Dir* Ernest B. Schoedsack   US

★ *Stars* Preston Foster, Basil Rathbone, Alan Hale, John Wood, Louis Calhern, Dorothy Wilson

Last Days of Pompeii is a spectacle picture, full of action and holds a good tempo throughout.

What is presented is a behind-the-scenes of Roman politics and commerce both of which are shown as smeared with corruption and intrigue.

Basil Rathbone comes very close to stealing the picture with his playing of Pontius Pilate. Jesus crosses the path of Marcus (Preston Foster) one time gladiator who is in Judea on a little business deal (horse stealing) which he carries out as the silent partner of Pilate.

Foster has the central role. He carries through from the boyish blacksmith of the opening sequence to the rich man who in the end sees his beloved son face probable death in the arena (just before the volcano erupts). On the way he is gladiator, slave trader, horse-stealer and general tough guy, but more the victim of a fierce semi-barbaric environment than of any personal cruelty trait.

THE LAST VALLEY

1971, 125 mins, ◇ Ⓥ *Dir* James Clavell   UK, US

★ *Stars* Michael Caine, Omar Sharif, Florinda Bolkan, Nigel Davenport, Per Oscarsson, Arthur O'Connell

The Last Valley is a disappointing 17th-century period melodrama about the fluid and violent loyalties attendant on major civil upheaval. Shot handsomely abroad for about $6 million and top-featuring Michael Caine and Omar Sharif in strong performances, James Clavell's film emerges as heavy cinematic grand opera in tab version format, too literal in historical detail to suggest artfully the allegories intended and, paradoxically, too allegorical to make clear the actual reality of the Thirty Years War.

Clavell adapted a J.B. Pick novel in which Sharif, neither peasant nor nobleman, is fleeing the ravages of war and finds a valley still spared from cross-devastation. Caine, hard-bitten leader of mercenaries, also discovers the locale. At

Sharif's urging Caine decides to live in peace for the winter with the residents, headed by Nigel Davenport and an uneasy truce develops.

The fatuous political and religious and social rationalizations of behavior get full exposition. But the whole entity doesn't play well together as Clavell's script often halts for declamations.

LE MANS

1971, 108 mins, ◇ *Dir* Lee H. Katzin, [John Sturges]   US

★ **Stars** Steve McQueen, Siegfried Rauch, Elga Andersen, Ronald Leigh-Hunt

Marked by some spectacular car-racing footage, *Le Mans* is a successful attempt to escape the pot-boiler of prior films on same subject. The solution was to establish a documentary mood. Steve McQueen stars (and races).

Filmed abroad on actual French locales, the project began under director John Sturges. Creative incompatibilities brought McQueen, his Solar Prods indie, and Cinema Center Films to the mat, and as the dust settled Sturges was out and Lee H. Katzin finished the film and gets solo screen credit.

The spare script finds McQueen returning to compete in the famed car race a year after he has been injured. Elga Andersen, wife of a driver killed in the same accident, also returns, somewhat the worse for emotional wear. Siegfried Rauch is McQueen's continuing rival in racing competition.

The film establishes its mood through some outstanding use of slow motion, multiple-frame printing, freezes, and a most artistic use of sound – including at times no sound. The outstanding racing footage not only enhances the effects, but stands proudly on its own four wheels in straight continuity.

LICENCE TO KILL

1989, 133 mins, ◇ Ⓥ *Dir* John Glen   UK

★ **Stars** Timothy Dalton, Carey Lowell, Robert Davi, Talisa Soto, Anthony Zerbe

The James Bond production team has found its second wind with *Licence to Kill*, a cocktail of high-octane action, spectacle and drama.

Presence for the second time of Timothy Dalton as the sauve British agent clearly has juiced up scripters, and director John Glen.

Out go the self-parodying witticisms and over-elaborate high-tech gizmos that slowed pre-Dalton pics to a walking pace. Dalton plays 007 with a vigor and physicality that harks back to the earliest Bond pics, letting full-bloodied actions speak louder than words.

The thrills-and-spills chases are superbly orchestrated as pic spins at breakneck speed through its South Florida and Central American locations. Bond survives a plethora of outstanding underwater and mid-air stunt sequences which

are above par for what has become expected of the series.

He's also pitted against a crew of sinister baddies (led by Robert Davi and Frank McRae) who give the British agent the chance to use all his wit and wiles. Femme elements in the guise of Carey Lowell and Talisa Soto add gloss but play second fiddle to the action.

THE LIGHT AT THE EDGE OF THE WORLD

1971, 120 mins, ◇ Ⓥ *Dir* Kevin Billington   US

★ **Stars** Kirk Douglas, Yul Brynner, Samantha Eggar, Jean Claude Drouot, Fernando Rey, Renato Salvatori

Jules Verne's *The Light at the Edge of the World* shapes up as good action-adventure escapism. The stars are Kirk Douglas, who produced on Spanish locations, as the sole survivor on an island captured by pirate Yul Brynner, with Samantha Eggar as a shipwrecked hostage.

Douglas is a bored assistant to lighthouse-keeper Fernando Rey on a rock off the tip of South America in 1865. Massimo Ranieri, a young man rounding out the group, is brutally killed along with Rey when Brynner's pirate ship takes over the island. Douglas escapes and ekes out a passive survival. When Brynner's men darken the regular beacon and erect a false light to snare Cape Horn vessels, Douglas rescues Renato Salvatori from slaughter and begins to fight back.

Eggar, saved from the shipwreck, is used by Brynner as a look-alike of Douglas' old secret love. From this point on, it's all downhill until the exciting confrontation between Douglas and Brynner atop the burning lighthouse.

THE LIGHTHORSEMEN

1987, 128 mins, ◇ Ⓥ *Dir* Simon Wincer   AUSTRALIA

★ **Stars** Jon Blake, Peter Phelps, Tony Bonner, Bill Kerr, John Walton

Toward the end of this epic about Aussie cavalry fighting in the Middle East in 1917, there's a tremendously exciting and spectacular 14-minute sequence in which soldiers of the Light Horse charge on German/Turkish-occupied Beersheba. It's a pity writer and co-producer Ian Jones couldn't come up with a more substantial storyline to build around his terrific climax.

Focus of attention is on Dave Mitchell, very well played by Peter Phelps. Opening sequence, which is breathtakingly beautiful, is set in Australia and involves young Dave deciding to enlist in the Light Horse after seeing wild horses being mustered for shipment to the Middle East.

Main story involves four friends (Jon Blake, John Walton, Tim McKenzie, Gary Sweet) who are members of the Australian cavalry, chaffing because the British, who have overall command of allied troops in the area, misuse the cavalry time and again, forcing the Australians to dismount before going into battle.

An Aussie soldier takes part in the spectacular cavalry charge on German/Turkish lines in The Lighthorsemen.

The principal leads are very well played, with Phelps a standout as the most interesting of the young soldiers. Walton scores as the quick-tempered leader of the group, while McKenzie creates a character out of very little material. Topbilled Blake is thoroughly charming as Scotty.

LIVE AND LET DIE

1973, 121 mins, ◇ ⓥ *Dir* Guy Hamilton   UK

★ *Stars* Roger Moore, Yaphet Kotto, Jane Seymour, Clifton James, Julius W. Harris, Geoffrey Holder

Live and Let Die, the eighth Cubby Broccoli-Harry Saltzman film based on Ian Fleming's James Bond, introduces Roger Moore as an okay replacement for Sean Connery. The script reveals that plot lines have descended further to the level of the old Saturday afternoon serial.

Here Bond's assigned to ferret out mysterious goings on involving Yaphet Kotto, diplomat from a Caribbean island nation who in disguise also is a bigtime criminal. The nefarious scheme in his mind: give away tons of free heroin to create more American dopers and then he and the telephone company will be the largest monopolies. Jane Seymour, Kotto's tarot-reading forecaster, loses her skill after turning on to Bond-age.

The comic book plot meanders through a series of hardware production numbers. These include some voodoo ceremonies; a hilarious airplane-vs-auto pursuit scene; a double-decker bus escape from motorcycles and police cars; and a climactic inland waterway powerboat chase. Killer sharks, poisonous snakes and man-eating crocodiles also fail to deter Bond from his mission.

THE LIVES OF A BENGAL LANCER

1935, 110 mins, ⓥ *Dir* Henry Hathaway   US

★ *Stars* Gary Cooper, Franchot Tone, Richard Cromwell, Guy Standing, C. Aubrey Smith

Academy Award 1935: Best Picture (Nomination)

Work on *Lancer* commenced four years earlier when Ernest Schoedsack went to India for exteriors and atmosphere. Some of the Schoedsack stuff is still in, but in those four years the original plans were kicked around until lost. Included in the scrapping was the Francis Yeats-Brown novel.

From the book only the locale and title have been retained. With these slim leads five studio writers went to work on a story, and they turned in a pip. In theme and locale *Lancer* is of the *Beau Geste* school. A sweeping, thrilling military narrative in Britain's desert badlands.

There is a stirring emotional conflict between father and son, the former a traditional British commander with

L

Above: *James Bond makes a spectacular escape from the deadly crocodile farm in* **Live and Let Die.**

Below: *Gary Cooper in* **The Lives of a Bengal Lancer,** *about British military stiff upper lip in the face of adversity.*

whom discipline and loyalty to the service come first, and the boy rebelling at his father's cold-blooded attitude.

Gary Cooper and Franchot Tone, as a pair of experienced military officers, are not directly involved in the main theme beyond being actuated by it. They are however the picture's two most important characters and provide the story with its dynamite.

Story concerns their rescue of the colonel's son after the latter's disillusionment over his father's reception of him makes him a setup for capture by a warring native chieftain.

Tone establishes himself as a first-rate light comedian. But in their own way Cooper, Sir Guy Standing, Richard Cromwell, C. Aubrey Smith and Douglas Dumbrille also turn in some first-rate trouping.

THE LIVING DAYLIGHTS

1987, 130 mins, ◇ Ⓥ   *Dir* John Glen   UK

★ *Stars* Timothy Dalton, Maryam d'Abo, Jeroen Krabbe, Joe Don Baker, John Rhys-Davies, Art Malik

Timothy Dalton, the fourth Bond, registers beautifully on all key counts of charm, machismo, sensitivity and technique. In *The Living Daylights* he's abetted by material that's a healthy cut above the series norm of super-hero fantasy.

There's a more mature story of its kind, too, this one about a phony KGB defector involved in gunrunning and a fraternal assassination plot.

There are even some relatively touching moments of romantic contact between Dalton and lead femme Maryam d'Abo as Czech concert cellist. Belatedly, the Bond characterization has achieved appealing maturity.

D'Abo, in a part meant to be something more than that of window-dressed mannikin, handles her chores acceptably. Able support is turned in by Joe Don Baker as a nutcase arms seller, Jeroen Krabbe and John Rhys-Davies as respective KGB bad and good types (a little less arch than the usual types), and Art Malik as an Oxford-educated Afghan freedom fighter.

THE LONG DUEL

1967, 115 mins, ◇ *Dir* Ken Annakin   UK

★ **Stars** Yul Brynner, Trevor Howard, Harry Andrews, Andrew Keir, Charlotte Rampling, Virginia North

Produced and directed by Ken Annakin at Pinewood and on location in Granada, Spain, this is an ambitious actioner which has plenty of punch.

But the yarn, though based on fact, unfolds with little conviction and is repeatedly bogged down by labored dialog and characterization in Peter Yeldham's screenplay [based on a story by Ranveer Singh].

Story is set on the Indian Northwest Frontier during the 1920s and basically hinges on the uneasy relationship and lack of understanding between most of the British top brass and the native tribes. Trevor Howard, an idealistic police officer, is very conscious of the need for tact and diplomacy when handling the touchy natives.

When he is ordered to track down the Bhanta tribe leader (Yul Brynner), who is trying to lead his people from the bondage of the British, Howard recognizes Brynner as a fellow idealist and an enemy to respect.

THE LONG SHIPS

1964, 124 mins, ◇ *Dir* Jack Cardiff   UK, YUGOSLAVIA

★ **Stars** Richard Widmark, Sidney Poitier, Russ Tamblyn, Rosanna Schiaffino, Beba Loncar, Oscar Homolka

Any attempt to put this into the epic class falls down because of a hodge-podge of a storyline, a mixture of styles and insufficient development of characterization.

The plot, which has obviously suffered in both editing and in censorial slaps, is a conglomeration of battles, double-crossing, sea-storms, floggings, unarmed combat with occasional halfhearted peeks at sex. Throughout there's a great deal of noise and the entire experience is a very long drag.

Film [based on the novel by Frans G. Bengtsson] concerns the rivalry of the Vikings and the Moors in search of a legendary Golden Bell, the size of three men and containing 'half the gold in the world'. Leaders of the rival factions are Richard Widmark, an adventurous Viking con man, who plays strictly tongue in cheek, and Sidney Poitier, dignified,

ruthless top man of the Moors. In contrast to Widmark, he seeks to take the film seriously. The clash in styles between these two is a minor disaster.

LORD JIM

1965, 154 mins, ◇ ⊛ *Dir* Richard Brooks   UK, US

★ **Stars** Peter O'Toole, James Mason, Curt Jurgens, Jack Hawkins, Eli Wallach, Dahlia Levi

Many may be disappointed with Richard Brooks' handling of the Joseph Conrad novel. The storyline is often confused, some of the more interesting characters emerge merely as shadowy sketches. Brooks, while capturing the spirit of adventure of the novel, only superficially catches the inner emotional and spiritual conflict of its hero. In this he is not overly helped by Peter O'Toole whose performance is self-indulgent and lacking in real depth.

The story concerns a young merchant seaman. In a moment of cowardice he deserts his ship during a storm and his life is dogged throughout by remorse and an urge to redeem himself. His search for a second chance takes him to South Asia. There he becomes the conquering hero of natives oppressed by a fanatical war lord.

Brooks has teetered between making it a fullblooded,

Peter O'Toole as Conrad's Lord Jim, a sailor dogged by a moment of cowardice and the search for redemption.

no holds-barred adventure yarn and the fascinating psychological study that Conrad wrote. O'Toole, though a fine, handsome figure of a man, goes through the film practically expressionless and the audience sees little of the character's introspection and soul searching.

Of the rest of the cast the two who stand out, mainly because they are provided with the best opportunities, are Eli Wallach and Paul Lukas.

THE MACOMBER AFFAIR

1947, 89 mins, *Dir* Zoltan Korda   US

★ **Stars** Gregory Peck, Robert Preston, Joan Bennett

The Macomber Affair, with an African hunt background, isn't particularly pleasant in content, even though action often is exciting and elements of suspense frequently hop up the spectator. Certain artificialities of presentation, too, and unreal dialog are further strikes against picture, [based on a short story by Ernest Hemingway], although portion of footage filmed in Africa is interesting.

Robert Preston enacts role of Francis Macomber, a rich American with an unhappy wife (Joan Bennett), who arrives at Nairobi and hires Gregory Peck, a white hunter, to take him lion hunting. On the safari, this time in cars, Macomber can't stand up under a lion charge and his wife sees him turn coward. The white hunter kills the lion. Thereafter, Macomber broods over his shame and his wife falls for the dashing hunter.

African footage is cut into the story with showmanship effect, and these sequences build up suspense satisfactorily. There are closeups of lions and other denizens of the veldt, and scenes in which lion and water buffalo charge, caught with telescopic lenses by camera crew sent to Africa from England, will stir any audience. These focal points of the story out-interest the human drama as developed in scripters' enmeshing trio of stars.

MALAYA

1949, 95 mins, *Dir* Richard Thorpe   US

★ **Stars** Spencer Tracy, James Stewart, Valentina Cortese, Sydney Greenstreet, John Hodiak, Lionel Barrymore

Malaya is a pulp-fiction, wartime adventure yarn, based on a factual incident early in the fighting, that takes the customer for a pretty fancy chimerical flight. Kickoff for the story is tied to a letter from President Roosevelt to Manchester Boddy, LA newspaper publisher, concerning the government's need to obtain rubber during the war.

James Stewart plays a roaming newspaper reporter who promises to steal rubber for his government, which supplies him with ships for transporting and gold for bribing. He effects the release from prison of Spencer Tracy to aid in the daring adventure.

Tracy and Stewart are at home in their toughie roles. Valentina Cortese appears very well as a jungle torch singer in the Malayan saloon. Sydney Greenstreet's character of a sharp operatorwho is wise in the ways of man, comes over excellently.

THE MAN FROM SNOWY RIVER

1982, 102 mins, ◇ ⓥ *Dir* George Miller   AUSTRALIA

★ **Stars** Kirk Douglas, Jack Thompson, Tom Burlinson, Sigrid Thornton, Lorraine Bayly

Here is a rattling good adventure story, inspired by a legendary poem [by A.B. 'Banjo' Paterson] which nearly every Australian had drummed into him as a child, filmed in the spectacularly rugged, mountainous terrain in the Great Dividing Ranges in Victoria.

Kirk Douglas plays two brothers who have had a terrible falling-out for reasons explained late in the narrative. While one brother, the wealthy autocratic landowner Harrison fits him like a glove, the actor is less believable as Spur, a gruff, grizzled, out-of-luck prospector.

Apparently, Douglas wrote or rewrote some of the dialog; hopefully not some of Spur's groaners like 'It's a hard country, made for hard men'.

Tom Burlinson shines in his first feature film role as Jim, well matched by Sigrid Thornton as Harrison's high-spirited daughter. Jack Thompson shares top billing with Douglas as Clancy, the crack horseman who becomes Jim's mentor.

THE MAN IN THE IRON MASK

1939, 110 mins, *Dir* James Whale   US

★ **Stars** Louis Hayward, Joan Bennett, Joseph Schildkraut, Alan Hale, Warren William

Alexander Dumas' classic, presented for the first time in film form, is a highly entertaining adventure melodrama. Story has a verve in its tale of dual heirship to the throne of France, used by Dumas as basis of his novel. D'Artagnan and the Three Musketeers reappear as stalwart supporters of Philippe, twin brother of Louis XIV, who is tossed into the Bastille with a fiendishly designed locked iron mask.

Louis Hayward, carrying the dual role of the arrogant Louis XIV and the vigorously self-assured Philippe, gives one of the finest dual characterizations of the screen. He vividly contrasts the king's personality, with its slight swish, with the manly and romantic attitude of twin brother Philippe.

Joan Bennett, is capably romantic. Warren William is carefree and colorful.

**Long Live Adventure...
and Adventurers!**

Columbia Pictures presents

Sean Connery and **Michael Caine**
Christopher Plummer

in the John Huston-John Foreman film **The Man Who Would Be King** A

Also starring Saeed Jaffrey and introducing Shakira Caine
Screenplay by John Huston and Gladys Hill based on a story by Rudyard Kipling Music composed and conducted by Maurice Jarre
Produced by John Foreman Directed by John Huston Services by Royal Service Company Panavision® A Persky-Bright/Devon Feature
A Columbia Pictures-Allied Artists Production Columbia Pictures

Action and adventure in the Himalayas, **The Man Who Would Be King** *with Sean Connery and Michael Caine.*

MAN ON A TIGHTROPE

1953, 105 mins, *Dir* Elia Kazan   US

★ *Stars* Fredric March, Terry Moore, Gloria Grahame, Cameron Mitchell, Adolphe Menjou, Richard Boone

Man on a Tightrope is a taut 'chase' [based on a story, *International Incident* by Neil Paterson]. The chase, in this instance, is an entire circus, a shabby enough troupe but, nonetheless, a burdensome commodity to sneak across any Iron Curtain frontier. But Fredric March does achieve this as he maneuvers his one-ring circus from Czechslovakia into freedom. Director Elia Kazan limns his characters with proper mood and shade, as the red-tape of the Reds becomes mountingly obstructive. He projects beaucoup romance against the general background, including a willful daughter (Terry Moore) and a flirtatious second wife (Gloria Grahame).

Moore is equally volatile in her affections for Cameron Mitchell, an itinerant deckhand whom March suspects as the spy for the Czech secret police. There is effective suspense in Adolphe Menjou's interrogation, as an officious propaganda ministry attache. Robert Beatty is a rival circus owner. The bold manner in which the circus, in full calliope style, parades right by the auxiliary frontier guards and plans its di-

version tactics for escape into the American zone is plausibly staged by Kazan. Much of this footage was shot in Austria and Germany.

THE MAN WHO WOULD BE KING

1975, 129 mins, ◇ *Dir* John Huston   UK

★ *Stars* Sean Connery, Michael Caine, Christopher Plummer, Saeed Jaffrey, Shakira Caine

Whether it was the intention of John Huston or not, the tale of action and adventure is a too-broad comedy, mostly due to the poor performance of Michael Caine.

As Peachy Carnehan, a loudmouth braggart and former soldier in the Indian army, Caine joins forces with another veteran, Daniel Dravot (Sean Connery), to make their fortunes in a mountain land beyond Afghanistan. Connery, in the title role, gives a generally credible, but not very sympathetic, portrayal of the man thrust into potential greatness.

The most redeeming aspect of the film is the performance of Christopher Plummer as Rudyard Kipling, from whose classic story pic is a variation. Despite the small amount of footage he well deserves his star billing.

THE MAN WITH THE GOLDEN GUN

1974, 123 mins, ◇ ⓥ *Dir* Guy Hamilton   UK

★ *Stars* Roger Moore, Christopher Lee, Britt Ekland, Maud Adams, Herve Villechaize, Clifton James

Screenwriters' mission this ninth time around was to give the James Bond character more maturity, fewer gadgetry gimmicks, and more humor. On the last item they fumbled badly; and the comparatively spare arrays of mechanical devices seem more a cost-cutting factor.

Story diverts Bond from tracking down a missing solar energy scientist towards the mission of locating mysterious international hit man (Christopher Lee) who uses tailor-made gold bullets on his contract victims. To nobody's surprise, Lee has the solar energy apparatus installed on his Hong Kong area island hideaway. Bond naturally conquers all obstacles, and finds some fadeout sack time for Britt Ekland, the local British intelligence charmer.

THE MARK OF ZORRO

1940, 93 mins, *Dir* Rouben Mamoulian   US

★ *Stars* Tyrone Power, Linda Darnell, Basil Rathbone, Gale Sondergaard, Eugene Pallette, J. Edward Bromberg

In the 1920s Douglas Fairbanks started his series of historical super-spectacles with *The Mark of Zorro*, a tale of early California under Spanish rule, adapted from Johnston

One of many versions of the masked bandit Zorro, **The Mark of Zorro** *sees Tyrone Power in the title role.*

McCulley's story, *The Curse of Capistrano.* In the remake 20th-Fox inducts Tyrone Power into the lead spot.

The colorful background, detailing Los Angeles as little more than a pueblo settlement under the Spanish flag, is utilized for some thrilling melodramatics unfolded at a consistently rapid pace. Picture consumes a third of its footage in setting the characters and period, and in the early portion drags considerably. But once it gets up steam, it rolls along with plenty of action and, despite its obvious formula of hooded Robin Hood who terrorizes the tax-biting officials of the district to finally triumph for the peons and caballeros, picture holds plenty of entertainment.

Power is not Fairbanks (the original screen Hood) but, fortunately, neither the script nor direction forces him to any close comparison. He's plenty heroic and sincere in his mission, and delays long enough en route for some romantic interludes with the beauteous Linda Darnell.

After an extensive education in the Spanish army in Madrid, Power returns to California to find his father displaced as Alcalde of Los Angeles by thieving J. Edward Bromberg. Latter, with aid of post captain Basil Rathbone and his command, terrorizes the district and piles on burdensome taxes. Power embarks on a one-man Robinhoodian campaign of wild riding and rapier-wielding to clean up the

situation and restore his father to his rightful position. And there's a sweet romance with Darnell, niece of Bromberg, who is unsympathetic to his policies.

Sword duel between Power and Rathbone, running about two minutes, is a dramatic highlight.

THE MASTER OF BALLANTRAE

1953, 88 mins, ◇ ⊛ *Dir* William Keighley   US

★ *Stars* Errol Flynn, Roger Livesey, Anthony Steel, Beatrice Campbell, Yvonne Furneaux, Felix Aylmer

Robert Louis Stevenson's novel provides a tailor-made vehicle for Errol Flynn. Picture was filmed mostly in Scotland, and the backgrounds are a colorful addition to the period values and escapism.

Character development in the plotting is elementary but the handling gets the most out of the script and the competent cast to sharpen the romantic values of the 18th-century adventure yarn.

Flynn's customary heroics are brought off with debonair dispatch, whether it's wooing the girls, duelling or engaging in mass battle. He's seen as Jamie Durrisdeer, heir to the Scottish estate of Ballantrae, who joins a Stuart rebellion against the King of England, becomes a fugitive after the rebels are put down and flees to the West Indies with Irish adventurer Roger Livesey, believing he had been betrayed to the British by his brother.

Livesey is colorful and humorous as Flynn's chief partner in the swashbuckling. Beatrice Campbell is gracious and beautiful as Lady Alison. Yvonne Furneaux, a girl with whom Flynn pitches some extra-curricular wooing, and Gillian Lynne, a pirate's dancing girl friend, also provide femme beauty.

THE MERCENARIES

1968, 106 mins, ◇   *Dir* Jack Cardiff   UK

★ **Stars** Rod Taylor, Yvette Mimieux, Peter Garsten, Jim Brown, Kenneth More, Andre Morell

Based on the Congo uprising, this is a raw adventure yarn [from a novel by Wilbur Smith] with some glib philosophizing which skates superficially over the points of view of the cynical mercenaries and the patriotic Congolese.

Rod Taylor plays a hardbitten mercenary major who's prepared to sweat through any task, however dirty, providing his fee is okay. He's given an assignment by the Congo's president to take a train through rebel Simba-held country and bring back fugitives and a load of uncut diamonds

The Mercenaries, a raw adventure yarn starring Rod Taylor as a major employed to help out in the Congo.

which are stashed away in a beleaguered town.

The action is taken care of effectively but the rapport between some of the characters is rarely smooth nor convincing enough. Pic was filmed in Africa and at Metro's British studios.

Acting is mostly of a straightforward nature for the script does not lend itself to a subtlety of characterization. Taylor makes a robust hero while Jim Brown brings some dignity and interest to the role of the Congolese native.

MISSING IN ACTION

1984, 101 mins, ◇ ⓥ   *Dir* Joseph Zito   US

★ **Stars** Chuck Norris, M. Emmet Walsh, Lenore Kasdorf, James Hong, Pierrino Mascarino, Ernie Ortega

With the Philippines filling in for Vietnam jungles, with Chuck Norris kicking and firing away, with a likable sidekick in the black marketeering figure of M. Emmet Walsh, and with a touch of nudity in sordid Bangkok bars, writer James Bruner and director Joseph Zito have marshalled a formula pic with a particularly jingoistic slant: even though the war is long over, the Commies in Vietnam still deserve the smack of a bullet.

Norris plays a former North Vietnamese prisoner, an American colonel missing in action for seven years, who escapes to the US and then returns to Vietnam determined to find MIAs and convince the world that Yanks are still imprisoned in Vietnam.

MISTER MOSES

1965, 115 mins, ◇ *Dir* Ronald Neame   US

★ *Stars* Robert Mitchum, Carroll Baker, Ian Bannen, Alexander Knox, Raymond St Jacques, Orlando Martins

The Biblical Moses, in a manner, has been updated for this Frank Ross production, switching the plot to an American diamond smuggler leading an African tribe to a promised land. Director Ronald Neame has taken every advantage of fascinating African terrain for his unusual adventure yarn from Max Catto's novel.

Film takes its motivation from orders by the district commissioner for a village, threatened by flood waters of a new dam being constructed, to evacuate. The religious-minded chief, who has heard the story of Moses from a missionary and his daughter who live with the tribe, refuses to take his people in helicopters to be provided for purpose, because the Bible says the children of Israel, when they went to their promised land, took their animals with them. No animals, no go.

Robert Mitchum, a medicine-man who smuggles diamonds, is set down in this ticklish situation, a guy known as Dr Moses. The chief hails him as the true Moses who will lead them to a special government preserve.

MOBY DICK

1930, 70 mins, *Dir* Lloyd Bacon   US

★ *Stars* John Barrymore, Joan Bennett, Lloyd Hughes, May Boley, Walter Long

The Sea Beast was a money picture for Warners in 1926. [This sound remake, using the title of Herman Melville's original novel], again stars John Barrymore.

Moby Dick is just as smart as ever, but Barrymore is smarter. He's got a better whale to work with this time. And Moby Dick deserves his finish, after Barrymore has chased him over seven seas for seven years because of that leg bite.

Back home the demure Joan Bennett, who could never grow old out in New Bedford, waits for her whaling boyfriend to return. *Moby Dick* is stirring, even if you don't believe in whales. And this one's said to have cost Warners $120,000, with or without teeth.

MOBY DICK

1956, 116 mins, ◇ ⓥ *Dir* John Huston   UK

★ *Stars* Gregory Peck, Richard Basehart, Leo Genn, Harry Andrews, Orson Welles, Bernard Miles

Costly weather and production delays on location in Ireland and elsewhere enlarged the bring-home price on John Huston's *Moby Dick* to as high as $5 million.

Moby Dick is interesting more often than exciting, owing to the fact that it is faithful to the time and text [of the Herman Melville novel] more than great theatrical entertainment. Essentially it is a chase picture and yet not escaping the sameness and repetitiousness which often dulls the chase formula.

It was astute of director Huston to work out a print combining color and black-and-white calculated to capture the sombre beauties of New Bedford, circa 1840, and its whaling ways.

Orson Welles appears early and briefly in the story as a local New Bedford preacher who delivers a God-fearing sermon on Jonah and the whale. Welles turns in an effective bit of brimstone exhortation, appropriate to time and place.

Gregory Peck hovers above the crew, grim-faced and hate-obsessed. He wears a stump leg made of the jaw of a whale and he lives only to kill the greatest whale of all, the white-hided super-monster, Moby Dick, the one which had chewed off his leg. Peck's Ahab is not very 'elemental'. It is not that he fails in handling the rhetoric. Actually he does quite well with the stylized speech in which Melville wrote and which Ray Bradbury and Huston have preserved in their screenplay. It's just that Peck often seems understated and much too gentlemanly for a man supposedly consumed by insane fury.

MOGAMBO

1953, 115 mins, ◇ ⓥ *Dir* John Ford   US

★ *Stars* Clark Gable, Ava Gardner, Grace Kelly, Donald Sinden, Eric Pohlmann, Laurence Naismith

The lure of the jungle and romance get a sizzling workout in *Mogambo* and it's a socko package of entertainment, crammed with sexy two-fisted adventure.

While having its origin in the Wilson Collison play [*Red Dust*], this remake is fresh in locale and characterizations switching from the rubber plantations of Indo-China to the African veldt and updating the period.

John Lee Mahin's dialog and situations are unusually zippy and adult. Ava Gardner feeding a baby rhino and elephant, and her petulant storming at a pet boa constrictor to stay out of her ber, are good touches.

The romantic conflict boils up between the principals during a safari into gorilla country, where an anthropologist and his wife plan to do research. Clark Gable is the great white hunter leading the party. Gardner is the girl on the prowl for a man, and who has now settled on Gable. To get him she has to offset the sweeter charms of Grace Kelly, the wife, who also has become smitten with the Gable masculinity and is ready to walk out on Donald Sinden, the unexciting anthropologist.

For the second time in Metro filmmaking history, a picture has been made without a music score (*King Solomon's Mines* was the first) and none is needed as the sounds of the jungle and native rhythms are all that are required.

MOONFLEET

1955, 86 mins, ◇ ⓥ *Dir* Fritz Lang   US

★ *Stars* Stewart Granger, George Sanders, Joan Greenwood, Viveca Lindfors, Jon Whiteley, Liliane Montevecchi

Costumed action, well-spiced with loose ladies and dashing rakehellies, is offered in *Moonfleet*. With mood and action the keynote of the John Houseman production, the direction by Fritz Lang plays both hard, developing considerable movement in several rugged action sequences without neglecting suspense. Period of the J. Meade Falkner novel is the 1750s.

Stewart Granger was a good choice for the dubious hero of the story, a high-living dandy who heads a gang of murderous smugglers headquartering in the English coastal village of Moonfleet. Yarn opens on a Macbeth note of cold, wild-swept moors, and scary, dark shadows, establishing an eerie flavor for the kickoff.

Later, it reminds of *Treasure Island* a bit when Granger and a small boy undergo some imaginative adventures.

MOONRAKER

1979, 126 mins, ◇ ⓥ *Dir* Lewis Gilbert   UK

★ *Stars* Roger Moore, Lois Chiles, Michael Lonsdale, Richard Kiel, Bernard Lee, Corinne Clery

Christopher Wood's script takes the characters exactly where they always go in a James Bond pic and the only question is whether the stunts and gadgets will live up to expectations. They do.

The main problem this time is the outer-space setting which somehow dilutes the mammoth monstrosity that 007 must save the world from. One more big mothership hovering over earth becomes just another model intercut with elaborate interiors.

The visual effects, stuntwork and other technical con-

tributions all work together expertly to make the most preposterous notions believable. And Roger Moore, though still compared to Sean Connery, clearly has adapted the James Bond character to himself and serves well as the wise-cracking, incredibly daring and irresistible hero.

THE MOSQUITO COAST

1986, 117 mins, ◇ ⓥ *Dir* Peter Weir   US

★ *Stars* Harrison Ford, Helen Mirren, River Pheonix, Jadrien Steele, Hilary Gordon, Rebecca Gordon

It is hard to believe that a film as beautiful as *The Mosquito Coast* [adapted from the novel by Paul Theroux] can also be so bleak, but therein lies its power and undoing. A modern variation of *Swiss Family Robinson*, it starts out as a film about idealism and possibilities, but takes a dark turn and winds up questioning the very values it so powerfully presents. There's a stunning performance by Harrison Ford with first-rate filmmaking by Peter Weir.

Ford's Allie Fox is a world-class visionary with the power to realize his vision. He rants and raves against pre-packaged, mass consumed American culture and packs up his wife and four kids and moves them to a remote Caribbean island –79 the Mosquito Coast.

Fox transforms a remote outpost on the island into a thriving community equipped with numerous Rube Goldberg-like gadgets to harness the forces of nature and make life better for the inhabitants. For a while it's an idylic little utopian community, but the seeds of its downfall are present even as it thrives.

As Fox starts to unravel so does the film. None of the outside antagonists supplied by Paul Schrader's screenplay are fitting adversaries for Fox' genius.

MOTHER LODE

1982, 101 mins, ◇ ⓥ *Dir* Charlton Heston   US

★ *Stars* Charlton Heston, Nick Mancuso, Kim Basinger, John Marley, Dale Wilson

As the title indicates, the consuming issue in *Mother Lode* is a search for gold. The picture is not without shortcomings, but is long on good performances, charismatic people in the three principal roles, compelling outdoor aerial sequences in the Cassiar Mountains of British Columbia and high-level suspense throughout.

The role of Silas McGee, the disreputable Scottish miner trying to protect his great secret find, is a switch to villainy for Charlton Heston, but he relishes the role and even makes a creditable pass at a thick Scottish brogue. Nick Mancuso, as the bush-pilot protagonist who would delve the

*Kim Basinger and Nick Mancuso in **Mother Lode**, searching for gold in British Columbia.*

secret location of the lode at any cost, is the character around which the suspense must swirl, and he manages to keep matters tense to the very end.

Kim Basinger, the only femme in the picture, provides the reason for some unusual plot twists, and comes across as a beauteous screen personality.

MOUNTAINS OF THE MOON

1990, 135 mins, ◇ Ⓥ *Dir* Bob Rafelson   US

★ *Stars* Patrick Bergin, Iain Glen, Fiona Shaw, Richard E. Grant, Peter Vaughan, Anna Massey

Bob Rafelson's *Mountains of the Moon* is an outstanding adventure film, adapted from William Harrison's book *Burton and Speke* and the journals of 19th-century explorers Richard Burton and John Hanning Speke. Without sacrificing the historical context this pic provides deeply felt performances and refreshing, offbeat humour.

Starting in 1854, pic documents duo's ill-fated first two expeditions to Africa, climaxing with Speke's discovery of what became named Lake Victoria, the true source of the Nile (though Speke could not prove same). Roger Deakins' gritty, realistic photography of rugged Kenyan locations contrasts with segments of cheery beauty back home in England between treks.

Rafelson brings expert detailing to the saga. The male bonding theme of the two explorers is forcefully and tastefully told. Besides its vivid presentation of the dangers posed by brutal, hostile African tribes, pic strongly develops its major themes of self-realization and self-aggrandizement.

As explorer Speke, Scots actor Iain Glen creates sympathy for a wayward character. He resembles David Bowie on screen, a reminder that the project originally was planned as a vehicle for British rock stars including Bowie until wiser heads prevailed.

THE NAKED EARTH

1958, 96 mins, *Dir* Vincent Sherman   UK

★ *Stars* Richard Todd, Juliette Greco, Finlay Currie, John Kitzmiller, Laurence Naismith, Christopher Rhodes

The Naked Earth is a thoroughly well-made film that peeks into the heart of Africa and comes out with a captivating actress in Juliette Greco. It also presents a twinkling performance by Richard Todd and excellent photography of a bird picking the teeth of a crocodile.

Tale is set in a forsaken section of the darkest continent at the end of the 19th century. It's a story of man's struggle against nature, a bout in which he loses every round but still wins the fight. Todd, an Irishman looking for new wealth, treks to the African hinterlands to launch a farming effort with an old friend he's to meet there. When he finds the friend has been devoured by one of the feared crocodiles, he and the dead friend's female companion get married for convenience, then plant tobacco for profit. Bad luck with his plants pushes Todd into the gloomy rivers to stalk the treacherous crocodiles for their valued skins.

Greco has the humor and sarcasm of an Anna Magnani, and, to top that, a totally sensuous appeal. John Kitzmiller, as the native friend, and Finlay Currie, as a missionary, are excellent. The Milton Holmes script, from his own story, is skilfully constructed and sustains interest with a minimum of involvement.

THE NAKED PREY

1966, 86 mins, ◇ Ⓥ *Dir* Cornel Wilde   US

★ *Stars* Cornel Wilde, Gert Van Der Bergh, Ken Gampu, Patrick Mynhardt, Bella Randels, Morrison Gampu

Filmed entirely in South Africa, *The Naked Prey* is a story of a white man's survival under relentless pursuit by primitive tribesman. Told with virtually no dialog, the story embodies a wide range of human emotion, depicted in actual on-scene photography which effects realism via semi-documentary feel.

Basic story is set in the bush country of a century ago, where safari manager Cornel Wilde and party are captured by natives offended by white hunter Gert Van Der Bergh. All save Wilde are tortured in some explicit footage – not for the squeamish, while he is given a chance to survive – providing he can exist while eluding some dedicated pursuers.

Action then roves between the macroscopic and the microscopic; that is, from long shots of the varying bush country, caught in beautiful soft tones by H.A.R. Thomson's camera, where man is a spot on the landscape, all the way down to minute animal life, in which the pattern of repose, pursuit, sudden death and then repose matches that of Wilde and the natives. Ken Gampu, film and legit actor in South Africa, is excellent as the leader of the pursuing warriors.

NARROW MARGIN

1990, 97 mins, ◇ Ⓥ *Dir* Peter Hyams   US

★ *Stars* Gene Hackman, Anne Archer, James B. Sikking, J.T. Walsh, M. Emmet Walsh, Susan Hogan

Spectacular stunt work and Canadian locations punch up the train thriller *Narrow Margin*, but feature remake is too cool and remote to grab the viewer. Richard Fleischer's trim 1952 classic for RKO had a negative cost of only $230,000, while the remake logs in at $21 million. That extra bread shows up on screen in impressive production values but filmmaker Peter Hyams fails to make his story involving.

Basic plotline is retained in the new version. In the Charles McGraw role, Gene Hackman plays a deputy d.a. delivering key witness Anne Archer to testify against gangster Harris Yulin. Hackman's teammate, cop M. Emmet Walsh, is killed leaving Hackman and Archer to escape from a helicopter of armed heavies. They flee to a train headed across remote stretches of Canada and have to play cat and mouse with the thugs (led by evil James B. Sikking) who've boarded the train to eliminate them.

Hackman adds panache to a one-dimensional role. Archer is stuck with a nothing part, given barely one monolog to express her character's feelings. Curiously there is no sex or suggestion of romance in the film.

NEVER SAY NEVER AGAIN

1983, 137 mins, ◇ Ⓥ *Dir* Irvin Kershner   US

★ *Stars* Sean Connery, Klaus Maria Brandauer, Max Von Sydow, Barbara Carrera, Kim Basinger, Alec McCowen

After a 12-year hiatus, Sean Connery is back in action as James Bond. The new entry marks something of a retreat from the far-fetched technology of many of the later Bonds in favor of intrigue and romance.

Although not acknowledged as such, *Never Say Never Again* is roughly a remake of the 1965 *Thunderball*. World-threatening organization SPECTRE manages to steal two US cruise missiles and announces it will detonate their nuclear warheads in strategic areas unless their outrageous ransom demands are met.

In short order, Bond hooks up with dangerous SPECTRE agent Fatima Blush (Barbara Carrera), who makes several interesting attempts to kill her prey, and later makes the acquaintance of Domino (Kim Basinger), g.f. of SPECTRE kingpin Largo (Klaus Maria Brandauer), who enjoys the challenge presented by the secret agent as long as he thinks he holds the trump card.

What clicks best in the film is the casting. Klaus Maria Brandauer makes one of the best Bond opponents since very early in the series. Carrera lets out all the stops, while the lovely Kim Basinger is luscious as the pivotal romantic and dramatic figure.

And then, of course, there's Connery, in fine form and still very much looking the part.

NIGHT OF THE JUGGLER

1980, 100 mins, ◇ Ⓥ *Dir* Robert Butler   US

★ *Stars* James Brolin, Cliff Gorman, Richard Castellano, Abby Bluestone, Dan Hedaya, Julie Carmen

Night Of The Juggler is a relentlessly preposterous picture which never gives its cast a chance to overcome director Robert Butler's passion for mindless action.

The film is supposed to relate the story [from a novel by William P. McGivern] of James Brolin's frantic and desper-

Remake of Thunderball, Never Say Never Again *sees Sean Connery reprise his role as James Bond 007.*

ate pursuit of a loony kidnapper who grabs his daughter and takes off with her in a car.

But who cares if the performers are never allowed to make the characters come true?

As a frustrated, racist psychotic seeking revenge for the deterioration of his Bronx neighborhood, Cliff Gorman is trapped by the script's needs for him to be so loony you might actually believe in him.

Technically each individual shot was approached with intense concentration on the craft of filmmaking. Which is exactly what's wrong with the picture.

NORTHERN PURSUIT

1943, 93 mins, *Dir* Raoul Walsh   US

★ *Stars* Errol Flynn, Julie Bishop, Helmut Dantine, John Ridgely, Gene Lockhart

This one combines the elements of Nazi spies with the lusty and vigorous adventures of a Canadian North-west mountie.

Yarn pits Errol Flynn as a heroic mountie against Nazi

flyer Helmut Dantine, who's been dropped in the Hudson Bay region by a sub for a war mission in Canada. But Dantine is captured in the wild snow country by Flynn and John Ridgely, with Flynn devising plan to gain confidence of the flyer to smash spy ring. Snow-blanketed north is a fresh background for staging a Nazi spy chase; and full advantage is taken to blend the scenery with the dramatics.

Particularly effective is the process photography with several spectacular shots. At opening is the surfacing of the sub in the ice-covered waters; later a snow avalanche. Both script [from a story by Leslie T. White], and direction by Raoul Walsh, are in keeping with the best traditions of outdoor melodramatics.

NORTH SEA HIJACK

1980, 99 mins, ◇ Ⓥ *Dir* Andrew V. McLaglen   UK

★ *Stars* Roger Moore, James Mason, Anthony Perkins, Michael Parks, Jack Watson

The biggest attraction is the banter between Roger Moore and the various types with whom he comes in conflict during his preparations to save a hijacked supply ship.

A misogynistic but dedicated frogman, whose private crew of frogmen are the only seeming rescuers of the ship, Moore is today's ideal male chauvinistic pig. And delights in it. He doesn't even mind telling the British Prime Minister (a lady, of course) what he thinks of the situation.

He's ably supported by James Mason as a by-the-book

Roger Moore as an eccentric counter-insurgency expert comes under attack in North Sea Hijack.

admiral. Mason is also given star billing and almost builds his role into deserving it but Anthony Perkins and especially Michael Parks certainly belong below the title.

NORTH WEST FRONTIER

1959, 129 mins, ◇ Ⓥ *Dir* J. Lee Thompson   UK

★ *Stars* Kenneth More, Lauren Bacall, Herbert Lom, Wilfrid Hyde White, I.S. Johar, Ursula Jeans

From a smash opening to quietly confident fade, *North West Frontier* is basically the ageless chase yarn, transferred from the prairie to the sun-baked plains of India and done with a spectacular flourish.

Handled with tremendous assurance by J. Lee Thompson, the film is reminiscent of the same director's *Ice Cold in Alex*, with an ancient locomotive replacing the ambulance in that desert war story and with hordes of be-turbaned tribesmen substituting for the Nazi patrols.

Time is the turn of the century when the English still held sway in India. Kenneth More plays an officer ordered to take a boy prince, sacred figurehead to the Hindus, to safety in the teeth of Moslems. In company with an assorted group, More makes his getaway from a besieged citadel in a makeshift coach drawn by a worn-out locomotive.

Throughout the pic, the cast serves the job expertly, More coming through as solid and dependable if a shade too unemotional. Lauren Bacall scores with a keen delineation of the prince's outspoken nurse. Herbert Lom is first-rate as a journalist. I.S. Johar is the hit of the picture as the Indian railroad man.

NORTHWEST PASSAGE

1940, 125 mins, ◇ ⑦ *Dir* King Vidor   US

★ *Stars* Spencer Tracy, Robert Young, Walter Brennan, Ruth Hussey, Nat Pendleton, Donald McBride

Northwest Passage, which hit a negative cost of nearly $2 million, is a fine epic adventure. The picture carries through only the first half of the novel [by Kenneth Roberts] and is so designated in the main title. The title is misleading from an historical standpoint as it only covers the one expedition through upper New York state to the St Lawrence territory where the village of a hostile tribe is wiped out.

Spencer Tracy is brilliantly impressive as the dominating and driving leader of Rogers' Rangers, a band of 160 trained settlers inducted into service to clean up the hostile tribes to make homes and families safe. Robert Young, as the Harvardian who joins the Rangers to sketch Indians, has a more virile role than others assigned him and turns in a fine performance. Walter Brennan provides a typically fine characterization as the friend of Young.

There's a peculiar fascination in the unfolding of the historical narrative and adventure of the inspired band on the march to and from the Indian village. It's a continual battle against natural hazards, possible sudden attacks by ambushing enemies, and a display of indomitable courage to drive through swamps and over mountains for days at a time without food. It's grim and stark drama of those pioneers who blazed trails through the wilderness to make living in this country safe for their families and descendants.

OCTOPUSSY

1983, 130 mins, ◇ ⑦ *Dir* John Glen   UK

★ *Stars* Roger Moore, Maud Adams, Louis Jourdan, Kristina Wayborn, Kabir Bedi, Steven Berkoff

Storyline concerns a scheme by hawkish Russian General Orlov (Steven Berkoff) to launch a first-strike attack with conventional forces against the NATO countries in Europe, relying upon no nuclear retaliation by the West due to weakness brought about by peace movement in Europe.

Orlov is aided in his plan by a beautiful smuggler

*Spencer Tracy and Robert Young as Rogers' Rangers, a band of trained settlers, in **Northwest Passage**.*

Octopussy (Maud Adams), her trader-in-art-forgeries underling Kamal (Louis Jourdan) and exquisite assistant Magda (Kristina Wayborn). James Bond (Roger Moore, in his sixth entry) is set on their trail when fellow agent 009 (Andy Bradford) is killed at a circus in East Berlin.

Trail takes Bond to India (lensed in sumptuous travelog shots) where he is assisted by local contact Vijay (tennis star Vijay Amritraj in a pleasant acting debut). Surviving an impromptu *Hounds of Zaroff* tiger hunt turned manhunt and other perils, Bond pursues Kamal to Germany for the hair-raising race against time conclusion.

Film's high points are the spectacular aerial stuntwork marking both the pre-credits teaser and extremely dangerous-looking climax.

OKLAHOMA CRUDE

1973, 108 mins, ◇ ⑦ *Dir* Stanley Kramer   US

★ *Stars* George C. Scott, Faye Dunaway, John Mills, Jack Palance, William Lucking, Harvey Jason

Oklahoma Crude is a dramatically choppy potboiler about oil wildcatting in 1913.

Faye Dunaway plays a bitter woman determined to bring in an oil well on her own, aided by Rafael Campos, an Indian laborer. John Mills aiming to help her out after years

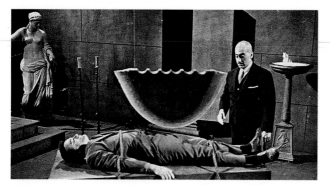

Robert Vaughn is the Man from U.N.C.L.E. in his first movie outing in **One Spy Too Many.**

of parental abandonment, recruits George C. Scott from the hobo jungles. The three of them (Campos is killed off early) joust with Jack Palance, snarling provocateur of the oil trust which wants Dunaway's property.

Since Oklahoma today does not resemble 1913, director Stanley Kramer found a great location in Stockton, California, but the solid impact of that choice is often negated by erratic special effects work.

Scott hunkers around chewing the scenery, but occasionally the interplay with Dunaway is momentarily touching. Mills does well, but Palance's caricature destroys the chance for a good, tough characterization.

ONE SPY TOO MANY

1966, 101 mins, ◇ *Dir* Joseph Sargent   US

★ **Stars** Robert Vaughn, David McCallum, Rip Torn, Dorothy Provine, Leo G. Carroll, Yvonne Craig

Expanded from a *Man from U.N.C.L.E.* TV two-parter, *One Spy Too Many* zips along at a jazzy spy thriller pace.

Action and gadgetry are hung on a slender plot. Alexander, played by Rip Torn, is out to take over the world in the fashion of his Greek namesake. He hoists from the US Army Biological Warfare Division a tankful of its secret 'will gas', leaving a Greek inscription in the lab. International espionage agents Robert Vaughn and David McCallum begin to pursue Alexander and are joined in their efforts by his wife (Dorothy Provine), who is attempting to reach her husband in order to have him sign her divorce papers.

ORCA

1977, 92 mins, ◇ Ⓥ *Dir* Michael Anderson   US

★ **Stars** Richard Harris, Charlotte Rampling, Will Sampson, Bo Derek, Keenan Wynn, Robert Carradine

Orca is man-vs-beast nonsense. Some fine special effects and underwater camera work are plowed under in dumb story-telling.

Richard Harris is a shark-hunting seafarer who incurs the enmity of a superintelligent whale after harpooning the whale's pregnant mate.

We learn all about the whales from Charlotte Rampling, ever at the ready with scientific exposition, occasional voiceover and arch posing.

Assorted supporting players include Will Sampson, who complements Rampling's pedantic dialog with ancient tribal lore; Peter Hooten, Bo Derek and Keenan Wynn, a part of the Harris boat crew; Scott Walker as menacing leader of village fishermen who wish Harris would just leave their whale-harassed town.

PAPER TIGER

1975, 101 mins, ◇ *Dir* Ken Annakin   UK

★ **Stars** David Niven, Toshiro Mifune, Hardy Kruger, Ando, Ivan Desny, Irene Tsu

Paper Tiger recalls the plots of vintage Shirley Temple vehicles in its cutesy relationship between English tutor David Niven and an 11-year-old Japanese moppet, (Ando), kidnapped together during turmoil in an unnamed Southeast Asian country.

Ando, like Temple, is dimpled, plucky, clever, and more resourceful than any of the adults in the story. He has a fresh, engaging personality, and it isn't his fault the camera moons over him at every opportunity.

Niven tries hard to breathe subtlety into his coward-turned-hero role, but is impeded by the lame screenplay and plodding direction. Toshiro Mifune, playing Ando's ambassador father, acts like his mind is elsewhere.

PAPILLON

1973, 150 mins, ◇ Ⓥ *Dir* Franklin J. Schaffner   US

★ **Stars** Steve McQueen, Dustin Hoffman, Victor Jory, Don Gordon, Anthony Zerbe, Robert Deman

Henri Charriere's story of confinement in, and escape from, the infamous French Guiana prison colony was that of an ordeal. So is Franklin J. Schaffner's film version. For 150 uninterrupted minutes, the mood is one of despair, brutality, and little hope.

The script is very good within its limitations, but there is insufficient identification with the main characters. Steve McQueen, for example, says he has been framed for murdering a pimp; we do not see the injustice occur, hence have insufficient empathy.

Dustin Hoffman plays an urbane counterfeiter, a white

collar criminal whose guilt is beyond question. Hoffman does an excellent job in portraying his character's adaptation to the corruptibilities of prison life.

The film begins with co-adaptor Dalton Trumbo (in an unbilled bit) addressing the latest shipload of prisoners consigned to the South American jungle horrors. He informs them they are henceforth nonhuman baggage. The oppressive atmosphere is so absolutely established within the first hour of the film that, in a sense, it has nowhere to go for the rest of the time.

The film cost $13 million and was shot mostly in Spain and in Jamaica.

PIRATES

1986, 124 mins, ◇ ⓥ *Dir* Roman Polanski

FRANCE, TUNISIA

★ *Stars* Walter Matthau, Damien Thomas, Richard Pearson, Cris Campion, Charlotte Lewis, Olu Jacobs

Roman Polanski's *Pirates* is a decidedly underwhelming comedy adventure adding up to a major disappointment.

Pirates first was announced as a 1976 Polanski feature to star Jack Nicholson and Isabelle Adjani, before finally being produced (commencing in 1984) in Tunisia, Malta and the Seychelles, costing in excess of $30 million.

Above: *Steve McQueen is* **Papillon,** *first prisoner to escape France's prison colony on Devil's Island.*

Below: *Walter Matthau as Captain Red, a peg-legged British pirate captain in Roman Polanski's* **Pirates.**

Shelley Winters, Red Buttons and Ernest Borgnine try to escape upside down ship in **The Poseidon Adventure.**

Walter Matthau gainfully essays the central role of Capt Thomas Bartholomew Red, a peg-legged British pirate captain with plenty of Long John Silver in his manner. Teamed with a handsome young French sailor (Cris Campion), Red is captured by Don Alfonso (Damien Thomas), captain of the Spanish galleon *Neptune*.

In a series of turnabout adventures, Red causes the *Neptune*'s crew to mutiny, takes the niece (Charlotte Lewis) of the governor of Maracaibo hostage, and steals a golden Aztec throne from the Spaniards.

Casting is unimpressive, with Matthau unable to carry the picture singlehandedly. Newcomer Campion projects a pleasant personality, more than can be said for Polanski's discovery Charlotte Lewis, thoroughly inexpressive here.

PLYMOUTH ADVENTURE

1952, 104 mins, ◇   *Dir* Clarence Brown   US

★ *Stars* Spencer Tracy, Gene Tierney, Van Johnson, Leo Genn, Lloyd Bridges, Dawn Adams

Metro has made *Plymouth Adventure*, the story of the Mayflower's perilous voyage to America [from a novel by Ernest Gebler], a large-scale sea spectacle.

The production, ably executed, puts more emphasis on the voyage itself and the attendant dangers than on developing the characters into flesh-and-blood people.

To Spencer Tracy falls the chore of enacting Captain Christopher Jones, the tough, earthy master of the Mayflower. Gene Tierney is the tragic Dorothy Bradford and Leo Genn her husband, the William Bradford later to become the first governor of the new colony. Van Johnson is John Alden, the carpenter who ships on the voyage and later marries Priscilla Mullins, played by Dawn Addams. They are all competent.

THE POSEIDON ADVENTURE

1972, 117 mins, ◇ ⓥ   *Dir* Ronald Neame   US

★ *Stars* Gene Hackman, Ernest Borgnine, Red Buttons, Carol Lynley, Roddy McDowall, Stella Stevens

The Poseidon Adventure is a highly imaginative and lustily-produced meller that socks over the dramatic struggle of 10 passengers to save themselves after an ocean liner capsizes when struck by a mammoth tidal wave created by a submarine earthquake.

It is a case of everything being upside down; in this reversed world of twisted ruin the principals' goal is the vessel's bottom where to break through may be some hope of survival for them.

The adaptation of the Paul Gallico novel plays up the tragic situation with a set of values which permits powerful action and building tension.

Chief protagonist is played by Gene Hackman, as a free-talking minister who keeps his cool and assumes leadership of the small group.

THE PRIDE AND THE PASSION

1957, 132 mins, ◇ ⓥ   *Dir* Stanley Kramer   US

★ *Stars* Cary Grant, Frank Sinatra, Sophia Loren, Theodore Bikel

This is Stanley Kramer's powerful production of C.S. Forester's sweeping novel, *The Gun*, about the Spanish 'citizens' army' that went to battle against the conquering legions of the French in 1810. The picture was in preparation and production in Spain for a year and a half.

It is the story of the band of guerillas who come upon

Cary Grant fires the oversized cannon that is the focus of **The Pride and the Passion,** *period pic set in Spain.*

an oversized cannon that is abandoned by the retreating Spanish army. All things revolve around the huge weapon; it becomes symbolic of the spirit and courage of the Spanish patriots and their leader (Frank Sinatra).

From this point on *Passion* focuses on this unlikely army seeking to make its way to the French stronghold at Avila against incredibly tall odds. Their ally is Cary Grant, a British naval officer assigned to retrieve the gun for use against Napoleon's forces.

Sophia Loren is Sinatra's sultry and inflammable mistress with beaucoup accent on the decollete. At first hostile toward Grant, she comes to recognize his pro-Spanish motives and veers to him romantically. They make for an engaging trio.

Top credit must go to the production. The panoramic, long-range views of the marching and terribly burdened army, the painful fight to keep the gun mobile through ravine and over waterway – these are major plusses.

PRINCE VALIANT

1954, 100 mins, ◇ ⓥ *Dir* Henry Hathaway   US

★ *Stars* James Mason, Janet Leigh, Robert Wagner, Debra Paget, Sterling Hayden, Victor McLaglen

The cartoon strip hero comes to the screen as a good offering for fans who dote on the fanciful derring-do of the Arthurian period.

Harold Foster's King Features strip gives an imaginative action basis for Robert L. Jacks' production guidance and the direction by Henry Hathaway. Although the picture comes in a bit overlength, the direction and Dudley Nichols' scripting combine to bring it off acceptably against some rather dazzling settings, including authentic castles and sites actually lensed in England.

Heading the star list is James Mason, who plays Sir Brack, pretender to King Arthur's throne. His dirty work is excellent, whether thinking up ambushes for Robert Wagner, in the title role, or engaging the young hero in joust or broadsword combat. The way he and Mason have at each other in the climaxing duel puts a topnotch action capper on the tale.

The plot finds Wagner in exile with his royal parents after their throne was seized by Primo Carnera. The Viking prince goes to King Arthur's court, becomes a squire to Sir Gawain, falls in love with Janet Leigh and, eventually, is able to put the finger on Mason as the mysterious Black Knight.

THE PRISONER OF ZENDA

1922, 130 mins, ⊗ *Dir* Rex Ingram   US

★ *Stars* Lewis Stone, Alice Terry, Robert Edeson, Stuart Holmes, Barbara La Marr, Lois Lee

To say that Rex Ingram and a remarkably good company of screen players have made the very utmost of the possibilities of Anthony Hope's novel about sums up this venture. It is the kind of romance that never stales – fresh, genuine, simple and wholesome. Indeed this screen translation is more profoundly interesting than either the novel or the Edward Rose stage play.

Ingram built a spacious ballroom with an atmosphere of unobtrusive splendor. For once you get the illusion that it is a royal ball and not a movie mob scene.

Another bit of finesse is the choice of the hero and heroine, in Lewis Stone, who makes no pretence to Apollo-like beauty, and Alice Terry who makes a Princess Flavia of surpassing blonde loveliness in her regal robes.

The close-ups of all the characters are done in a misty dimness that gives them a remoteness that inspires the imagination. Some of the landscapes are handled in like manner and throughout the photography is marked.

THE PRISONER OF ZENDA

1937, 100 mins, ⓥ *Dir* John Cromwell   US

★ *Stars* Ronald Colman, Madeleine Carroll, Douglas Fairbanks Jr, Mary Astor, C. Aubrey Smith, Raymond Massey

Zenda is hokum of the 24-carat variety [from Anthony Hope's novel, dramatized by Edward Rose]; a sheer piece of romantic nonsense about a mythical European kingdom, a struggle for possession of a throne between a dissolute true heir and an ambitious step-brother with larcenous inclinations; a lovely blonde princess; a swashbuckling duke, who bends with the political wind, and a young Englishman, on his annual outing, who is persuaded to impersonate the king.

Cromwell's direction is excellent. His opening scenes in the Balkan capital are as casual as a travelog, and his players assume lifelike characterizations through a series of intimate, human situations.

Colman (who plays the dual role of Englishman and King) has the ability to make a full dress court uniform appear as comfortable as a suit of pajamas. He never trips over his sword, or loosens his collar for air. Madeleine Carroll in all her blonde loveliness is quite receptive to impassioned protestations, so the romance has a touch of verity.

It's a close race between Colman and Fairbanks Jr, who plays Rupert of Hentzau for top acting honours. Best femme part is the scheming Antoinette, which Mary Astor is inclined to underplay.

THE PRISONER OF ZENDA

1952, 100 mins, ◇ ⓥ *Dir* Richard Thorpe   US

★ *Stars* Stewart Granger, Deborah Kerr, James Mason, Louis Calhern, Jane Greer, Lewis Stone

Fanciers of costumed swashbucklers will find this remake of the venerable *Prisoner of Zenda* a likeable version. The third time around for the yarn [adapted by Wells Root from

C. Aubrey Smith, David Niven and Ronald Colman in splendid costume swashbuckler, **The Prisoner of Zenda.**

the novel by Anthony Hope] this time it wears Technicolor dress, and has lavish physical appurtenances.

Plot deals with an Englishman who goes on a holiday to the small kingdom of Ruritania and gets involved in a royal impersonation and a love affair with a beautiful princess. Stewart Granger is the hero, dualing as the Englishman and the king he impersonates, and gives the roles the proper amount of dashing heroics.

Opposite him is Deborah Kerr, the lovely princess, and her looks and ability to wear period gowns are just what the part requires. James Mason scores as Rupert of Hentzau, making the character a rather likeable heavy.

Lewis Stone, who played the dual role in the original 1922 version of the story, appears briefly in this one as the cardinal.

THE PUNISHER

1990, 90 mins, ◇ Ⓥ *Dir* Mark Goldblatt   US, AUSTRALIA

★ **Stars** Dolph Lundgren, Louis Gossett Jr, Jeroen Krabbe, Kim Miyori, Bryan Marshall, Nancy Everhard

With origins in a Marvel Comics character, *The Punisher* is, as might be expected, two-dimensional. The Punisher has killed 125 people before the film even begins, and the ensuing 90 minutes are crammed with slaughters of every conceivable kind. Pic was the only product of the New World offshoot Down Under.

Story involves an ex-cop whose wife and children were murdered by the mafia in New York. He hides from civilization in the city's sewers and for five years he's been killing the various heads of the mob families in nonstop vengeance.

Another party comes to play – the Japanese mafia headed by the glamorous, stony cold Lady Tanaka. The

Dolph Lundgren is **The Punisher,** *a ex-cop who wages war, single-handed, against the Japanese Mafia in New York.*

Punisher is quite content to see his enemies slaughter each other until the Japanese kidnap the locals' children.

Dolph Lundgren looks just as if he's stepped out of a comic book. Thankfully, he breezes through the B-grade plot with tongue firmly placed in cheek.

PUPPET ON A CHAIN

1971, 98 mins, ◇ ⑨ *Dir* Geoffrey Reeve   UK

★ *Stars* Sven-Bertil Taube, Barbara Parkins, Alexander Knox, Patrick Allen, Vladek Sheybal, Penny Casdagli

Puppet on a Chain could be remembered as the film with the speedboat chase. Don Sharp, who was engaged specially to direct this sequence, has in no way spared the boats as the hero relentlessly pursues the villain through the canals of Amsterdam. Regrettably the standard of this sequence is not reflected in the rest of the film.

Sven-Bertil Taube plays a US narcotics agent seeking the headquarters of a drug syndicate in Amsterdam aided by his undercover assistant, Maggie (Barbara Parkins). Wherever they go sudden death is never far behind. The trail leads to a religious order and an island castle.

Alistair MacLean scripted his own story. There is all the action, implausible happenings, violent rough housing and mystery that distinguishes so much of his work, but he has created little sympathy for the characters.

QUEST FOR FIRE

1981, 97 mins, ◇ *Dir* Jean-Jacques Annaud
                                          FRANCE, CANADA

★ *Stars* Everett McGill, Rae Dawn Chong, Ron Perlman, Nameer El Kadi, Gary Schwartz, Kurt Schiegel

Jean-Jacques Annaud's *Quest for Fire* is an engaging prehistoric yarn that happily never degenerates into a club and lion-skin spinoff of *Star Wars* and resolutely refuses to bludgeon the viewer with facile or gratuitous effects.

Despite four years of effort, a $12 million budget, grueling location shooting in Kenya, Scotland, Iceland and Canada, hundreds of masks and costumes and a herd of difficult elephants (making their screen appearance as mammoths), Annaud and his collaborators have brought off a polished entertainment.

Technical advisor Anthony Burgess invented special primitive jargons for the occasion, which are used in moderation and don't jar comically on the ears.

Gerard Brach's screenplay is loosely based on Jean-Henri Rosny the Elder's *La guerre du feu* (1911), a classic of

Primitive homo sapiens search for protection against unfriendly Neanderthals in **Quest For Fire.**

French language popular literature. He also introduces a female character as a major dramatic and emotional pivot.

Three warriors of a primitive homo sapiens tribe are sent out to find a source of fire after their old pilot lights are extinguished during an attack by a group of unneighborly Neanderthals. After numerous adventures they not only find a fire amongst a cannibal tribe, but also learn how to produce it when they are led to an advanced human community by a young girl whom they've saved from the cannibals.

Annaud wisely uses mimes, dancers, acrobats and stuntmen for many of the secondary and extra roles. Under the guidance of anthropologist Desmond Morris, they provide credible physical expression under their excellent masks and makeup.

Everett Gill, New York stage actor Ron Perlman, and Turkish-born Nameer El Kadi etch engaging portraits as the three early homo sapiens, but the best performance comes from 20-year-old Rae Dawn Chong (daughter of comic Tommy Chong), unaffectedly radiant as the tribal nymphet who teaches them how to make a fire and eventually mates with Gill (after showing him how to make love face-to-face).

RAIDERS OF THE LOST ARK

1981, 115 mins, ◇ *Dir* Steven Spielberg   US

★ *Stars* Harrison Ford, Karen Allen, Denholm Elliott, Paul Freeman, Alfred Molina

Raiders of the Lost Ark is the stuff that raucous Saturday matinees at the local Bijou once were made of, a crackerjack fantasy-adventure.

Steeped in an exotic atmosphere of lost civilizations, mystical talismans, gritty mercenary adventurers, Nazi arch-

P Q R

villians and ingenious death at every turn, the film is largely patterned on the serials of the 1930s, with a large dollop of Edgar Rice Burroughs.

Story [by George Lucas and Philip Kaufman] begins in 1936 as Indiana Jones (Harrison Ford), an archeologist and university professor who's not above a little mercenary activity on the side, plunders a South American jungle tomb. He secures a priceless golden Godhead, only to have it snatched away by longtime archeological rival Paul Freeman, now employed by the Nazis.

Back in the States, Ford is approached by US intelligence agents who tell him the Nazis are rumored to have discovered the location of the Lost Ark of the Covenant (where the broken 10 Commandments were sealed). The ark is assumed to contain an awesome destructive power. Ford's mission is to beat the Germans to the ark.

Director Steven Spielberg has deftly veiled proceedings in a sense of mystical wonder that makes it all the more easy for viewers to suspend disbelief and settle back to watch the fun.

THE RAINS CAME

1939, 100 mins, *Dir* Clarence Brown   US

★ **Stars** Myrna Loy, Tyrone Power, George Brent, Jane Darwell, Brenda Joyce, Maria Ouspenskaya

Liberties have been taken with [Louis Bromfield's] original novel, resulting in switching some of the original

Harrison Ford as adventure-seeking archaeologist Indiana Jones in Steven Spielberg's Raiders of the Lost Ark.

characterizations or intent, but under production code restrictions, and to conform with the mass market of film entertainment, it merges as a competent job.

Newcomer Brenda Joyce, cast as the daughter of so- cial- climbing missionaries, rings the bell throughout with a consistent performance as a forthright romantic adolescent, stuck on George Brent. Latter is the wastrel, of good British family, who has been dawdling in Ranchipur for years on an art assignment.

His best friend is the enlightened young Dr-Major Rama Safti, who is blind to any romantic deviations, in his intensive medical duties, until Myrna Loy comes on the scene.

THE RAINS OF RANCHIPUR

1955, 104 mins, ◇ *Dir* Jean Negulesco   US

★ **Stars** Lana Turner, Richard Burton, Fred MacMurray, Joan Caulfield, Michael Rennie

Louis Bromfield's *The Rains Came*, brought to the screen once before by 20th-Fox in 1939, is filmed this time with Lana Turner as the titled trollop.

However, the cast itself hardly be less lifeless. The only sturdy performances are those turned in by Richard

Burton and Eugenie Leontovich.

Turner, as Edwina (Lady Esketh) has the role of a temptress down pat, perhaps too much so. She's good in a couple of scenes, indifferent in most of them and almost embarrassing in some. Burton's portrayal of Dr Safti, the dedicated Indian doctor, who falls in love with Turner, has strength and conviction and is underplayed intelligently. As the Maharani, Leontovich has dignity, and the scenes between her and Burton are definite assets to the picture.

RAISE THE TITANIC

1980, 102 mins, ◇ Ⓥ *Dir* Jerry Jameson   UK

★ **Stars** Jason Robards, Richard Jordan, Alec Guinness, David Selby, Anne Archer, M. Emmet Walsh

Raise the Titanic wastes a potentially intriguing premise with dull scripting, a lackluster cast, laughably phony trick work, and clunky direction. Half of the running time (at least) is devoted to underwater miniature shots of submarines and other apparatus trying to dislodge the long-lost luxury liner *Titanic* from its deepsea resting place.

The ridiculously expository screenplay [adapted by Eric Hughes from the novel by Clive Cussler] repeatedly explains what will happen, why it's happening, and how it's going to happen.

The actors adopt various strategies for coping with their unspeakable dialog and cardboard characterizations. Alec Guinness provides a dramatic highlight with a lovely scene as a retired old salt who had served as a member of the *Titanic*'s crew.

RAMBO FIRST BLOOD PART II

1985, 95 mins, ◇ Ⓥ *Dir* George Pan Cosmatos   US

★ **Stars** Sylvester Stallone, Richard Crenna, Charles Napier, Julia Nickson, Steven Berkoff, Martin Kove

This overwrought sequel to the popular *First Blood* (1982) is one mounting fireball as Sylvester Stallone's special operations veteran is sprung from a prison labor camp by his former Green Beret commander (Richard Crenna) to find POWs in Vietnam.

That the secret mission is a cynical ruse by higher-ups which is meant to fail heightens Stallone's fury while touching off a provocative political theme: a US government that wants to forget about POWs and accommodate the public at the same time.

The charade on the screen, which is not pulled off, is to accept that the underdog Rambo character, albeit with the help of an attractive machine-gun wielding Vietnamese girl (Julia Nickson), can waste hordes of Vietcong and Red Army contingents enroute to hauling POWs to an air base in Thailand in a smoking Russian helicopter with only a facial scar (from a branding iron-knifepoint) marring his tough physique.

Steven Berkoff is a twisted and nominally chilly Russian advisor, but his performance is essentially the same nasty thing he did in *Octopussy* and *Beverly Hills Cop*.

Slyvester Stallone in second outing for Viet vet and all-round tough hombre Rambo in **Rambo First Blood Part II.**

Patrick Swayze, Charlie Sheen and C. Thomas Howell form part of teenage guerrilla outfit in **Red Dawn.**

RAMBO III

1988, 101 mins, ◇ Ⓥ *Dir* Peter Macdonald US

★ *Stars* Sylvester Stallone, Richard Crenna, Marc de Jonge, Kurtwood Smith, Spiros Focas

Rambo III stakes out a moral high ground for its hero missing or obscured in the previous two pictures. In the Soviets' heinous nine-year occupation of Afghanistan, this mythic commando and quintessential outsider is enlisted in a cause that – glasnost notwithstanding – is indisputably righteous.

Indeed, as this chapter opens, the character of John Rambo has been demilitarized and transported to exotic self-exile in Thailand, where he lives in a Buddhist monastery and supports himself by engaging in slam-bang mercenary martial arts contests.

Richard Crenna has come halfway around the world to Bangkok to ask Stallone for payback – Rambo's participation in a clandestine operation to destroy a 'brutal' Russian general who rules a remote province in occupied Afghanistan.

The battle scenes in *Rambo III* are explosive and conflagratory tableaux that make for wrenching, frequently terrifying viewing. Always at ground zero in the chaos is Rambo – gloriously, inhumanly impervious to fear and danger – whose character is inhabited by Stallone with messianic intensity.

REAP THE WILD WIND

1942, 124 mins, Ⓥ *Dir* Cecil B. DeMille US

★ *Stars* Ray Milland, John Wayne, Paulette Goddard, Raymond Massey, Robert Preston, Susan Hayward

Reap the Wild Wind is a melodrama of Atlantic coastal shipping in the windjammer days, 100 years ago. It is a film possessing the spectacular sweep of colorful backgrounds which characterize the Cecil DeMille type of screen entertainment.

After a short foreword by DeMille, the picture opens with scenes of a hurricane, shipwreck and struggle for bounty among the salvage workers. This melodramatic tempo is too swift to be maintained. Various angles of plot and contest necessarily must be introduced. The pacing is uneven.

Towards the end, however, the action quickens. There is a unique filming of an undersea battle between a giant squid, of octopus descent, and the two male protagonists. Despite its obvious make-believe, it is shrewd filming, realistic and thrilling.

The production is a visual triumph. Some of the marine scenes are breathtaking. There is skilful blending of process photography.

RED DAWN

1984, 114 mins, ◇ Ⓥ *Dir* John Milius US

★ *Stars* Patrick Swayze, C. Thomas Howell, Ron O'Neal, William Smith, Powers Booth, Charlie Sheen

Red Dawn charges off to an exciting start as a war picture and then gets all confused in moralistic handwriting, finally sinking in the sunset.

Sometime in the future, the United States stands alone and vulnerable to attack, abandoned by its allies. Rather than an all-out nuclear war Soviet and Cuban forces bomb selectively and then launch a conventional invasion across the southern and northwest Boleroborders.

Dawn takes place entirely in a small town taken by surprise by paratroopers. Grabbing food and weapons on the run, a band of teens led by Patrick Swayze and C. Thomas Howell makes it to the nearby mountains as the massacre continues below.

Swayze, Howell and the other youngsters are all good in their parts.

RED LINE 7000

1965, 118 mins, ◇ *Dir* Howard Hawks US

★ *Stars* James Caan, Laura Devon, Gail Hire, Charlene Holt, John Robert Crawford, Marianna Hill

Script by George Kirgo, based on a story by director Howard Hawks, centers on three sets of characters as they go about their racing and lovemaking. Trio of racers are members of a team operating out of Daytona, Fla, their individual lives uncomplicated until three femmes fall in love with them. In a thrilling climax, one of the drivers, overcome with jealousy, causes another to crash but miraculously his life is saved.

Making excellent impressions are Laura Devon, Gail Hire and Marianna Hill, as girlfriends of the three daredevils of the track. James Caan, John Robert Crawford and James Ward in these roles are effective.

Hawks is on safe ground while his cameras are focused on race action. His troubles lie in limning his various characters in their more intimate moments. Title refers to an engine speed beyond which it's dangerous to operate a race car, perhaps symbolic of what Hawks wanted to achieve in the emotions of his players.

REDS

1981, 200 mins, ◇ *Dir* Warren Beatty   US

★ *Stars* Warren Beatty, Diane Keaton, Jerzy Kosinski, Jack Nicholson, Maureen Stapleton, Edward Herrmann

Warren Beatty's *Reds* is a courageous and uncompromising attempt to meld a high-level socio-political drama of ideas with an intense love story, but it is ultimately too ponderous.

More than just the story of American journalist-activist John Reed's stormy romantic career with writer Louise Bryant, a kinetic affair backdropped by pre-World War I radicalism and the Russian Revolution, the film is also, to its eventual detriment, structured as a Marxist history lesson.

First half of the film, though it takes an inordinant amount of time and detail to do it, does an intelligent job of setting both the political and emotional scene. Beginning in 1915, Reed (Beatty) is introduced as an idealistic reporter of decidedly radical bent who meets Portland writer Bryant (Diane Keaton) and persuades her to join him in New York within a tight-knit radical intellectual salon that includes the likes of playwright Eugene O'Neill (Jack Nicholson), anarchist-feminist Emma Goldman (Maureen Stapleton) and radical editor Max Eastman (Edward Herrmann).

Their on-again, off-again affair – which challenges their respective claims of emotional liberation – survives Keaton's brief fling with Nicholson and they marry.

But Beatty's inability to resist the growing socialist bandwagon strains them yet again and Keaton ships off to cover the French battlefront and begin life afresh. En route to cover the upcoming conflagration in Russia, Beatty persuades her to join him – in professional, not emotional status – and in Petrograd, the revolutionary fervor rekindles their romantic energies as well.

Reds bites off more than an audience can comfortably chew. Constant conflicts between politics and art, love and social conscience, individuals versus masses, pragmatism against idealism, take the form of intense and eventually exhausting arguments that dominate the script by Beatty and British playwright Trevor Griffiths.

As director, Beatty has harnessed considerable intensity into individual confrontations but curiously fails to give the film an overall emotional progression.

RED SONJA

1985, 89 mins, ◇ Ⓥ *Dir* Richard Fleischer   US

★ *Stars* Brigitte Nielsen, Arnold Schwarzenegger, Sandahl Bergman, Paul Smith, Ernie Reyes Jr, Ronald Lacey

Red Sonja [based on stories by Robert E. Howard] returns to those olden days when women were women and the menfolk stood around with funny hats on until called forth to be whacked at. Except, of course, for Arnold Schwarzenegger, whose Kalidor creation has just enough muscles to make him useful to the ladies, but not enough brains to make him a bother, except that he talks too much.

To her credit in the title role, Brigitte Nielsen never listens to a word he has to say, perhaps because he has an unfortunate tendency to address her as 'Sony-uh.' Nielsen wants to revenge her sister and find the magic talisman all on her own with no help from Kalidor, though she does think it's kind of cute when he wades into 80 guys and wastes them in an effort to impress her.

THE RED TENT

1971, 121 mins, ◇ Ⓥ *Dir* Mikhail Kalatozov   ITALY, USSR

★ *Stars* Sean Connery, Claudia Cardinale, Hardy Kruger, Peter Finch, Massimo Girotti, Luigi Vannucchi

This first Italo-Russian co-production deals with the 1928 rescue of an Italian Polar expedition stranded by a dirigible crash. Beautiful Arctic footage, plus a personal story of survival, make the production compelling and suspenseful.

Framework of the script is metaphysical; a sort of rugged adventure yarn in a Jean-Paul Sartre setting. Peter Finch plays General Nobile, an Italian Arctic explorer who is lost in the North Atlantic wastes.

Sean Connery plays Roald Amundsen, a fellow explorer who died in search for Finch; Claudia Cardinale plays a nurse who was in love with one of Finch's crew; and Hardy Kruger is a daredevil rescue pilot whose motivations in rescuing Finch before his men creates an international scandal.

Connery plays an aged man very convincingly. Kruger and Cardinale supply key plot motivations, but the heaviest burden is on Finch; he is excellent in a characterization which demands many moods, many attitudes.

THE RETURN OF THE MUSKETEERS

1989, 94 mins, ◇ Ⓥ *Dir* Richard Lester   UK, FRANCE, SPAIN

★ *Stars* Michael York, Oliver Reed, Frank Finlay, C. Thomas Howell, Richard Chamberlain, Kim Cattrall

In 1974 Richard Lester boosted his then-flagging career with *The Three Musketeers* and its sequel *The Four Musketeers,*

lavish swashbucklers with a comic touch. His attempt at a comeback is, sadly, a stillborn event which looks as tired as its re-assembled cast.

It's 20 years since the four musketeers ordered the execution of the evil Milady De Winter. But now King Charles is dead, and his son Louis, a 10-year-old, reigns with his mother (a reprise by Geraldine Chaplin).

D'Artagnan (Michael York) is assigned to bring together his three former comrades to fight for the Queen and Cardinal. He quickly recruits Porthos (Frank Finlay) and Athos (Oliver Reed), together with the latter's son, Raoul (C. Thomas Howell); however, Aramis (Richard Chamberlain), now a womanizing Abbe, is reluctant to join the band.

There follows a complicated and sometimes hard to follow plot [from Alexandre Dumas' *Twenty Years After*] involving a failed attempt to rescue King Charles I of England from execution. According to this, the executioner of the king was actually Justine (Kim Cattrall), evil daughter of Milady, who's intent on avenging herself on the four musketeers who she blames for the death of her mother.

Pic is dedicated to Roy Kinnear, whose accidental death during production cast a pall over the entire project.

Above: *Michael York, Frank Finlay, Oliver Reed and Richard Chamberlain in* **Return of the Musketeers.**

Below: *Poster for* **The Right Stuff,** *the compelling story of the US space program and the training of its astronauts.*

THE RIGHT STUFF

1983, 192 mins, ◇ ⦵ *Dir* Philip Kaufman   US

★ **Stars** Sam Shepard, Scott Glenn, Ed Harris, Dennis Quaid, Fred Ward, Barbara Hershey

Academy Award 1983: Best Picture (Nomination)

The Right Stuff is a humdinger. Full of beauty, intelligence and excitement, this big-scale look at the development of the US space program and its pioneering aviators provides a

A ROBERT CHARTOFF-IRWIN WINKLER Production of A PHILIP KAUFMAN Film "THE RIGHT STUFF" CHARLES FRANK · SCOTT GLENN · ED HARRIS · LANCE HENRIKSEN · SCOTT PAULIN · DENNIS QUAID SAM SHEPARD · FRED WARD · KIM STANLEY · BARBARA HERSHEY · VERONICA CARTWRIGHT PAMELA REED Music by BILL CONTI Director of Photography CALEB DESCHANEL Based on the Book by TOM WOLFE Produced by IRWIN WINKLER and ROBERT CHARTOFF Written for the Screen and Directed by PHILIP KAUFMAN

fresh, entertaining look back at the recent past. Film version of Tom Wolfe's best selling revisionist history was some three years in the making.

Tale spans 16 years, from ace test pilot Chuck Yeager's breaking of the sound barrier over the California desert to Vice-President Johnson's welcoming of the astronauts to their new home in Houston with an enormous barbecue inside the Astrodome. Telling takes over three hours, but it goes by lickity-split under Philip Kaufman's direction and is probably the shortest-seeming film of its length ever made.

Emblematic figure here is Yeager, played by a taciturn Sam Shepard. As the ace of aces who was passed by for astronaut training due to his lack of college degree, Yeager, for Kaufman as for Wolfe, is the embodiment of 'the right stuff', that ineffable quality which separates the men from the boys, so to speak.

ROAR

1981, 102 mins, ◇ *Dir* Noel Marshall   US

★ **Stars** Tippi Hedren, Noel Marshall, John Marshall, Melanie Griffith, Jerry Marshall, Kyalo Mativo

The noble intentions of director-writer-producer Noel Marshall and his actress-wife Tippi Hedren shine through the faults and short-comings of *Roar*, their 11-year, $17 million project – touted as the most disaster-plagued pic in Hollywood history.

Given the enormous difficulties during production – a devastating flood, several fires, an epidemic that decimated the feline cast and numerous injuries to actors and crew, it's a miracle that the pic was completed.

Here is a passionate plea for the preservation of African wildlife meshed with an adventure-horror tale which aims to be a kind of *Jaws* of the jungle. If it seems at times more like *Born Free* gone berserk, such are the risks of planting the cast in the bush (actually the Marshalls' ranch in Soledad Canyon in California), surrounded by 150 untrained lions, leopards, tigers, cheetahs and other big cats, not to mention several large and ill-tempered elephants.

Thin plot has Hedren and her three children trekking to Africa to reunite with Marshall, an eccentric scientist who's been living in the jungle with his feline friends, an experiment to show that humans and beasts can happily coexist.

Hedren and her daughter Melanie Griffith have proved their dramatic ability elsewhere: here they and their co-stars are required to do little more than look petrified.

ROBIN HOOD

1922, 120 mins, ⊗ *Dir* Allan Dwan   US

★ **Stars** Douglas Fairbanks, Wallace Beery, Sam De Grasse, Enid Bennett, Paul Dickey, William Lowery

Archery, and when knights were bold while villains were cold, and that is *Robin Hood*.

Robin Hood is a great production but not a great picture. It just misses being great through a slow long opening. In the days of Richard the Lionheart and his First Crusade. The prettiness of the sets of Robin Hood's lair in Sherwood Forest, the picturesqueness of his band of outlaws who were for their King and against his villainous brother, Prince John; the breadth of the settings throughout; the stunts by Douglas Fairbanks when he gets going; the superb supporting cast, the castle – that's *Robin Hood* and why it is a good picture. It holds you tense in the Robin Hood portion and lets you down badly when it's about Richard.

ROBIN HOOD PRINCE OF THIEVES

1991, 138 mins, ◇ ▼ *Dir* Kevin Reynolds   US

★ **Stars** Kevin Costner, Morgan Freeman, Mary Elizabeth Mastrantonio, Christian Slater, Alan Rickman, Sean Connery

Kevin Costner's *Robin Hood* is a Robin of wood. Murky and uninspired, this $50 million rendition bears evidence of the

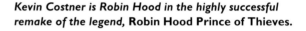

*Kevin Costner is Robin Hood in the highly successful remake of the legend, **Robin Hood Prince of Thieves**.*

rushed and unpleasant production circumstances that were much reported upon. At the same time, this seriously intended, more realistically motivated revision of the Robin Hood myth may have diminished the hero, but it hasn't destroyed him.

Lackluster script, from a story by Pen Densham, begins in the year 1194 in Jerusalem, where Robin leads a prison uprising and escapes with a Moor, Azeem (Morgan Freeman). Retreating from the Crusades, the pair head for England, where they find that Robin's father has been slain by the Sheriff of Nottingham (Alan Rickman), who is attempting to eliminate all resistance and perhaps make a play for the throne in the absence of King Richard.

To avenge his father's death, Robin joins up with Little John and the latter's band of outsiders who live in a safe enclave in Sherwood Forest. Major setpiece is the sheriff's attack on the outlaws' hippie-like compound, which decimates the group. But Robin is able to lead a counterattack on Nottingham Castle.

The best that can be said for Costner's performance is that it is pleasant. At worst, it can be argued whether it is more properly described as wooden or cardboard.

Looking beautiful and sporting an accent that comes and goes, Mary Elizabeth Mastrantonio makes a sprightly, appropriately feisty Marian. Of the Americans, Christian Slater is most successful at putting on an English accent, and he has some spirited moments as Will Scarlett.

As the 'painted man' who accompanies Robin in gratitude for his life having been saved, Freeman is a constant, dominant presence. As the sheriff, Rickman goes way over the top, emoting with facial and vocal leers. It's a relief whenever this resourceful thesp is on-screen, such is the energy and brio he brings to the proceedings.

An unbilled Sean Connery shows up at the very end as King Richard in time to give his blessing to Robin and Marian's marriage.

ROMANCING THE STONE

1984, 105 mins, ◇ ⓥ *Dir* Robert Zemeckis   US

★ *Stars* Michael Douglas, Kathleen Turner, Danny DeVito, Zack Norman, Alfonso Arau, Manuel Ojeda

Living alone with her cat, Kathleen Turner writes romantic novels and cries over the outcome, assuring friend Holland Taylor that one day the writer's life will pick up for real.

Naturally, Turner receives a package mailed from South America just ahead of her sister's phone call that she's been kidnapped and will die if Turner doesn't deliver the contents of the package south of the border as soon as possible.

Heading for the jungles in her high heels, Turner is like a lot of unwitting screen heroines ahead of her, guaranteed that her drab existence is about to be transformed – probably by a man, preferably handsome and adventurous. Sure enough, a dashing Michael Douglas pops out of the jungle.

The expected complications are supplied by the kidnappers, Danny DeVito and Zack Norman.

THE ROOTS OF HEAVEN

1958, 130 mins, ◇ *Dir* John Huston   US

★ *Stars* Errol Flynn, Juliette Greco, Trevor Howard, Eddie Albert, Orson Welles, Herbert Lom

The Roots of Heaven has striking pictorial aspects, some exciting performances and builds to a pulsating climax of absorbing tension. Unfortunately, these plus factors almost all come in the second half of the picture.

The locale of the screenplay, from Romain Gary's novel, is French Equatorial Africa. Trevor Howard, whose presence is never completely explained, is launching a campaign to save the elephants of Africa. He believes they are threatened with extinction from big game hunters, ivory poachers and the encroachment of civilization. When he tries to get signers of his petition to outlaw the killings, he is rebuffed on all fronts.

Howard gets only two signatures. One is from Errol Flynn, an alcoholic British ex-officer, and the other is from Juliette Greco, a prostitute. So Howard decides on a campaign of harassment of the hunters and his counter-attack attracts the attention of a safari-ing American TV personality, Orson Welles; a Danish scientist, Friedrich Ledebur; a German nobleman, Olivier Hussenot, and some natives who propose to use Howard as a symbol of their own resistance to colonial law and practice.

Kathleen Turner and Michael Douglas come up against a South American drug smuggler in **Romancing the Stone.**

Director John Huston has staged his exterior scenes superbly. Full advantage is taken here of the arduous African locations. Howard gives a fine performance and is responsible for conveying as much as comes across of the tricky theme. Flynn plays the drunken officer competently but without suggesting any latent nobility or particular depth. Greco is interesting without being very moving. Orson Welles in a brief bit (reportedly done as a favor to producer Darryl F. Zanuck) is a pinwheel of flashing vigor, his evil to be lamented.

ROYAL FLASH

1975, 121 mins, ◇ *Dir* Richard Lester UK

★ *Stars* Malcolm McDowell, Alan Bates, Florinda Bolkan, Oliver Reed, Britt Ekland, Lionel Jeffries

Royal Flash is a royal pain. Richard Lester's formula period comedy style [adapted by George MacDonald Fraser from his novel], as enduring as it is not particularly endearing, achieves its customary levels of posturing silliness.

Malcolm McDowell, fleeing a bordello raid, falls in with Florinda Bolkan, playing Lola Montez, in turn alienating Oliver Reed's Otto von Bismarck. The latter, with accomplice Alan Bates and hit-men Lionel Jeffries and Tom Bell, force McDowell to impersonate a Prussian nobleman for purposes of marriage to duchess Britt Ekland. Complex political, sexual and survival strategies lurch the plot forward.

The players are as competent as the film allows, and their work in other films is proof of their talent.

RUNAWAY TRAIN

1985, 111 mins, ◇ ⓥ *Dir* Andrei Konchalovsky US

★ *Stars* Jon Voight, Eric Roberts, Rebecca DeMornay, Kyle T. Heffner, John P. Ryan, T.K. Carter

Runaway Train is a sensational picture. Wrenchingly intense and brutally powerful, Andrei Konchalovsky's film rates as a most exciting action epic and is fundamentally serious enough to work strongly on numerous levels.

An exercise in relentless, severe tension, tale begins with a prison drama, then never lets up as it follows two escaped cons as they become inadvertent passengers on some diesel units that run out of control through the Alaskan wilderness.

The two desperate men who find themselves joined by a young lady, are tracked throughout their headlong journey by railroad officials bent on avoiding a crash.

Jon Voight brilliantly portrays a two-time loser determined never to return to prison after his third breakout.

The film is based upon [an unfilmed] screenplay by Akira Kurosawa, and bears imprint of the renowned Japanese director.

Younger con Eric Roberts impressively manages to hold his own under the demanding circumstances, and

Rebecca DeMornay works herself well into the essentially all-male surroundings.

RUN FOR THE SUN

1956, 98 mins, ◇ *Dir* Roy Boulting US

★ *Stars* Richard Widmark, Trevor Howard, Jane Greer, Peter Van Eyck, Carlos Henning, Juan Garcia

Run for the Sun is a chase feature in practically all its phases. Jane Greer, a news mag staffer, comes to Mexico to find Richard Widmark, writer-adventurer, to find out why he's given up writing. She falls for her news quarry and then the plane in which she is flying with him crashes in the jungle.

The couple is rescued by Trevor Howard and Peter Van Eyck, a mysterious pair. When Widmark discovers their true identities as war criminals hiding out from trial and punishment, it becomes a murderous game through the jungle.

The four principals enact their roles exceptionally well. Pic is based on Richard Connell's story *The Most Dangerous Game* [filmed in 1932], but there is virtually no resemblance to that old thriller in the final results.

SAHARA

1983, 104 mins, ◇ ⓥ *Dir* Andrew V. McLaglen US

★ *Stars* Brooke Shields, Lambert Wilson, Horst Buchholz, John Rhys-Davies, Ronald Lacey, John Mills

Co-producer Menahem Golan reportedly hatched the idea for *Sahara* when Mark Thatcher, son of the British prime minister, disappeared in the desert during an international car rally.

An old fashioned B-grade romantic adventure, directed in pedestrian fashion by Andrew V. McLaglen, *Sahara* is lamentably low on excitement, laughs and passion.

Screenplay, set in 1927, has Brooke Shields as heiress to a car company who promises her dying daddy that she'll win the world's toughest endurance rally driving the car he designed. Wily Brooke disguises herself as a man, complete with wig and moustache.

Soon after the race starts, she discards her disguise and reverts to Brooke the beautiful, only to receive a beating and a mouthful of sand when she's captured by Arab thug John Rhys-Davies. Handsome sheikh Lambert Wilson saves her from his clutches and falls mildly in love with her.

Director McLaglen and most everyone else treat it all tongue in cheek.

SAIGON

1988, 102 mins, ◇ Ⓥ *Dir* Christopher Crowe   US

★ *Stars* Willem Dafoe, Gregory Hines, Fred Ward, Amanda Pays, Kay Tong Lim, Scott Glenn

Saigon [also known as *Off Limits*] is a well-crafted story by Christopher Crowe and Jack Thibeau that explores the underbelly of Saigon well enough as two undercover detectives (Willem Dafoe and Gregory Hines) go about to solve a string of prostitute murders by a high ranking Army officer. While the plot and characterizations are well worked out, production lacks pizzazz to distinguish it from others in this genre.

Dafoe and Hines stick together like glue, working diligently in the sticky Saigon heat with equally racist attitudes about 'gooks' and 'slopes', trying to find which Army officer

Left: *John Rhys-Davies and Brook Shields in old-fashioned romantic adventure* **Sahara.**

Below: *Willem Dafoe is an undercover cop searching for a high-ranking officer who is murdering prositutes in* **Saigon.**

is cavorting with whores and then wasting them.

Director Crowe has tried to make a tough picture with sensitivity, though it's the former that mostly prevails.

SANDERS OF THE RIVER

1935, 98 mins, 🎬 *Dir* Zoltan Korda   UK

★ *Stars* Leslie Banks, Paul Robeson, Nina Mae McKinney, Robert Cochran, Martin Walker, Allan Jeayes

Story of an African colony is an immense production, done for the greater part with deft direction, played with distinction by two main characters. Leslie Banks and Paul Robeson carry the greater part of this tale of a British commissioner who rules an African sector through commanding both fear and respect.

The story [from an original by Edgar Wallace] is simple. Sanders (Banks) is in charge of a large section in the British African possessions. He makes a minor chief of Bosambo (Robeson), an engaging fugitive from prison, revealing the excellence of his judgment of men. Mofolabo, known as 'the old king', is in an inaccessible section of the district and gives much trouble. When Sanders goes out on leave to get married, rum runners send word through the district that Sanders is dead. But Sanders has gone only as far as the coast when he hears of the trouble, and comes back.

There are some nicely staged mob scenes, mostly ceremonials, with a remarkable male muscle dancer and a small regiment of natives who appear to be genuine. Robeson gets two of the songs [lyrics by Arthur Wimperis], with the third going to Nina Mae McKinney, a lullaby set against a humming harmonic background.

SANDS OF THE KALAHARI

1965, 119 mins, ◇ *Dir* Cy Endfield   UK

★ *Stars* Stuart Whitman, Stanley Baker, Susannah York, Harry Andrews, Theodore Bikel, Nigel Davenport

Cy Endfield, co-producer, director and scripter of the long film (made almost entirely on location in Africa), wisely makes the camera as important as anyone in the cast, emphasizing the savagery that is throughout. Although Endfield has been lucky with his casting, some members too quickly betray symptoms of scenery chewing.

A planeload of assorted types crashes in the desert and the rest of the film deals with their efforts to survive. It's some time before a villain is unveiled and, even then, the viewer's faith gets a few shakes. Susannah York, as the only female in the cast, gets plenty of exposure. Stuart Whitman, a gunhappy survivalist, and Stanley Baker, a nondescript loser, are the only main characters. Unbilled but colorful are assorted natives, animals and insects.

Entertainment, pure and simple [from a novel by William Mulvihill], was evidently what the filmmakers aimed for and that's the target they hit.

SAN FRANCISCO

1936, 115 mins, 🎬 *Dir* W.S. Van Dyke   US

★ *Stars* Clark Gable, Jeanette MacDonald, Spencer Tracy, Jack Holt, Jessie Ralph, Ted Healy

Academy Award 1936: Best Picture (Nomination)

An earthquake noisy and terrifying, is *San Francisco*'s forte. Quake occurs after more than an hour and up to then the picture is distinguished chiefly for its corking cast and super-fine production.

Story basically follows the outline traced previously by Warner's *Frisco Kid* and Goldwyn's *Barbary Coast* [both 1935] although this one tends more to the musical through the constant singing of Jeanette MacDonald.

Lone incongruous note is the remarkable survival of Clark Gable after a whole wall has toppled over on him. His survival is necessary, to complete the picture, but it might have been made easier to believe.

As were James Cagney and Edward G. Robinson before him, Gable is 'king' of the Barbary Coast, and like his predecessors, his reformation is the essence of the plot [story by Robert Hopkins]. Only this guy is tougher; it takes the earthquake to cure him. As Blackie Norton he operates a prosperous gambling joint and beer garden. The closest friend of this godless soul is a priest, who doesn't try to reform Blackie but always hopes for the best. MacDonald enters as a Denver choir singer, in Frisco looking for work. From the show at Blackie Norton's she graduates to grand opera under the sponsorship of Blackie's political rival.

Spencer Tracy plays a priest, and it's the most difficult role in the picture. His slang – he calls Gable 'mug' and 'sucker' good naturedly – is the sort usually associated with men of lesser spiritual quality.

THE SATAN BUG

1965, 114 mins, ◇ 🎬 *Dir* John Sturges   US

★ *Stars* George Maharis, Richard Basehart, Anne Francis, Dana Andrews, Edward Asner, Frank Sutton

The Satan Bug is a superior suspense melodrama and should keep audiences on the edge of their seats despite certain unexplained, confusing elements which tend to make plot at times difficult to follow.

Based on a novel by Ian Stuart (nom de plume for Britisher Alistair MacLean), producer-director John Sturges builds his action to a generally chilling pace after a needlessly-slow opening which establishes America's experiments in bacteriological warfare at a highly-secret top-security research installation in the desert. The scientist who develops the deadly virus known as the Satan Bug, so lethal it can cause instant death over great areas, is murdered and flasks containing the liquid mysteriously spirited out of the lab.

Script projects George Maharis as a former Army

S

Intelligence officer recalled to find the virus before it can be put to the use threatened by a millionaire paranoiac who master-minded the theft and claims to hate war.

Maharis makes a good impression as the investigator, although his character isn't developed sufficiently – a fault also applying to other principals – due to overspeedy editing in an attempt to narrate story at fever pitch.

SCARAMOUCHE

1952, 115 mins, ◇ Ⓥ *Dir* George Sidney   US

★ *Stars* Stewart Granger, Eleanor Parker, Janet Leigh, Mel Ferrer, Henry Wilcoxon, Nina Foch

Metro's up-to-date version of *Scaramouche* bears only the most rudimentary resemblance to its 1923 hit or to the Rafael Sabatini novel on which they both were based. Pic never seems to be quite certain whether it is a costume adventure drama or a satire on one.

The highly-complex Sabatini plot has been greatly simplified for present purposes. It finds the French Revolution all but eliminated from the story, because of the inevitable Red analogy were the hero allowed to spout the 1789 theme of 'Liberty, Equality, Fraternity'.

Granger is a brash young man who is determined to avenge the death of a friend at the hand of nobleman Mel Ferrer, the best swordsman in France. Stewart Granger has to keep under cover until he gets in enough lessons with the weapon to take on Ferrer. Just in the nick, (a) he's elected to the French assembly, so he doesn't have to hide out anymore; (b) he discovers Miss Leigh is not his sister, so he can grab her, and (c) the marquis is really his brother. That leaves everyone mildly happy except Miss Parker, who, when last seen is being hauled into a bedroom by Napoleon.

SCOTT OF THE ANTARCTIC

1948, 111 mins, ◇ Ⓥ *Dir* Charles Frend   UK

★ *Stars* John Mills, Harold Warrender, Derek Bond, Reginald Beckwith, James Robertson Justice, Kenneth More

Scott of the Antarctic should be not only a magnificent eye-filling spectacle but also a stirring adventure. But the director's affinity to the documentary technique robs the

Reginald Beckwith as Bowers, John Mills as Scott and Harold Warrender as Wilson in **Scott of the Antarctic.**

Ealing Studios present
JOHN MILLS *IN* **SCOTT of the ANTARCTIC**   Ⓤ Ⓖ
COLOUR BY TECHNICOLOR
with **DEREK BOND · HAROLD WARRENDER · JAMES ROBERTSON JUSTICE · REGINALD BECKWITH**
A MICHAEL BALCON PRODUCTION · *Directed by* CHARLES FREND · *Associate Producer* SIDNEY COLE
Screenplay by WALTER MEADE *and* IVOR MONTAGU   GENERAL FILM DISTRIBUTORS LIMITED

subject of much of its intrinsic drama and suspense.

Pic's greatest asset is the superb casting of John Mills in the title role. Obviously playing down the drama on directorial insistence, Mills' close resemblance to the famous explorer makes the character come to life.

Scott's discovery that he has been beaten in the race to the South Pole should be a piece of poignant and moving drama. Instead, the five members of the expedition look very resolute, and very British, and philosophically begin the long trail home. Although depicted with fidelity, the agonies of the explorers on their homeward trek are presented with inadequate dramatization, with the result that the audience isn't emotionally affected.

THE SEA HAWK

1924, 129 mins, ⊗ *Dir* Frank Lloyd   US

★ *Stars* Milton Sills, Enid Bennett, Lloyd Hughes, Wallace MacDonald, Marc MacDermott, Wallace Beery

This picture has no end of entertainment value. It is just as thrilling and gripping as reading one of Rafael Sabatini's books; all of the punch of that author's writings has been brought to the screen.

There's action aplenty. It starts in the first reel and holds true to the last minute. Milton Sills, who is featured together with Enid Bennett, comes into his own in this production, and Bennett also scores tremendously. One must, however, not overlook Wallace Beery, a low comedy ruffian, who wades right through the story.

Frank Lloyd, who directed, is to be considered with the best that wield a megaphone. *The Sea Hawk* cost around $800,000. The properties used alone cost $135,000. The picture looks it.

THE SEA HAWK

1940, 127 mins, ⊘ *Dir* Michael Curtiz   US

★ *Stars* Errol Flynn, Brenda Marshall, Claude Rains, Flora Robson, Donald Crisp, Alan Hale

The Sea Hawk retains all of the bold and swashbuckling adventure and excitement of its predecessor, turned out for First National by Frank Lloyd in 1923. But the screenplay of the new version is expanded to include endless episodes of court intrigue during the reign of Queen Elizabeth that tend to diminish the effect of the epic sweep of the high seas dramatics. When the script focuses attention on the high seas and the dramatic heroics of the sailors who embarked on daring raids against Spanish shipping, the picture retains plenty of excitement.

Story traces the adventures of the piratical sea fighter (Errol Flynn), commander of a British sailing ship that preys on Spanish commerce in the late 16th century. Colorful and exciting sea battle at the start, when Flynn's ship attacks and sinks the galleon of the Spanish ambassador, comes too

early and is never topped by any succeeding sequences. Then follows extensive internal politics of Elizabeth's court, with the queen secretly condoning the Sea Hawk's buccaneering activities.

Little credit can be extended to the overwritten script, with long passages of dry and uninteresting dialog, or to the slow-paced, uninspiring direction by Michael Curtiz. Errol Flynn fails to generate the fire and dash necessary to successfully put over the role of the buccaneer leader, although this lack might partially be attributed to the piloting. Flora Robson gets attention in the role of Queen Elizabeth.

The Sea Hawk is a big budget production with reported cost set around $1.75 million. Expenditure is easily seen in the large sets, sweeping sea battles and armies of extras used with lavish display. From a production standpoint, the picture carries epic standards, but same cannot be said for the story.

SEARCH FOR PARADISE

1957, 120 mins, ◇ *Dir* Otto Lang   US

★ *Stars* Lowell Thomas, James S. Parker, Christopher Young

The fourth Cinerama sticks almost slavishly to established formulae. Once more strange lands are 'seen' by two selected 'tourists' this time a make-believe air force major (Christopher Young) and sergeant (James S. Parker) who, at the payoff, decide that they'll sign up for another hitch, the air force itself being the ultimate paradise.

The beginning of the picture is cornily contrived. An Associated Press newsmachine is seen ticking out a bulletin that Lowell Thomas is one of three ambassadors just appointed to represent Washington at the coronation durbar of King Mahendra of Nepal.

The several stops of *Search* are all way-stations en route to Nepal. The picture centres upon the approach to and environs of the Himalayas, world's greatest peaks, truthfully described as a region of mystery, age, mysticism and Communistic intrigue.

Lowell picks up the major and the sarge in the Vale of Kashmir, a plausible paradise indeed, especially its Shalimar Gardens. The visit at Nepal is the big sequence. And a stunning display of oriental pomp it is. This segment is a genuine peep into dazzling fantasy and a true coup for Cinerama and Thomas.

THE SEA WOLF

1941, 98 mins, ⊕ *Dir* Michael Curtiz   US

★ *Stars* Edward G. Robinson, Ida Lupino, John Garfield, Alexander Knox, Barry Fitzgerald

Jack London's famous hellship sails for another voyage over the cinematic seas in this version of *The Sea Wolf*. Edward G. Robinson steps into the role of the callous and inhuman skipper, Wolf Larsen.

John Garfield signs on to the sailing schooner to escape the law. Ida Lupino (also a fugitive) and the mild-mannered novelist (Alexander Knox) are rescued from a sinking ferryboat in San Francisco bay. Robinson is the dominating and cruel captain who takes fiendish delight in breaking the spirits of his crew and unwilling passengers.

Robinson provides plenty of vigor and two-fisted energy to the actor-proof role of Larsen, and at times is over-directed. Garfield is the incorrigible youth whose spirit cannot be broken, and is grooved to his familiar tough characterization of previous pictures. Lupino gives a good account of herself in the rough-and-tumble goings on, but the romantic angle is under-stressed in this version.

Michael Curtiz directs in a straight line, accentuating the horrors that go on during the voyage of the *Ghost*.

SECRET COMMAND

1944, 81 mins, *Dir* Eddie Sutherland   US

★ *Stars* Pat O'Brien, Carole Landis, Chester Morris, Ruth Warrick

This is a lusty melodrama of counter-espionage around a large shipyard, with expert blending of action and suspense with spontaneous good humor resulting in solid entertainment.

Naval intelligence gets wind of Nazi sabotage plans at the large shipyard, and Pat O'Brien is sent in to get a job as a secret agent. He starts as a pilebuck on shift bossed by brother Chester Morris, and latter is not sold on O'Brien's tale of wife (Carole Landis) and two youngsters in bungalow – with family and housing conveniently supplied by Intelligence. Yarn weaves between the dramatics of tracing the Nazi saboteurs at the shipyards, and intimacies at home with O'Brien's newly-acquired family setup.

O'Brien turns in a fine performance in the lead, with Landis and Ruth Warrick sharing femme spots in good style. Strong support is provided by Morris, Barton MacLane, Tom Tully and Wallace Ford.

THE 7TH DAWN

1964, 123 mins, ◇   *Dir* Lewis Gilbert   UK

★ *Stars* William Holden, Susannah York, Capucine, Tetsuro Tamba, Michael Goodliffe, Allan Cuthbertson

Set in the Malayan jungle, circa 1945, the pic uses as its background a three-way struggle between Communist-inspired Malayan terrorists, British governors and the people of Malaya along with outsiders who have vested interests in the country. All are interested in freedom for the place but their motives vary considerably.

Pivotal characters in the film each represent a faction, a fact which leads to some rather predictable problems and solutions as time passes. Personal relationships aren't helped much either by co-producer Karl Tunberg's screenplay,

based on Michael Keon's novel *The Durian Tree*. Although the script moves fairly fluently through the action passages, harmful slowdowns develop during personal moments between the characters.

William Holden handles himself in credible fashion as a Yank co-leader of local guerilla forces during World War II who stays on after the war's end to become a major local land owner and who gets involved in the new politics because of his old time friendship for the leader of the Red terrorists, played by Tetsuro Tamba. Holden is further involved because of his mistress, a Malayan loyalist portrayed by Capucine. These three had worked together on the same side during the previous combat. For further plot there's the blonde and attractive daughter of the British governor, a role essayed by Susannah York.

SHE

1965, 104 mins, ◇   *Dir* Robert Day   UK

★ *Stars* Ursula Andress, Peter Cushing, Bernard Cribbins, John Richardson, Christopher Lee, Andre Morell

Fourth filming of H. Rider Haggard's fantasy adds color and widescreen to special effects, all of which help overcome a basic plot no film scripter has yet licked.

Ursula Andress is sole-starred as the immortal She, cold-blooded queen Ayesha of a lost kingdom who pines for return of the lover she murdered eons ago. In David T. Chantler's okay script, it turns out that John Richardson is the look-alike lover, footloose in Palestine after the First World War with buddies Peter Cushing and Bernard Cribbins.

High priest Christopher Lee and servant girl Rosenda Monteros are emissaries who spot Richardson's resemblance, triggering a desert trek by the three men to Kuma land. Cushing and Cribbins keep their senses, while Richardson falls under Andress' spell.

Director Robert Day's overall excellent work brings out heretofore unknown depths in Andress' acting. Role calls for sincere warmth as a woman in love, also brutal cruelty as queen, and she convinces.

SHOOT TO KILL

1988, 110 mins, ◇ ◉   *Dir* Roger Spottiswoode   US

★ *Stars* Sidney Poitier, Tom Berenger, Kirstie Alley, Clancy Brown, Richard Masur

Everybody, including the audience, gets a good workout in *Shoot to Kill*, a rugged, involving manhunt [story by Harv Zimmel] in which a criminal leads his pursuers over what is perhaps the most challenging land route out of the U.S.

Sidney Poitier establishes his authority immediately as a veteran FBI man in San Francisco who, despite handling the crisis with calm assuredness, cannot prevent the getaway of a thief who kills hostages on a foggy night on Frisco Bay.

Another shooting of a similar type takes Poitier up to

the Pacific Northwest, where he is forced to engage the services of tough backwoodsman Tom Berenger to lead him up into the mountains to apprehend the villain before he makes it over the border into Canada.

A self-styled macho hermit, Berenger considers Poitier a cityfied softy incapable of making it in the mountains. This sets up a cliched enmity between the two men that one knows will have to be broken down, but not without some predictable jibes at Poitier's awkwardness outdoors and some revelations of Berenger's own vulnerabilities.

Poitier, 63 when the film was shot, looks little more than 40. The actor's directness and easiness on the screen are refreshing, his humor self-deprecating and understated.

Berenger solidly fills the bill as the confident mountain man, and Kirstie Alley, despite the extreme limitations of her role, proves entirely believable as his female counterpart. British Columbia locations give the film tremendous scenic impact.

SHOUT AT THE DEVIL

1976, 147 mins, ◇ Ⓥ *Dir* Peter Hunt   UK

★ *Stars* Lee Marvin, Roger Moore, Barbara Parkins, Ian Holm, Rene Kolldehoff, Horst Janson

A nice sprawling, basic, gutsy and unsophisticated film, which displays its reported $7 million budget on nearly every frame. Based on a Wilbur Smith [*Gold*] novel, script is a pastiche of almost every basic action-suspense ingredient known to the cinema.

Exotic tropical settings, man-eating crocodiles, air and sea combat, shipwreck, big game hunting, natives on a rampage, ticking time bombs, rape and fire, malaria, they're all there and then some. Basic ingredients have to do with a successful attempt to put permanently out of action a crippled World War I German battle cruiser holed up for repairs in a remote South East African river delta.

The oddball opposites-attract relationship between Lee Marvin and Roger Moore generally works very well indeed, and the constantly imbibing Irisher and the contrastingly 'straight' Britisher make good foils. The motivating love story linking Moore and Barbara Parkins is rarely involving and convincing.

SIGN OF THE PAGAN

1954, 91 mins, ◇ *Dir* Douglas Sirk   US

★ *Stars* Jeff Chandler, Jack Palance, Ludmilla Tcherina, Rita Gam, Jeff Morrow, George Dolenz

Unlike most screen spectacles, *Sign of the Pagan*'s running time is a tight 91 minutes, in which the flash of the Roman Empire period is not permitted to slow down the telling of an interesting action story.

Plot deals with Attila the Hun, the Scourge of God, and his sweep across Europe some 1,500 years ago.

Particularly noteworthy is the treatment of the barbarian in writing and direction, and in the manner in which Jack Palance interprets the character. Instead of a straight, all-evil person, he is a human being with some good here and there to shade and make understandable the bad.

Douglas Sirk's direction of the excellent script catches the sweep of the period portrayed without letting the characters get lost in spectacle. Representing good in the plot is Jeff Chandler, centurion made a general by his princess, Ludmilla Tcherina, to fight off Attila's advancing hordes.

With Palance scoring so solidly in his role of Attila, he makes the other performers seem less colorful, although Chandler is good as Marsian.

THE SILVER CHALICE

1954, 142 mins, ◇ Ⓥ *Dir* Victor Saville   US

★ *Stars* Virginia Mayo, Pier Angeli, Jack Palance, Paul Newman, Natalie Wood, Joseph Wiseman

Like the Thomas B. Costain book, the picture is overdrawn and sometimes tedious, but producer-director Victor Saville still manages to instill interest in what's going on, and even hits a feeling of excitement occasionally.

The picture introduces Newman who handles himself well before the cameras. Helping his pic debut is Pier Angeli, and it is their scenes together that add the warmth to what might otherwise have been a cold spectacle.

The plot portrays the struggle of Christians to save for the future the cup from which Christ drank at the Last Supper. On the side of the Christians is a Greek sculptor, played by Newman, who is fashioning a silver chalice to hold the religious symbol. On the side of evil are the decadent Romans, ruled over by an effete Nero, and Simon, the magician (a real character), played by Jack Palance, who wants to use the destruction of the cup to further his own rise to power.

SILVER DREAM RACER

1980, 111 mins, ◇ Ⓥ *Dir* David Wickes   UK

★ *Stars* David Essex, Beau Bridges, Cristina Raines, Harry H. Corbett, Diane Keen, Lee Montague

It's about motorcycle racing. But among all the biking footage in a yarn about a 'revolutionary' prototype which challenges and, natch, licks all world championship comers, there's not one memorable shot of the machine in action.

That's a big pity, as the model – a genuine prototype built by Britisher Barry Hart – will certainly whet the appetites of two-wheel fans. But the film's action sequences prove generally disappointing.

Plot is routine, but no worse than many, and the acting does favors for the dialog. Popstar David Essex is a natural as the ingenuous-looking Cockney fellow who can turn on a sneer when needed. Beau Bridges is fine as the loud-

S

mouthed American Goliath against whom David pits his derided British mount.

SITTING TARGET

1972, 93 mins, ◇ *Dir* Douglas Hickox   UK

★ **Stars** Oliver Reed, Jill St John, Ian McShane, Edward Woodward, Frank Finlay, Freddie Jones

Sitting Target is a picture of brutish violence. Its story of a British prison break by a hardened, jealousy-ridden convict to kill the wife he believes unfaithful has been recounted with no holds barred.

The screenplay [from a novel by Laurence Henderson] sometimes is difficult to follow, but Douglas Hickox' tense direction keeps movement at top speed. Obsession of con to get to his wife, who has revealed she is pregnant and wants a divorce, is a motivating theme. Jill St John becomes the sitting target for Oliver Reed as the convicted murderer who smashes his way to freedom and stalks his prey.

Actual scenes lensed in two Irish prisons give film a grimly authentic atmosphere and the escape of Reed and two other cons is spectacularly depicted.

SKYJACKED

1972, 100 mins, ◇ *Dir* John Guillermin   US

★ **Stars** Charlton Heston, Yvette Mimieux, James Brolin, Claude Akins, Jeanne Crain, Susan Dey

Charlton Heston and Yvette Mimieux star as pilot and stewardess respectively of a jetliner seized by James Brolin. John Guillermin's fast-paced direction makes the most of a large group of top performers.

Stanley R. Greenberg's adaptation of David Harper's novel, *Hijacked*, establishes early and sustains throughout the diverse personal interactions of literally dozens of characters. The dramatic device of trapping a motley group is a venerable but effective blue-print, herein made all the more compelling by a contemporary social phenomenon.

Heston is an effective leader as the captain suddenly faced with a lipstick-scrawled demand for a course change to Alaska, where Claude Akins as a ground controller heightens the suspense of a delicate landing maneuver.

SKY RIDERS

1976, 91 mins, ◇ Ⓥ *Dir* Douglas Hickox   US

★ **Stars** James Coburn, Susannah York, Robert Culp, Charles Aznavour, Werner Pochath, Zou Zou

Hang gliding stunts provide most of the interest in *Sky Riders* filmed in Greece. The political terrorism story line is a familiar one and the screenplay is synthetic formula stuff, but the stunt work is good.

Simple plot has footloose pilot James Coburn masterminding the rescue of Susannah York and her two children after bungling police operation led by Charles Aznavour doesn't produce results.

The film provoked an international incident when a Greek electrician died in an explosion accident. Ironically, no one was seriously injured in the aerial scenes. Producer Terry Morse Jr was arrested, exec producer Sandy Howard was detained in Greece for several weeks, and a $250,000 out-of-court settlement was made.

SLAVE SHIP

1937, 90 mins, *Dir* Tay Garnett   US

★ **Stars** Warner Baxter, Wallace Beery, Elizabeth Allan, Mickey Rooney, George Sanders, Jane Darwell

While a lot of the acting and motivation reeks of the phoney, *Slave Ship* is so effectively mounted and shot through with action that it stands up.

Director Tay Garnett passes up no known artifice for intensifying the gymnastic implications of ship fighting. He has his bullet-struck sailors popping off from the halyards, the crow's nest and where not. The dives these extras take make an Olympiad in themselves.

As a couple of the last of the slave runners, Warner Baxter and Wallace Beery move along elementary grooves, the former going from one tight spot to another, and the latter playing his dumb, sentimental scalawag to the hilt. Elizabeth Allan carves out a telling performance where it has to do with romantic interludes. Mickey Rooney also bats out a neat score, accounting for most of the film's scanty allotment of comedy as the cabin boy. Most of the action [from the novel by George S. King] is laid aboard the barque Albatross. Ill-fated from the day she is launched, the ship finally comes into the ownership of Baxter who, with Beery as his first mate and partner, puts her in the trade of smuggling slaves from Africa to America.

THE SNOWS OF KILIMANJARO

1952, 113 mins, ◇ Ⓥ *Dir* Henry King   US

★ **Stars** Gregory Peck, Susan Hayward, Ava Gardner, Hildegarde Neff, Leo G. Carroll, Torin Thatcher

A big, broad screen treatment has been given to Ernest Hemingway's *The Snows of Kilimanjaro*. The script broadens the 1927 short story considerably without losing the Hemingway penchant for the mysticism behind his virile characters and lusty situations.

Ava Gardner makes the part of Cynthia a warm, appealing, alluring standout. Gregory Peck delivers with gusto the character of the writer who lies dangerously ill on the plain at the base of Kilimanjaro, highest mountain in Africa,

S

and relives what he believes is a misspent life. Susan Hayward is splendid, particularly in the dramatic closing sequence, in the less colorful role of Peck's wife.

The location-lensed footage taken in Paris, Africa, the Riviera and Spain add an important dress to the varied sequences. The Paris street and cafe scenes, the music and noise, are alive. The African-lensed backgrounds are brilliant, as are those on the Riviera and in Spain.

SOLDIERS THREE

1951, 91 mins, *Dir* Tay Garnett   US

★ **Stars** Stewart Granger, Walter Pidgeon, David Niven, Robert Newton, Cyril Cusack, Greta Gynt

Three scripters worked on the story, loosely based on Rudyard Kipling, but come up with nothing more than a string of incidents involving three soldiers in India (Stewart Granger, Robert Newton and Cyril Cusack). Trio's off-limits antics, such as drunken brawling, add to the hot water in which their colonel (Walter Pidgeon) finds himself and do nothing to calm the colonel's aide (David Niven). Antics do, however, enliven the film's footage.

Granger is very likeable in his comedy role, and his two cohorts, Newton and Cusack, do their full share in getting laughs. Niven also is good as the slightly stuffy aide who leads the pants-losing patrol. Pidgeon, as a colonel with worries, forgets his broad British bumbling occasionally, but this fits with general development.

SON OF FURY

1942, 98 mins, ⬥ *Dir* John Cromwell   US

★ **Stars** Tyrone Power, Gene Tierney, George Sanders, Frances Farmer, Roddy McDowall, Elsa Lanchester

Laid in England during the reign of King George III, the story [from a novel by Edison Marshall] is that of Benjamin Blake (Tyrone Power) who undergoes great hardships and reverses in an attempt, ultimately successful, to establish the birthright that had been snatched from him nefariously by a scheming uncle of the upper crust. However, on regaining

Tyrone Power and George Sanders in Son of Fury, *a tale of disinheritance in the time of George III.*

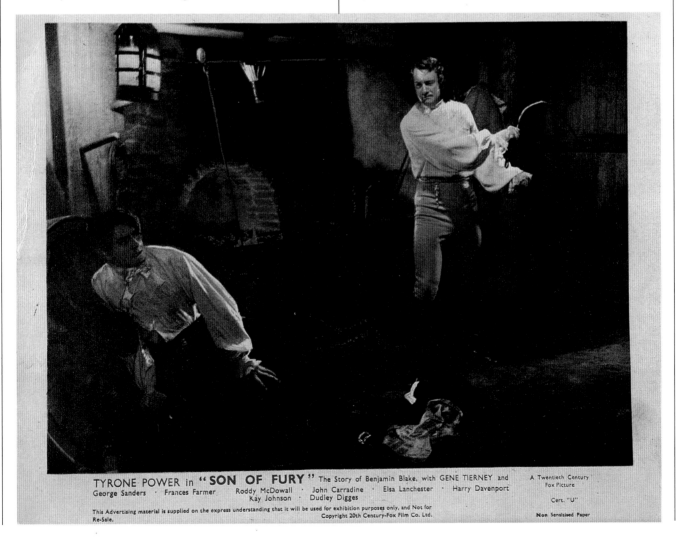

TYRONE POWER in "SON OF FURY" The Story of Benjamin Blake, with GENE TIERNEY and
George Sanders · Frances Farmer   Roddy McDowall · John Carradine · Elsa Lanchester · Harry Davenport
Kay Johnson · Dudley Digges

A Twentieth Century Fox Picture

Cert. "U"

This Advertising material is supplied on the express understanding that it will be used for exhibition purposes only, and Not for Re-Sale.
Copyright 20th Century-Fox Film Co. Ltd.

Non Sensitised Paper

title to the fortune that was rightfully his, he parcels it out to servants of the estate and others in order to return to the tropic isle where he made himself independently rich from oyster pearls and, in the process, met Gene Tierney.

Running time is a little long, with some sequences slowing the action down, but generally the story commands rapt attention and, on the whole, emerges as sound, compelling entertainment. There is virtually no comic relief. It could have been used here and there to fine advantage because of the general heaviness of the action.

THE SOUND BARRIER

1952, 118 mins, *Dir* David Lean   UK

★ **Stars** Ralph Richardson, Ann Todd, Nigel Patrick, John Justin, Dinah Sheridan, Joseph Tomelty

Technically, artistically and emotionally, this is a topflight British offering.

Dwarfing the individual performers, good though they are, are the magnificent air sequences, with impressive and almost breathtaking dives by the jet as it attempts to crash the sound barrier.

The visionary in the film is superbly played by Ralph Richardson. His ambition to make the first faster-than-sound plane has brought him nothing but grief and disaster. He sees his only son killed on his first solo try; he accepts the estrangement of his daughter (Ann Todd) when his son-in-law (Nigel Patrick) crashes while making the first attempt to crash the barrier.

Ann Todd's portrayal of the daughter correctly yields the emotional angle.

David Lean's direction is bold and imaginative.

THE SPANISH MAIN

1945, 101 mins, ◇ Ⓥ *Dir* Frank Borzage   US

★ **Stars** Paul Henreid, Maureen O'Hara, Walter Slezak, Binnie Barnes, John Emery, Barton MacLane

Robust saga of swaggering pirates and beautiful girls. Story concentrates on action melodrama but occasionally takes a satirical slant on such high adventure doings, thus bringing nifty chuckles.

Plot [from an original story by Aeneas MacKenzie] concerns a group of Dutchmen whose ship is wrecked by a storm on the shore of Spanish-held Cartagena. Spanish governor orders the survivors into slavery and the ship's captain to be hung.

The captain and several others escape and take up piracy against all Spanish ships. One ship seized is carrying the governor's betrothed, daughter of Mexico's viceroy. The captain-turned-buccanneer forces the girl into marriage but reckons not of jealousy and treachery among his fellow pirates who fear marriage will result in Spaniards arising in force against Tortuga, the buccaneer colony.

Paul Henreid does well by the dashing Dutchman who becomes the Spaniards' sea-scourge and will please his following. Maureen O'Hara hasn't much opportunity to show off her acting ability but fulfills the role's other requirements with lush beauty. Walter Slezak's cruel Spanish governor character is showy.

SPAWN OF THE NORTH

1938, 105 mins, *Dir* Henry Hathaway   US

★ **Stars** George Raft, Henry Fonda, Dorothy Lamour, Akim Tamiroff, John Barrymore, Louise Platt

Impressive scenes of the Alaskan waters, backgrounded by towering glaciers which drop mighty icebergs into the sea, imperiling doughty fishermen and their frail craft, lift *Spawn of the North* into the class of robust out-of-door films where the spectacular overshadows the melodrama.

The plot [story by Barrett Willoughby] recounts the battles between licensed fishermen and pirates who steal the catch from the traps which are set for salmon at spawning time. George Raft and Henry Fonda, boyhood friends, are members of opposing factions, the former having fallen in with Russian thieves.

Merit of the film is in the persuasive and authentic photographic record of Alaskan life and customs. Akim Tamiroff is a truly menacing pirate with a black heart and no regard for law and order. John Barrymore is an amusing small town editor and Lynne Overman makes a cynical role standout by his gruff humor.

SPHINX

1981, 117 mins, ◇ *Dir* Franklin J. Schaffner   US

★ **Stars** Lesley-Anne Down, Frank Langella, Maurice Ronet, John Gielgud, Saeed Jaffrey

This film is an embarrassment. Contempo *Perils of Pauline* sees earnest, dedicated Egyptologist Lesley-Anne Down through countless situations of dire jeopardy as she travels from Cairo to Luxor's Valley of the Kings in pursuit of a mysterious tomb of riches, which also holds great interest for black marketeers.

Along the way, lovely Lesley-Anne is almost murdered after witnessing John Gielgud's demise, caught off guard not once, not twice, but three times in her hotel room, shot at as a matter of course, nearly raped by a prison guard, held at knifepoint, thrown into a dark dungeon inhabited by decomposed corpses, attacked by bats, chased by a car, shot at again and finally nearly buried as the tomb's ceiling comes crashing down.

In all, she screams gasps and exclaims 'My God!' more often than any heroine since Jamie Lee Curtis in her collected horror films.

Franklin J. Schaffner's steady and sober style is helpless in the face of the mounting implausibities.

THE SPIRIT OF ST. LOUIS

1957, 135 mins, ◇ Ⓥ *Dir* Billy Wilder   US

★ *Stars* James Stewart, Murray Hamilton, Patricia Smith, Bartlett Robinson

Although lacking the elaborate production trappings that would automatically mirror a multi-million dollar budget, an extensive shooting schedule and painstaking care went into this picture. It's Class A picturemaking yet doesn't manage to deliver entertainment wallop out of the story about one man in a single-engine plane over a 3,610-mile route.

Spirit is a James Stewart one-man show. He portrays Charles Lindbergh with a toned-down performance intended as consistent with the diffident nature of the famed aviator. The story development tends to focus on the personal side as much as it does on the flight itself, and Stewart comes off with sort of an appropriate, shy amiability.

The flashback technique is used frequently to convey some of Lindbergh's background, such as his days as a mail pilot, an amusing bit re his first encounter with the air force, his barnstorming stunts, etc.

THE STORM

1930, 76 mins, *Dir* William Wyler   US

★ *Stars* Lupe Velez, Paul Cavanaugh, William Boyd, Alphonz Ethier, Ernie S. Adams

The Storm served on two former occasions as a silent, in 1916 for Paramount and in 1922 for U. Lupe Velez is a French smuggler's daughter who is left with a friendly trapper by her father just before a bullet from a mountie's gun lays him low. She plays with an accent that is a cross between Spanish and French, half the time doing a flashing Spanish senorita, the other half a piquant young demoiselle.

Story [from a play, *Men without Skirts*, by Langdon McCormick] is that of a trapper-miner and his best friend who develop a bad jealousy between each other for the girl ward left with the former. They both lean heavily toward the girl, finally hating each other. Shots of the girl in the river attempting to rescue her father from Mounties are very cleverly done. The old man's leap from a cliff, and their race down the river until the canoe capsizes, is also thrilling stuff.

STORM OVER THE NILE

1955, 107 mins, ◇ Ⓥ *Dir* Terence Young, Zoltan Korda   UK

★ *Stars* Anthony Steel, Laurence Harvey, Mary Ure, Ronald Lewis, Ian Carmichael, James Robertson Justice

The Four Feathers ranked high among Alexander Korda's pre-war successes and, in this remake of the A.E.W. Mason story, his brother Zoltan assumes some producer credit as well as sharing the directorial chore with Terence Young. Use of the widescreen process is probably the main justification for the remake, particularly as it enhances the vivid battle scenes in which Kitchener's troops rout the native armies at Khartoum, while imprisoned British officers capture the enemy arsenal. These spectacular sequences are the main highlight of the picture, which in other ways is outmoded in spirit and story content. Battle sequences filmed in the Sudan have a convincing look.

Generally, the acting hardly matches the lavish and spectacular qualities of the production. Laurence Harvey as a fellow officer who gets blinded by an overdose of sun, appears miscast. Only James Robertson Justice, as a veteran of the Crimea and father of Steel's fiancee, fits happily into the story.

THE STORY OF ROBIN HOOD

1952, 83 mins, ◇ Ⓥ *Dir* Ken Annakin   UK

★ *Stars* Richard Todd, Joan Rice, Peter Finch, James Hayter, James Robertson Justice, Martita Hunt

For his second British live-action production, Walt Disney took the legend of Robin Hood and translated it to the screen as a superb piece of entertainment, with all the action of a western and the romance and intrigue of a historical drama.

Despite his modest stature, Richard Todd proves to be a first-rate Robin Hood, alert, dashing and forceful, equally convincing when leading his outlaws against Prince John as he is in winning the admiration of Maid Marian. Although a comparative newcomer to the screen, Joan Rice acts with charm and intelligence.

James Hayter as Friar Tuck, Martita Hunt as the queen, Peter Finch as the sheriff, James Robertson Justice as Little John, Bill Owen as the poacher, and Elton Hayes as the minstrel are in the front rank.

THE STUNT MAN

1980, 129 mins, ◇ Ⓥ *Dir* Richard Rush   US

★ *Stars* Peter O'Toole, Steve Railsback, Barbara Hershey, Allen Goorwitz, Alex Rocco, Sharon Farrell

Offbeat tale, based on Paul Brodeur's 1970 novel, has Vietnam vet Steve Railsback on the lam and accepting refuge from film director Peter O'Toole, who puts the fugitive through some highly dangerous paces as a stunt man while shielding him from the cops.

Lawrence B. Marcus and adaptor-director Richard Rush are least successful in making fully credible the relationship between Railsback and film-within-the-film star Barbara Hershey, with his disillusionment upon discovering that she once had a fling with O'Toole playing as particularly unconvincing.

S

Robert Shaw and Genevieve Bujold in Swashbuckler, an attempt to emulate the great adventure yarns of the past.

O'Toole is excellent in his best, cleanest performance in years. He smashingly delineates an omnipotent, godlike type whose total control over those around him makes him seem almost unreal.

STUNTS

1977, 90 mins, ◇ ⦿ *Dir* Mark L. Lester   US

★ **Stars** Robert Forster, Fiona Lewis, Joanna Cassidy, Darrell Fetty, Bruce Glover, Jim Luisi

Robert Forster is excellent as an ace stuntman who thwarts a maniac stalking a film crew making a police actioner on an ocean-side location in San Luis Obispo, Calif.

This is a tight-lipped actioner about a male group involved in a dangerous trade, with sexy female camp followers admitted to the group once they accept the code of grace under pressure.

There is much emphasis on expertise, emotional control, and the details of the craft, which are shown in docu-like style. The action scenes alternate with more relaxed character interplay in a motel and a bar, where the concept of expertise is translated into personal relationships.

Fiona Lewis is the prime romantic interest, a groupie journalist who initially causes friction in the group.

SWASHBUCKLER

1976, 101 mins, ◇ *Dir* James Goldstone   US

★ **Stars** Robert Shaw, James Earl Jones, Peter Boyle, Genevieve Bujold, Beau Bridges, Anjelica Huston

An uneven picture which is splotchy in the form it tries to emulate, and vacuous in the substance.

Jeffrey Bloom is given sole screenplay credit and Paul Wheeler sole story credit, for the coloring-book plot and formula characters as follows: genial lead pirates, Robert Shaw (a few years past his optimum dash in the role) and James Earl Jones; wicked colonial governor, Peter Boyle; wronged noblelady, Genevieve Bujold; wronged noblelady's noble father, Bernard Behrens; and foppish soldier, Beau Bridges; supporting rogues, Avery Schreiber, Tom Clancy and Geoffrey Holder.

There's no sincerity in *Swashbuckler*. There's not even a consistent approach. This tacky pastepot job can't make up its mind whether it is serious, tongue-in-cheek, satirical, slapstick, burlesque, parody or travesty; but be assured it's all of the above.

Shoehorn several action sequences into 101 minutes, sprinkle with assorted crowd noises and mob types, and add some location work. That's all there is.

TARAS BULBA

1962, 123 mins, ◇ ⦿ *Dir* J. Lee Thompson   US

★ **Stars** Tony Curtis, Yul Brynner, Christine Kaufmann, Sam Wanamaker, Brad Dexter, Guy Rolfe

For many minutes of the two hours it takes director J. Lee Thompson to put Gogol's tale of the legendary Cossack hero on the screen, the panorama of fighting men and horses sweeping across the wide steppes (actually the plains of Argentina) provides a compelling sense of pageantry and grandeur.

As powerful as they are, the spectacular features of *Taras Bulba* do not quite render palatable the wishy-washy subplot, seemingly devised to give Tony Curtis as much screen time as the far more colorful title-role of Yul Brynner. Even avid action-seekers are likely to find hard swallowing a hoary love story of an uncivilized Cossack lad and a polished Polish maiden.

Curtis, an excellent actor when properly supervised or motivated, was seemingly neither inspired nor irritated suffi-

the picture has a strange sort of power that overcomes the total lack of logic.

Tarzan No. 1 ended with Tarz and the white girl from England at peace in their jungle kingdom. They're again at peace as No. 2 ends, but in the 92 minutes between the two fade-outs they're almost in pieces, several times. Trouble starts soon as the domain of Mr and Mrs Tarzan (Weissmuller and Maureen O'Sullivan) is trespassed upon by Neil Hamilton and Paul Cavanagh, a couple of heels from Mayfair. Boys are after the fortune in ivory which lies in a pachyderm graveyard.

Tarzan and his mate spend most of their time swinging through the branches. The Tarzans also do some fancy swimming, particularly during a tank sequence when Weissmuller and a lady swimmer doubling for O'Sullivan, perform some artistic submarine formations. The lady is brassiere-less, but photographed from the side only.

TARZAN AND THE SLAVE GIRL

1950, 74 mins, *Dir* Lee Sholem   US

★ *Stars* Lex Barker, Vanessa Brown, Robert Alda, Denise Darcel, Hurd Hatfield, Arthur Shields

Lex Barker, as Tarzan, takes to the jungle on the trail of some femme natives who are being held prisoners by a group of lost tribesmen [led by Hurd Hatfield]. With him on the trek are a doctor (Arthur Shields), searching for the source of a jungle disease; a comely half-breed nurse with a yen for men; a drunken jungle beachcomber (Robert Alda), and sundry native carriers. Enroute, the safari fights off natives disguised as bushes and armed with deadly blowguns.

Vanessa Brown makes her bow in the Jane role and fills the bill on all counts. Denise Darcel is the nurse, adding plenty of s.a. spice.

TARZAN ESCAPES

1936, 90 mins, *Dir* Richard Thorpe   US

★ *Stars* Johnny Weissmuller, Maureen O'Sullivan, John Buckler, Benita Hume, William Henry, Herbert Mundin

This plot permits Tarzie's idyllic romance with his mate (Maureen O'Sullivan) to be rudely interrupted by a couple of the missus' relatives from London. Mrs Tarzan has unknowingly become the heir to a late uncle's large fortune, and the relatives try to bring her back to civilization so that she may grab the coin and help them grab some of it also.

It so happens, however, that their jungle guide is a dastardly rat who sees in Tarzan a cinch freak show attraction for up north, and it takes not only Tarz himself but also a big zoo full of animal friends to clear up the mess, save the lives of the white folks, give the villyan his just dues, and restore Tarzan's mate to Tarzan.

Johnny Weissmuller again looks good as the jungle

ciently by his talented credits-sharer to do more than kiss and kill on cue.

Brynner's Taras Bulba is an arrogant, proud, physically powerful Cossack chief. Even though the actor follows the habit of running his lines together, his actions are always unmistakably clear. He's allowed plenty of space in which to chew the scenery and there's precious little of it in which he doesn't leave teethmarks.

The battle sequences and, to a lesser extent, the Cossack camp scenes, are the picture's greatest assets. Some of cameraman Joseph MacDonald's long shots of hordes of horsemen sweeping across the plains, as countless others pour over every hillside, are breathtakingly grand and fully utilize the wide screen. Franz Waxman's score, Russian derived, for the battles and his czardas-like themes for the Cossacks are among his best work.

TARZAN AND HIS MATE

1934, 92 mins, *Dir* Cedric Gibbons   US

★ *Stars* Johnny Weissmuller, Maureen O'Sullivan, Neil Hamilton, Paul Cavanagh, Forrester Harvey, Nathan Curry

In *Tarzan and His Mate*, second of the Metro series with Johnny Weissmuller, the monkeys do everything but bake cakes and the very human elephants always seem on the verge of sitting down for a nice, quiet game of chess; yet

boy. And O'Sullivan is also okay once more as the loving wife, but considerably more covered up in clothing this time. A female ape called Cheetah is the Tarzans' pet and house-worker, and some expert handling of the monk provides the picture with its most legitimately comical and best moments.

TARZAN FINDS A SON

1939, 81 mins, *Dir* Richard Thorpe   US

★ *Stars* Johnny Weissmuller, Maureen O'Sullivan, Johnnie Sheffield, Ian Hunter, Laraine Day, Frieda Inescort

Tarzan Finds a Son carries more credulity and believable jungle adventure than the long list of preceding Tarzan features.

Tarzan and the Missus save a baby in plane that crashes in the jungle. Tarzan is proudly teaching his accepted son the jungle lore, when a searching party arrives to establish death of the baby, who has come into heavy inheritance. Ian Hunter and Frieda Inescort are out to grab the inheritance for themselves, and start plotting death of Tarzan and snatch of the youngster. Johnny Weissmuller athletically runs and swims through as the ape-man in okay fashion. Maureen O'Sullivan is the jungle wife, and gets in some good dramatic work in battling against herself to give up the youngster. Tarzan's boy, little Johnnie Sheffield, does nicely and performs his athletic chores satisfactorily.

TARZAN, THE APE MAN

1932, 70 mins, ⚑ *Dir* W. S. Van Dyke   US

★ *Stars* Johnny Weissmuller, Maureen O'Sullivan, Neil Hamilton, C. Aubrey Smith, Doris Lloyd, Forrester Harvey

A jungle and stunt picture, done in deluxe style, with tricky handling of fantastic atmosphere, and a fine, artless performance by the Olympic athlete that represents the absolute best that could be done with the character [created by Edgar Rice Burroughs].

Footage is loaded with a wealth of sensational wild animal stuff. Suspicion is unavoidable that some of it is cut-in material left over from the same producer's *Trader Horn* (by the same director).

Some of the stunt episodes are grossly overdone, but the production skill and literary treatment in other directions compensates. Tarzan (Johnny Weissmuller) is pictured as achieving impossible feats of strength and daring. One of them has him battling single-handed, and armed only with an inadequate knife, not only with one lion but with a panther and two lions, and saved at the last minute from still a third big cat only by the friendly help of an elephant summoned by a call of distress in jungle language.

Story that introduces the Tarzan character is slight. An English trader (C. Aubrey Smith) and his young partner (Neil Hamilton) are about to start in search of the traditional elephants' graveyard where ivory abounds, when the elder

Publicity still of Johnny Weissmuller, the quintessential Tarzan, for Tarzan, the Ape Man.

man's daughter from England (Maureen O'Sullivan) appears at the trading post and insists upon going along. The adventures grow out of their travels.

TARZAN'S GREATEST ADVENTURE

1959, 90 mins, ◇ *Dir* John Guillermin   US

★ *Stars* Gordon Scott, Anthony Quayle, Sara Shane, Niall MacGinnis, Sean Connery, Scilla Gabel

Tarzan finally steps away from Hollywood's process screens to pound his chest amid authentic terrors in the heart of Africa. Death and trauma are the stars, and the supporting players are bullets, arrows, knives, hatchets, dynamite, neck-choking paraphernalia, crocodiles, lions, snakes, spiders, boulders, spikes, pits, quicksand and prickly cactus. It's a furious affair, with an exciting chase or two.

Tarzan (Gordon Scott) is a modern he-man, still adorned in loincloth but more conversational than Edgar Rice Burroughs pictured him. Scott puts little emotion into his greatest adventure, but he swings neatly from tree to tree, takes good care of a crocodile, even if it does appear dead from the start, deciphers with ease the sounds of his animal friends and, more than anything else, looks the part.

Film's storyline has Tarzan and another white man as

mortal enemies. The antagonist (Anthony Quayle) is leading a five-member boat expedition upriver to get rich in diamonds, and Tarzan, knowing of his bestial attitude, follows in hot pursuit. An approximately beautiful female (Sara Shane), drops out of the sky to tag along with Tarzan and turns out to be quite handy in helping the apeman through one or two bad times.

Quayle is excellent as the scarfaced villain, and Niall MacGinnis as a nearly blind diamond expert is equally fine. Sean Connery and Al Mulock, the two other male members of the expedition, are okay, and Scilla Gabel, looking like a miniature Sophia Loren, is easy to look at.

TARZAN'S PERIL

1951, 79 mins, *Dir* Byron Haskin, Phil Brandon   US

★ *Stars* Lex Barker, Virginia Huston, George Macready, Douglas Fowley, Glenn Anders, Alan Napier

This latest entry in the *Tarzan* series has the familiar ingredients of jungle adventure, plus good background footage actually lensed in Africa.

Lex Barker is a capable hero in his Tarzan character. Script could have made him even more of a superman, but otherwise does not let down the fans of the Edgar Rice Burroughs creation. Tarzan is called upon to mete out jungle justice to a gun-runner who supplies forbidden weapons to a tribe of would-be warriors. The script has the hero swinging through trees, swimming rivers, surviving a plunge over a waterfall and taking on a whole tribe in battle before establishing peace and quiet again in his native heath.

Virginia Huston has only a few scenes as Tarzan's mate, Jane, in the footage. There's more emphasis on

Burt Lancaster (left) and nine other Foreign Legionnaires volunteer to foil an attack by the Riffs in Ten Tall Men.

Dorothy Dandridge, queen of a tribe that is saved by Tarzan from its warring rivals. George Macready is the able villain.

TEN TALL MEN

1951, 97 mins, ◇ *Dir* Willis Goldbeck   US

★ *Stars* Burt Lancaster, Jody Lawrance, Gilbert Roland, Kieron Moore, George Tobias, John Dehner

Yarn [from a story by James Warner Bellah and Willis Goldbeck] is tailor-made for the burly Burt Lancaster. Cast as a Foreign Legion sergeant, he picks up a tip while in jail that the Riffs plan an invasion of the city. With nine fellow prisoners he volunteers to harass the would-be invaders. Mission succeeds all expectations when the group manages to seize a sheik's daughter (Jody Lawrance), a key to the whole attack.

Proceedings come off at a crisp pace under Willis Goldbeck's breezy direction. Lancaster, Lawrance and a lengthy list of supporting players handle their roles broadly, which at times achieves almost a satiric effect. Whether that was intentional or not is tough to determine.

THEY CAME TO CORDURA

1959, 123 mins, ◇ Ⓥ *Dir* Robert Rossen   US

★ *Stars* Gary Cooper, Rita Hayworth, Van Heflin, Tab Hunter, Richard Conte

A bitter and realistic drama of the wry twists life can work on men when they are thrown into situations beyond their control – in this case the 1916 border action between US troops and Pancho Villa's Mexican rebels.

The screenplay, from Glendon Swarthout's book, takes

its theme from the title. Cordura is the name of the Texas town the principals are bound for. It is also the Spanish word for courage. The moral is that what's called courage is sometimes a question of interpretation, of accident, or of momentary aberration. Gary Cooper is the US Army officer detailed to lead five Medal of Honor candidates back from the front lines of the war. Cooper has been made Awards Officer after showing cowardice in battle. The son of an army general and himself a career officer, Cooper is desperately interested in the five heroes because they have what he lacks – or so he thinks. Also on the party is Rita Hayworth, the disillusioned and dissolute daughter of a disgraced politician. Gary Cooper is very good as the central figure, although he is somewhat too old for the role. Hayworth, looking haggard, drawn and defeated, gives the best performance of her career.

Van Heflin does a brilliantly evil job as one of the 'heroes', and Richard Conte, as his malevolent sidekick, is almost equally impressive.

THEY MET IN BOMBAY

1941, 92 mins, *Dir* Clarence Brown   US

★ **Stars** Clark Gable, Rosalind Russell, Peter Lorre, Reginald Owen, Matthew Boulton, Jessie Ralph

This is an actionful adventure yarn [based on a story by John Kafka] unfolded in a Far East setting. Story picks up Clark Gable and Rosalind Russell in Bombay, both bent on lifting a famous jewel during Empire Day celebration. Pair meet, Gable tabs girl's purpose immediately, and then proceeds to let her grab the gem so he can conveniently take it from her after the theft. But his scheming is discovered by Russell, and pair take it on the lam in front of Scotland Yard pursuers, grabbing a tramp steamer bound for Hong Kong.

Logic prevails in the early episodes which present much rapid-fire and sparkling by-play between Gable and Russell. But when the pair reach Hong Kong, story strays through fields of corn in an attempt to reform the pair.

Gable is swaggering, resourceful and adventurous to the danger point – and capably gets over these phases of the character. Russell is fine in the early section, but drops into a groove in the second half. Clarence Brown directs at a consistent pace, and manages to hold attention throughout.

THE THIEF OF BAGDAD

1924, 155 mins, ◇⊗ ⓥ *Dir* Raoul Walsh   US

★ **Stars** Douglas Fairbanks, Snitz Edwards, Julanne Johnston, Anna May Wong, Charles Belcher, Sojin

Douglas Fairbanks comes forth with an absorbing, interesting picture, totally different than any of its predecessors. Nearly all of it is fairytale-like or fantasy, and so well is it done that the picture carries its audience along

in the spirit of the depiction. *The Arabian Nights* are classic stories in book form. *The Thief of Bagdad* is a classic in pictures.

There is a magic rope thrown into the air up which the thief climbs high walls. There is a magic carpet upon which he sails with his princess away into the land of happiness. There is a magic chest which the favored one retrieves after heroic struggles through the valley of fire, the vale of dragons, even to the depths of the seas. It is the thief, now a prince who returns at the coming of the seventh moon to win his princess against the wiles of Oriental potentates seeking her hand. He wraps her in his invisible cloak and whisks her away.

The cast has been brightly selected. At the head of those players is Sojin in the role of the Mongol prince, a really fine characterization. Anna May Wong as the little slave girl who is a spy for the Mongol prince, proves herself a fine actress. Julanne Johnston as the princess is languorous, being more decorative than inspiring.

THE THIEF OF BAGDAD

1940, 106 mins, ◇ ⓥ *Dir* Ludwig Berger, Michael Powell, Tim Whelan, Geoffrey   UK

★ **Stars** Conrad Veidt, Sabu, June Duprez, John Justin, Rex Ingram, Miles Malleson

The Thief of Bagdad is a colorful, lavish and eye-appealing spectacle. It's an expensive production accenting visual appeal, combining sweeping panoramas and huge sets, amazing special effects and process photography, and vivid magnificent Technicolor. These factors completely submerge the stolid, slow and rather disjointed fairytale which lacks any semblance of spontaneity in its telling.

Alexander Korda retains only the Bagdadian background and title in presenting his version of the picture first turned out by Douglas Fairbanks in 1924. But while Fairbanks presented dash and movement to his story, to have the latter dominate his spectacular settings, Korda uses the reverse angle. As result, audience interest is focused on the production and technical displays of the picture, and the unimpressive story and stagey acting of the cast fail to measure up to the general production qualities.

The story combines many imaginative incidents culled from Arabian Nights fables. There's the mechanical horse that flies through the air; the giant genie of the bottle; the huge spider that guards the all-seeing eye; the six-armed dancing doll; the evil magic of the villain; and the famous magic carpet.

Korda spent two years in preparation and production of *Thief of Bagdad*. All of the large sets, including the city of Bagdad and seaport of Basra, were shot in England, in addition to most of the dramatic action. With the war stopping production in England Korda moved to Hollywood to complete the picture, substituting the American desert and the Grand Canyon for sequences that he originally intended to shoot in Arabia and Egypt. Conrad Veidt is most impressive as the sinister grand vizier, sharing honors with Sabu, who capably carries off the title role.

Above: *Sabu, the youthful star of Alexander Korda's The Thief of Bagdad, a classic tale from The Arabian Nights.*

THE 39 STEPS

1935, 86 mins, ◇ Ⓥ   *Dir* Alfred Hitchcock   UK

★ *Stars* Robert Donat, Madeleine Carroll, Godfrey Tearle, Peggy Ashcroft, Lucie Mannheim, Wylie Watson

Gaumont has a zippy, punchy, romantic melodrama in *The 39 Steps*. Story is by John Buchan. It's melodrama and at times it is far-fetched and improbable, but the story twists and spins artfully from one high-powered sequence to another while the entertainment holds like steel cable from start to finish.

Story places a Canadian rancher (Robert Donat) in the centre of an English military secrets plot. He is simultaneously flying from a false accusation of murder and hunting down the leader of the spies, of whom he has learned from a lady who becomes a corpse early in the story. In the course of his wanderings through Scotland's hills and moors he has a series of spectacular escapes and encounters. If the story were less ably written, directed and acted, the hero's facility of extrication from tight spots would be absurd but the tempo carries all before it. Criticism is cancelled in pleasure.

It's a creamy role for Donat and his performance, ranging from humor to horror, reveals acting ability behind that good-looking facade. Teamed with Madeleine Carroll, who enters the footage importantly only toward the latter quarter

Below: *Robert Donat and Lucie Mannheim in* **The 39 Steps,** *a tale of spies and murder set in Scotland.*

section of the film, the romance is given a light touch which nicely colors an international spy chase.

THE 39 STEPS

1959, 93 mins, ◇ Ⓥ *Dir* Ralph Thomas   UK

★ **Stars** Kenneth More, Taina Elg, Brenda de Banzie, Barry Jones, Reginald Beckwith, James Hayter

Though somewhat altered from Alfred Hitchcock's original, the main idea remains unchanged and the new version of John Buchan's novel stands up very well.

When a strange young woman is stabbed to death in his flat, Kenneth More finds himself involved in a mysterious adventure involving espionage and murder. Before her death the girl tells him that she is a secret agent and gives him all the clues she knows about a spy organization seeking to smuggle some important plans out of the country. All he knows is that the top man is somewhere in Scotland and that the tangle is tied up with strange words told him by the victim - 'The 39 Steps.' Suspected of the murder of the girl, More has just 48 hours to find out the secret of the 39 Steps, expose the gang and so clear himself of the murder rap.

Film starts off brilliantly with tremendous tension and suitably sinister atmosphere. After a while that mood wears off as the pic settles down to an exciting and often amusing chase yarn, set amid some easy-on-the-eye Scottish scenery.

More's performance is a likeable mixture of humor and toughness while Taina Elg is appealing as the pretty schoolmistress who is dragged into the adventure against her will. Then there are Barry Jones, as a sinister professor; Brenda de Banzie, as a fake spiritualist who with her eccentric husband (Reginald Beckwith) helps More's getaway; James Hayter as a vaude memory man' who is a tool of the gang; and Faith Brook, whose murder sparks off the drama, all pitch in splendidly in a well acted picture.

THE 300 SPARTANS

1962, 108 mins, ◇ *Dir* Rudolph Mate   US

★ **Stars** Richard Egan, Ralph Richardson, Diane Baker, Barry Coe, David Farrar, Donald Houston

The hopeless but ultimately inspiring defense of their country by a band of 300 Spartan soldiers against an immense army of Persian invaders in 480 B.C. – known to history as the Battle of Thermopylae – is the nucleus around which St. George's screenplay is constructed. The inherent appeal and magnitude of the battle itself virtually dwarfs and sweeps aside all attempts at romantic byplay.

An international cast has been assembled for the enterprise, primarily populated with Britishers, Greeks and Americans. Richard Egan, as King Leonidas of Sparta, is physically suitable for the character, but the heroic mold of his performance is only skin deep – more muscle than corpuscle. Ralph Richardson, as might be expected, does the

best acting in the picture, but no one is going to list this portrayal as one of the great achievements in his career.

Diane Baker is glaringly miscast. The fragile actress has been assigned the part of a Spartan girl who knocks two large men off their feet, bodily. As written, it's a role that required an actress of at least Lorenesque proportions.

THE THREE MUSKETEERS

1939, 71 mins, *Dir* Allan Dwan   US

★ **Stars** Don Ameche, Ritz Brothers, Binnie Barnes, Lionel Atwill, Pauline Moore

Utilizing the broadest strokes of comedy technique, this version of Dumas' romantic adventure presents Don Ameche as a rather personable D'Artagnan, and the Ritz Bros as a helter-skelter trio hopping in and out frequently to perform their standard screwball antics.

There is little seriousness or suspense generated in the slender story, and not much interest in the adventures of D'Artagnan and his pals to regain the queen's brooch in the possession of the Duke of Buckingham. Main excuse for the yarn apparently is to provide Ameche with an opportunity to be a dashing hero while the freres Ritz clown through the footage as phoney musketeers.

Romance between Ameche and Pauline Moore is sketchily presented, developing little interest or sincerity.

THE THREE MUSKETEERS

1948, 126 mins, ◇ Ⓥ *Dir* George Sidney   US

★ **Stars** Gene Kelly, Lana Turner, June Allyson, Van Heflin, Angela Lansbury, Vincent Price

The Three Musketeers is a swaggering, tongue-in-cheek treatment of picturesque fiction, extravagantly presented.

The fanciful tale is launched with a laugh, and quickly swings into some colorful and exciting sword duels as the pace is set for the imaginative adventures that feature the lives and loves of D'Artagnan and his three cronies. It is the complete Dumas novel.

There are acrobatics by Gene Kelly that would give Douglas Fairbanks pause. His first duel with Richelieu's cohorts is almost ballet, yet never loses the feeling of swaggering swordplay. It is a masterful mixture of dancing grace, acro-agility and sly horseplay of sock comedic punch.

Lana Turner is a perfect visualization of the sexy, wicked Lady de Winter, sharply contrasting with the sweet charm of June Allyson as the maid Constance. The three king's musketeers of the title are dashingly portrayed by Van Heflin, Gig Young and Robert Coote as Athos, Porthos and Aramis. They belt over their parts in keeping with the style Kelly uses for D'Artagnan.

Another aid in making the film top entertainment is the score by Herbert Stothart, using themes by Tchaikovsky. Score bridges any gap in movement without intruding itself.

THE THREE MUSKETEERS

1973, 105 mins, ◇ Ⓥ *Dir* Richard Lester   PANAMA

★ *Stars* Oliver Reed, Charlton Heston, Raquel Welch, Faye Dunaway, Richard Chamberlain, Michael York

The Three Musketeers take very well to Richard Lester's provocative version that does not send it up but does add comedy to this adventure tale [by Alexandre Dumas].

Here D'Artagnan, played with brio by Michael York, is a country bumpkin; the musketeers themselves are more interested in money, dames and friendship than undue fidelity to the King, a simple-minded type, and their fight scenes are full of flailing, kicks and knockabout. They are not above starting a fight at an inn to steal victuals when they run out of money. Behind it, however, is a look at an era of poverty and virtual worker slavery to fulfill the King's flagrantly rich whims.

Musketeers are played with panache by Richard Chamberlain as the haughty ladies' man, Oliver Reed as the gusty one and Frank Finlay as the dandyish type. Raquel Welch has comedic timing as the maladroit girl of D'Artagnan while Faye Dunaway has less to do as the perfidious Milady.

THUNDER AND LIGHTNING

1977, 93 mins, ◇ Ⓥ *Dir* Corey Allen   US

★ *Stars* David Carradine, Kate Jackson, Roger C. Carmel, Sterling Holloway, Ed Barth, Ron Feinberg

Thunder and Lightning, has just about everything in the action department but Dracula loping after Frankenstein's monster, packing thrills and fast movement as stunt drivers have their day in some wild pic mileage.

Film picks up in tempo and ends on a socko note as David Carradine, an irrepressible booze runner, competes with girlfriend Kate Jackson's pop in his chosen field. Script laces comedy with the action, and director Corey Allen expertly maneuvers his chase sequences with stunting both with Everglade buggies and fast cars on the highways.

Carradine shows he has the stuff of which action stars are made, and distaffer Jackson lends a distracting note as an actress who doesn't mind getting her hair mussed.

THUNDERBALL

1965, 130 mins, ◇ Ⓥ *Dir* Terence Young   UK

★ *Stars* Sean Connery, Claudine Auger, Adolfo Celi, Luciana Paluzzi, Rik van Nutter, Bernard Lee

Sean Connery plays his indestructible James Bond for the fourth time in the manner born, faced here with a $280 million atomic bomb ransom plot. Action, dominating element of three predecessors, gets rougher before even the credits flash on. Richard Maibaum (who co-scripted former entries) and John Hopkins' screenplay is studded with inventive play and mechanical gimmicks. There's visible evidence that the reported $5.5 million budget was no mere publicity figure; it's posh all the way.

Underwater weapon-carrying sea sleds provide an imaginative note, as does a one-man jet pack used by Bond in the opening sequence, reminiscent of the one-man moon vehicle utilized by Dick Tracy in the cartoon strip.

Connery is up to his usual stylish self as he lives up to past rep, in which mayhem is a casual affair.

Adolfo Celi brings dripping menace to part of the swarthy heavy who is nearly as ingenious – but not quite – as the British agent, whom, among other means, he tries to kill with man-eating sharks.

Terence Young takes advantage of every situation in his direction to maintain action at fever-pitch.

THUNDER BAY

1953, 103 mins, ◇ Ⓥ *Dir* Anthony Mann   US

★ *Stars* James Stewart, Joanne Dru, Gilbert Roland, Dan Duryea, Jay C. Flippen, Marcia Henderson

A modern plot that deals with offshore oil drilling gives this regulation outdoor actioner an interesting switch. James Stewart and Dan Duryea, as a couple of ex-GIs with a dream of extracting oil from the bottom of the Gulf of Mexico off the coast of Louisiana, carry the principal story load. Having talked Jay C. Flippen, head of an oil company, into backing the offshore exploration, the two adventurers plunge into their work against the wishes of the shrimp fishermen, who see their livelihood ruined.

Stewart moves easily through his role as the stalwart, steadfast member of the adventuring pair. Duryea supplies likeable color to his wise-cracking heroics and comes over strongly. Joanne Dru's character as the daughter of fisherman Antonio Moreno needed more clarity to be effective.

Anthony Mann's direction manages considerable action to balance a script tendency towards talkiness. The water sequences have punch.

TOP GUN

1986, 110 mins, ◇ Ⓥ *Dir* Tony Scott   US

★ *Stars* Tom Cruise, Kelly McGillis, Val Kilmer, Anthony Edwards, Tom Skerritt, Meg Ryan

Set in the world of naval fighter pilots, pic has strong visuals and pretty young people in stylish clothes and a non-stop soundtrack.

Cinematographer Jeffery Kimball and his team have assembled some exciting flight footage.

Tom Cruise is Maverick, a hot-shot fighter pilot with a

Tom Cruise is Maverick, a Navy pilot who gets to go to the top training School, Top Gun.

mind of his own and something to prove, assigned to the prestigious Top Gun training school.

Along for the ride as a romantic interest is Kelly McGillis, a civilian astrophysicist brought in to teach the boys about negative Gs and inverted flight tanks. Cruise, however, has his sights set on other targets.

McGillis is blessed with an intelligent and mature face that doesn't blend that well with Cruise's one-note grinning. There is nothing menacing or complex about his character. Tom Skerritt turns in his usual nice job as the hardened but not hard flight instructor.

THE TOWERING INFERNO

1974, 165 mins, ◇ Ⓥ *Dir* John Guillermin, Irwin Allen   US

★ *Stars* Steve McQueen, Paul Newman, William Holden, Faye Dunaway, Robert Vaughn, Richard Chamberlain

Academy Award 1974: Best Picture (Nomination)

The Towering Inferno is one of the greatest disaster pictures made, a personal and professional triumph for producer Irwin Allen. The $14 million cost has yielded a truly magnificent production which complements but does not at all overwhelm a thoughtful personal drama.

The strategy of casting expensive talent pays off handsomely. Steve McQueen, as the fireman in charge of extinguishing the runaway fire in a 130-storey San Francisco building, Paul Newman, as the heroic and chagrined architect of the glass and concrete pyre, William Holden as its builder, and Faye Dunaway, as Newman's fiancee, get and deserve their star billing.

Both 20th and WB pooled their finances and their separate but similar book acquisitions – Richard Martin Stern's *The Tower* and *The Glass Inferno*, by Thomas N. Scortia and Frank M. Robinson respectively– to effect a true example of synergy.

The Towering Inferno, one of the best disaster pics ever made, about a 130 storey building that goes up in flames.

TRADER HORN

1931, 123 mins, *Dir* W.S. Van Dyke   US

★ *Stars* Harry Carey, Edwina Booth, Duncan Renaldo, Mutia Omoolu, Olive Golden, C. Aubrey Smith

Academy Award 1930/31: Best Picture (Nomination)

A good-looking animal picture. The story doesn't mean anything other than a connecting link for a series of sequences which, at one point, become nothing more than an out-and-out lecture tour, as various herds of animals are described by the voice of Harry Carey, in the title role. Studio has simply interpreted the original novel [by Aloysius Horn and Ethelreda Lewis] as it saw fit, lifting a couple of characters therefrom and putting them through a succession of narrow escapes from four-footed enemies and a tribe of hungry cannibals.

Light love vein is introduced between Carey's young companion, Duncan Renaldo, and Edwina Booth as the queen of a tribe from whom she and the men escape when

her followers turn on her after she countermands an order of death by torture for Carey, Renaldo and Rencharo, the former's native gun boy.

Booth, very easy to look at, prances through the jungle in scanty raiment, knowing only the gutteral language of the blacks. The escape of the quartet immediately goes into a chase, during which Carey doubles back to act as decoy so the boy and girl can get away. Finish is the successful reaching of a river settlement where the youth and former tribal queen board a small river steamer bound for civilization, while Carey, as Trader Horn, prepares to go back into the jungle once more.

Sound effects are outstanding. Andy Anderson, the sound man, accompanied director W.S. Van Dyke's unit to Africa. The camera work is also swell marksmanship.

THE TRAP

1966, 106 mins, ◇ ⓥ *Dir* Sidney Hayers   UK, CANADA

★ *Stars* Rita Tushingham, Oliver Reed, Rex Sevenoaks, Barbara Chilcott, Linda Goranson, Blain Fairman

This Anglo-Canadian get together deals with an earthy adventure yarn, a struggle for survival, and an offbeat battle of the sexes.

Story is set in the mid-1890s when British Columbia was wild and untamed and only the strong came out on top. Jean La Bete (Oliver Reed), a huge, lusty French-Canadian trapper, returns to the trading post too late for the once-a-year 'auction' of harlots, thieves and femme riff-raff sent away from civilization for this purpose. So he settles for a young mute orphan, a servant in the trader's house, sold to him by the grasping wife.

He hauls the protesting girl into a canoe and sets off for the wastes. There follows an edgy Taming of the Shrew situation as the hunter tries to win her affection by cajoling, bullying, threatening, and occasionally sweet-talking.

Reed is larger-than-life as the crude, brawling trapper yet also has moments of great sensitivity with his co-star. Tushingham, sans benefit of dialog has to depend on her famous eyes, and wistful mouth to put over a tricky role embracing many emotions, from spitfire to waif, and she does marvels.

TREASURE ISLAND

1934, 105 mins, *Dir* Victor Fleming   US

★ *Stars* Wallace Beery, Jackie Cooper, Lionel Barrymore, Otto Kruger, Lewis Stone, Nigel Bruce

It's pretty dangerous to put an old classic as popular as this Robert Louis Stevenson yarn on the screen. It is hard to imagine anyone else in the Long John Silver role than Wallace Beery. It is hard to think of anyone who might have replaced Jackie Cooper as Jim Hawkins. Yet neither of the two completely convinces.

Best performance honors are really split between Lionel Barrymore and Chic Sale. Former, as Billy Bones, and latter as Ben Gunn, seem most thoroughly to have caught the Stevenson spirit. They overact almost to mugging but it's in keeping with the manner of the story.

Treasure Island as a story is a grand, blood-curdling adventure yarn. In portions where it is so played it's genuinely thrilling and good entertainment.

TREASURE ISLAND

1950, 96 mins, ◇ ⓥ *Dir* Byron Haskin   UK

★ *Stars* Bobby Driscoll, Robert Newton, Basil Sydney, Walter Fitzgerald, Dennis O'Dea, Finlay Currie

Treasure Island, Robert Louis Stevenson's classic, has been handsomely mounted by Walt Disney. Settings are sumptuous and a British cast headed by American moppet Bobby Driscoll faithfully recaptures the bloodthirsty 18th-century era when pirates vied for the supremacy of the seas. It was made in Britain with Disney and RKO frozen pounds.

Stevenson yarn revolves around a squire and a doctor who fit out a ship to search for South Seas treasure on the strength of a chart obtained from a dying pirate.

Robert Newton racks up a virtual tour de force as Long John Silver. Likewise, Driscoll smashes across with a vital portrayal of Jim Hawkins, the saloonkeeper's son who falls heir to a map leading the way to pirate treasure.

There's no dearth of action in the footage.

TREASURE OF THE GOLDEN CONDOR

1953, 93 mins, ◇ ⓥ *Dir* Delmer Daves   US

★ *Stars* Cornel Wilde, Constance Smith, Finlay Currie, Anne Bancroft, George Macready, Fay Wray

A moderate round of entertainment is offered in this adventure-swashbuckler that lays its action in early France and Guatemala. Ancient Mayan ruins, particularly the earthquake-wrecked city of Antigua, supply a picturesque touch.

Delmer Daves directed and scripted from a novel by Edison Marshall. Plot deals with Cornel Wilde's efforts to oust a cruel uncle who has usurped his French estates and title. Needing money to prove his rights, Wilde joins forces with Finlay Currie, possessor of a map to a fabulous Mayan treasure. Escaping the bondage under which his uncle has held him since childhood, Wilde takes off with Currie for the jungles of Guatemala and the treasure.

Wilde is likable as the dashing hero and has some good swash-buckling moments in the latter portions of the footage. He also has more than one man's share of comely femmes with whom to clinch in the persons of Constance Smith and Anne Bancroft. – both of whom look good in their costumes. Fay Wray has only a few brief scenes as Macready's suffering wife.

THE TREASURE OF THE SIERRA MADRE

1948, 124 mins, ⊗ *Dir* John Huston   US

★ **Stars** Humphrey Bogart, Walter Huston, Tim Holt, Bruce Bennett

Academy Award 1948: Best Picture (Nomination)

Sierra Madre, adapted from the popular novel by B. Traven, is a story of psychological disintegration under the crushers of greed and gold. The characters here are probed and thoroughly penetrated, not through psychoanalysis but through a crucible of human conflict, action, gesture and expressive facial tones.

Huston, with an extraordinary assist in the thesping department from his father, Walter Huston, has fashioned this standout film with an unfailing sensitivity for the suggestive detail and an uncompromising commitment to reality, no matter how stark ugly it may be.

Except for some incidental femmes who have no bearing on the story, it's an all-male cast headed by Bogart, Huston and Tim Holt. They play the central parts of three gold prospectors who start out for pay dirt in the Mexican mountains as buddies, but wind up in a murderous tangle at the finish.

Lensed for most part on location, the film has, at least, a physical aspect of rugged beauty against which is contrasted the human sordidness.

Bogart comes through with a performance as memorable as his first major film role in *The Petrified Forest*. In a remarkable controlled portrait, he progresses to the edge of madness without losing sight of the subtle shadings needed to establish persuasiveness.

TWILIGHT FOR THE GODS

1958, 120 mins, ◇ *Dir* Joseph Pevney   US

★ **Stars** Rock Hudson, Cyd Charisse, Arthur Kennedy, Leif Erickson, Charles McGraw, Richard Haydn

Twilight for the Gods emerges as a routine sea adventure drama, bolstered by the marquee names of Rock Hudson and Cyd Charisse. Novelist Ernest Gann, who also wrote the screenplay, has employed the familiar technique [from his successful *The High and the Mighty*] of assembling a group of passengers of different personalities and backgrounds, including several with shady pasts, and studies their reactions to the dangers encountered during a long sea voyage.

There's Hudson, a court-martialed ship's captain fighting alcoholism, as the skipper of the battered sailing ship; Charisse as a Honolulu call girl running away from the authorities; Arthur Kennedy as a bitter and treacherous second mate; Leif Erickson as a down-and-out showman; Judith Evelyn as a has-been opera singer; Vladimir Sokoloff and Celia Lovsky as an elderly refugee couple; Ernest Truex as a

missionary, and Richard Haydn as a British beachcomber.

Filmed on location in the Hawaiian islands, the photography is a delight to the eyes as it captures the sailing ship in motion, a sea village, various beaches and sites on a chain of islands, Honolulu harbor, and Waikalulu Falls.

TWO YEARS BEFORE THE MAST

1946, 96 mins, *Dir* John Farrow   US

★ **Stars** Alan Ladd, Brian Donlevy, William Bendix, Barry Fitzgerald, Howard da Silva

Chief credit for this one [based on R.H. Dana's famous book] belongs to director John Farrow. With the emphasis on action throughout, Farrow keeps his cast thesping to the hilt and achieves several little bits of suspense.

Although Alan Ladd and the other stars top the cast, it's Howard da Silva, as the pitiless ship's captain, who walks off with the blue ribbon.

Rest of cast, from leads to minor bit parts perform excellently. Ladd does a nice job as the fop who finds his regeneration while fighting to get human treatment for the merchant seamen of that day. Bendix gives a restrained reading to his role as the tough but necessarily sympathetic first mate, and Barry Fitzgerald adds the comedy touches as the ship's cook.

ULYSSES

1954, 104 mins ◇ ⊗ *Dir* Mario Camerini   ITALY

★ **Stars** Kirk Douglas, Silvana Mangano, Anthony Quinn, Rossana Podesta, Jacques Dumesnil

A lot, perhaps too much, money went into the making of *Ulysses*, but expense shows. Besides the epic Homeric peg, pic has an internationally balanced cast, with Yank, French and Italian elements predominant.

Only a few of the w.k. Homeric episodes have been included in the already lengthy pic, and are told in flashback form as remembered by the hero. Featured are his love for Nausicaa; the cave of Polyphemus, the one-eyed monster; the Siren Rocks; the visit to Circe's Island cave and the return to Penelope. But material covered makes for plenty of action, dominated by a virile performance by Kirk Douglas.

Others include costar Silvana Mangano, a looker, as both Circe and Penelope, but unfortunately limited by both parts to expressing monotonous unhappiness until the finale. Anthony Quinn handles his bits well. For a spectacle, the pic runs too many closeups, with longish stretches of dialog between the two principals, or soliloquized.

Kirk Douglas wrestles with Umberto Silvestri in the Italian-produced **Ulysses,** *featuring a selection of Homeric tales.*

UNCOMMON VALOR

1983, 105 mins, ◇ Ⓥ   *Dir* Ted Kotcheff   US

★ **Stars** Gene Hackman, Robert Stack, Fred Ward, Reb Brown, Randall 'Tex' Cobb, Patrick Swayze

All of the top talent involved - especially Gene Hackman - is hardly needed to make *Uncommon Valor* what it is, a very common action picture.

Hackman does as much as he can as a grieving father obsessed with the idea that his son remains a prisoner 10 years after he was reported missing-in-action in Vietnam. Financed by oil tycoon Robert Stack, whose son is also missing, Hackman puts together his small invasion force and two-thirds of *Valor* is consumed introducing the characters and putting them through various practice drills for the rescue which will predictably be tougher than they planned on.

True to a long tradition of war films, by the time the tough really get going it's only a question of who won't come back from the dangerous mission. But at least each of the main characters in *Valor* does his best to make you care whether it's him.

UNCONQUERED

1947, 135 mins, ◇   *Dir* Cecil B. DeMille   US

★ **Stars** Gary Cooper, Paulette Goddard, Howard DaSilva, Boris Karloff, Ward Bond, Katherine DeMille

Cecil B. DeMille's *Unconquered* is a $4 million Technicolor spectacle; it's a pre-Revolutionary western with plenty of Injun stuff which, for all the vacuousness and shortcomings, has its gripping moments. The redskins are ruthless scalpers and the British colonials alternatively naive and brave, patriotic and full of skullduggery to give substance to the melodramatic heroics and knavery of the most derring-do school.

Howard DaSilva is the arch-knave whose marriage to Injun chief Boris Karloff's daughter (Katherine DeMille) puts him plenty in the black with the redskins on fur-trading and the like. Paulette Goddard is the proud slave-girl whose freedom Gary Cooper purchases on the British slaveship, only to cross paths with the heavy (DaSilva) and his No. 2 menace (Mike Mazurki).

It is not a generally known fact that in that 1763 period English convicts facing imprisonment in gaol had the alternative of being sold into limited slavery in the American colonies. Although a bond slave, Goddard spurns DaSilva and sufficiently attracts Cooper to make for the pic's romantic angle.

Despite the ten-twent-thirt meller-dramatics and the frequently inept script, the performances are convincing, a great tribute to the cast because that dialog and those situations try the best of troupers.

Gene Hackman heads up a team of vets who return to Vietnam to rescue prisoners of war in **Uncommon Valor.**

UNDER FIRE

1983, 100 mins, ◇ Ⓥ *Dir* Roger Spottiswoode   US

★ *Stars* Nick Nolte, Gene Hackman, Joanna Cassidy, Jean-Louis Trintignant, Ed Harris, Richard Masur

The American media are strongly taken to task in *Under Fire*. This is the story of two correspondents (one working for *Time*, the other Public Radio) and an on-the-scenes war photographer. The action begins in the African bush of Chad, then moves on to Nicaragua – and a feature-film rehearsal of that tragic televised killing of the ABC correspondent by a Somoza government soldier in the late 1970s as he was covering the fighting with the winning Sandinista rebels.

Three individuals cover the Chad conflict in the late 1960s: the 30-year-old photog Russell Price (Nick Nolte), the 50-year-old senior correspondent for *Time* mag Alex Grazier (Gene Hackman), and the circa 40-year-old radio newslady Claire Stryder (Joanna Cassidy). All are tough professionals.

There's a fourth individual who surfaces now and then: he's a hired mercenary, a killer by trade, whom lenser Nolte meets from time to time, in Chad and in Nicaragua.

In the course of covering the events Nolte and Cassidy opt to search for a certain rebel leader named Rafael among the revolutionary Sandinistas, for Rafael has never been photographed nor interviewed by the American press.

Further, Nolte's photos of the rebels play into the hands of a double-agent, the Frenchman (Jean-Louis Trintignant), who uses them to hunt down and kill the key Sandinista leaders. These factors are the core of the action.

UNDER TWO FLAGS

1936, 111 mins, *Dir* Frank Lloyd   US

★ *Stars* Ronald Colman, Claudette Colbert, Victor McLaglen, Rosalind Russell, Gregory Ratoff, Nigel Bruce

The classic *Under Two Flags*, in book [by Ouida], play and through two silent filmizations [1916 and 1922], is still sturdy fare, talkerized. A pioneer saga of the Foreign Legion, Darryl Zanuck and 20th-Fox have further fortified it by a four-ply marquee ensemble (Ronald Colman, Claudette Colbert, Victor McLaglen and Rosalind Russell).

Not the tempestuous Cigarette of the Theda Bara vintage [1916 version] when *Under Two Flags* was a highlight in that silent film vamp's career, Colbert nonetheless makes the somewhat bawdy cafe hostess stand up. It's not exactly in her metier. Twixt the native Cigarette and Rosalind Russell as the English lady, Colman does all right on the romance interest, with the desert as a setting.

Victor McLaglen turns in an expert chore as the scowling Major Doyle, lovesick for and jealous of Cigarette's two-timing. Gregory Ratoff is planted well for comedy relief with his plaint that he's already forgotten just what he joined the Legion to forget.

The production highlight is the pitched battle on the desert [directed by Otto Brower, photographed by Sidney Wagner] between the marauding Arabs and the handful of legionnaires defending the fort.

UTU

1983, 120 mins, ◇ Ⓥ *Dir* Geoff Murphy   NEW ZEALAND

★ *Stars* Anzac Wallace, Bruno Lawrence, Kelly Johnson, Wi Kuki Kaa, Tim Eliot, Ilona Rodgers

In a NZ western of the North American Indian–white settler school, Geoff Murphy has fashioned a fast-moving visual tale of archetypal passion and action. 'Utu' is the Maori word for 'revenge'.

Central figure is rebel leader Te Wheke (Anzac Wallace) during the wars between European settlers and the native Maoris in the late 19th century.

At first sympathetic to the European (pakeha) cause, Te Wheke turns guerilla when his village is wiped out by British soldiers protecting the settlers. He retaliates in kind while recruiting supporters. As his actions become more despotic and cruel, he is hunted, captured and finally shot.

Murphy has produced powerful images and strong performances, particularly from Wallace, Wi Kuki Kaa (as Wirimu) and a big cast of Maori actors. Action sequences, special effects, and visual exploitation of a rugged, high country location in central New Zealand are superb.

VALLEY OF THE KINGS

1954, 85 mins, ◇ *Dir* Robert Pirosh   US

★ *Stars* Robert Taylor, Eleanor Parker, Carlos Thompson, Kurt Kasznar, Victor Jory, Leon Askin

The story is one dealing with robbers of the tombs of the Pharaohs in Egypt, with a side angle having to do with the establishment that Old Testament accounts of Joseph in Egypt are literally true.

Some good suspense action and thrills are whipped up in the screenplay [suggested by historical data in *Gods, Graves and Scholars* by C.W. Ceram] on the robber score during the first 70 minutes. The side angle to the plot is wrapped up in the concluding 15 minutes and, while quite interesting, is anti-climactic.

Robert Taylor plays a rugged American archaeologist who agrees to help Eleanor Parker, married to Carlos Thompson, search for the tomb of the Pharaoh, Ra-hotep. She wants to prove that her late father was right in believing the tomb will prove his theory about Joseph in Egypt. Clues turn up indicating the tomb already has been robbed and a mysterious gang, seemingly headed by sinister Kurt Kasznar, puts obstacles in the way of the search.

VANISHING POINT

1971, 107 mins, ◇ Ⓥ *Dir* Richard C. Sarafian   US

★ *Stars* Barry Newman, Cleavon Little, Charlotte Rampling, Dean Jagger, Victoria Medlin, Paul Koslo

If the viewer believes what Guillermo Cain's screenplay is trying to say in this lowercase action effort, the 'wasteland' between Denver and the California border is peopled only with uniformed monsters, aided and abetted by an antagonistic citizenry with the only 'good' people the few hippies, motorcycle gangs and dope pushers.

The action is almost entirely made up of one man driving a car at maximum speed from Denver to, hopefully, San Francisco, against various odds, including the police who try to intercept him, and the oddball individuals he meets along the way.

Barry Newman is the ex-marine who tackles the 15-hour drive sans rest or reason, kept awake by pep pills. A Negro disk jockey (Cleavon Little), tucked away on a tiny radio station in what is close to being a ghost town becomes his collaborator, warning him over the radio when he's near a police trap. This leads, naturally, to the now screen cliche of his being attacked and beaten by racists.

Also seen briefly is Dean Jagger as a Death Valley prospector who tries to befriend Newman and, very briefly, Charlotte Rampling, as a hitchhiker with whom Newman beds down for the night.

VIETNAM, TEXAS

1990, 85 mins, ◇ Ⓥ *Dir* Robert Ginty   US

★ *Stars* Robert Ginty, Haing S. Ngor, Tim Thomersen, Kiev Chinh, Tamlyn Tomita

Good intentions are roughly served in this uneven actioner that displays some compassion for the stateside Vietnam community while exploiting its violent elements.

Robert Ginty, who also directed, stars as Father Thomas McCain, a Vietnam vet turned priest who still suffers guilt about the Vietnamese woman he abandoned – pregnant with his child – when he returned to the United States. Fifteen years later, he tracks them down in Houston's Little Saigon and forces himself into their lives, despite the fact that his former flame Mailan (Kieu Chinh) is now comfortably established as the wife of a vicious drug runner, Wong (Haing S. Ngor).

Ginty hooks up with his old soldier buddy Max (Tim Thomerson), now a dissolute bar owner, and they set out to reach Mailan and her teenage daughter Lan (Tamlin Tomita), setting off beatings and murders as they run up against Wong's henchmen.

Christopher Walken and Grace Jones, the two baddies who confront James Bond in **A View to a Kill.**

Among its plusses, pic features numerous Asian roles, with Tomita a standout as the spirited teenage daughter. Ngor (*The Killing Fields*) is suitably chilling as Wong.

A VIEW TO A KILL

1985, 131 mins, ◇ Ⓥ *Dir* John Glen   UK

★ *Stars* Roger Moore, Christopher Walken, Tanya Roberts, Grace Jones, Patrick Macnee, Patrick Bauchan

Bond's adversary this time is the international industrialist Max Zorin (Christopher Walken) and his love-hate interest, May Day (Grace Jones). Bond tangles with them at their regal horse sale and uncovers a profitable scheme in which microchips are surgically implanted in the horse to assure an easy victory.

Horse business is moderately entertaining, particularly when Patrick Macnee is on screen as Bond's chauffeur accomplice. Action, however, jumps abruptly to San Francisco to reveal Zorin's true motives. He's hatching some master plan to pump water from the sea into the San Andreas fault causing a major earthquake, destroying the Silicon Valley and leaving him with the world's microchip monopoly.

While James Bond pics have always traded heavily on the camp value of its characters, *A View to a Kill* almost attacks the humor, practically winking at the audience with every move.

As for Roger Moore, making his seventh appearance as Bond, he is right about half the time. He still has the suave and cool for the part, but on occasion he looks a bit old and his womanizing seems dated when he does.

THE VIKINGS

1958, 114 mins, ◇ Ⓥ *Dir* Richard Fleischer   US

★ *Stars* Kirk Douglas, Tony Curtis, Ernest Borgnine, Janet Leigh, Alexander Knox, Frank Thring

The Vikings is spectacular, rousing and colorful. Blood flows freely as swords are crossed and arrows meet their mark in

Battle scene from **The Vikings,** *the story of a marauding Norse army, led by Kirk Douglas and Tony Curtis.*

barbarian combat. And there's no hesitance about throwing a victim into a wolf pit or a pool of crabs.

There is some complication at the start, however, as the various characters are brought into view – as the Viking army of 200 raids the Kingdom of Northumbria, in England, and elements of mystery and intrigue are brought into the story. But it is not too long before the screenplay [from the novel by Edison Marshall] and director Richard Fleischer have their people in clear focus.

History is highly fictionalized. It starts with the raid, the death of the English leader, the succession to the throne of Frank Thring who's strictly the heavy. The queen is with child, the father being Ernest Borgnine, head of the marauding Vikings. To escape the new king's wrath she flees to another land and with the proper passage of time the child, now a young man (Tony Curtis), turns up in the Viking village as a slave whose identity is not known.

It is at this point that Curtis encounters Kirk Douglas, latter as heir to the Viking throne. Neither is aware of the fact that the other is his brother. They clash. Janet Leigh participates as daughter of the king of Wales who is to be taken as a bride by the sadistic English king. Douglas falls for Leigh in a big way but she comes to favor Curtis, and thus is established the romantic triangle.

It's the production that counts and producer Jerry Bresler, working with Douglas' indie outfit, has done it up big and with apparent authenticity. Lensing was in the Norse fjord area and various parts of Europe, including the Bavarian Studios.

Douglas, doing a bangup, freewheeling job as the ferocious and disfigured Viking fighter, fits the part splendidly. Borgnine's Viking chief is a conqueror of authority.

VILLA RIDES

1968, 125 mins, ◇ ⊕   *Dir* Buzz Kulik   US

★ *Stars* Yul Brynner, Robert Mitchum, Grazia Buccella, Charles Bronson, Robert Viharo, Frank Wolff

Villa Rides is a pseudo-biopic of a portion of the bandit career of Mexico's folk hero, Pancho Villa, with Yul Brynner in title role.

Ted Richmond's handsome exterior production, filmed in 1967 in Spain, is competently, if leisurely and routinely, directed with the accent on violent death.

Script fails to establish clearly the precise political framework, while over-developing some lesser details. This, plus overlength, adds up to dramatic tedium.

Film concerns itself with Villa's own aggressive acts. With the aid of Charles Bronson and Robert Viharo, Brynner is responsible for the on-screen deaths of literally dozens of men, most explicitly detailed.

Brynner makes Villa sympathetic at times, as a man fighting for human rights, though that's a bit hard to swallow since his philosophy does not get spelled out for 105 min-

utes into the film. His rationalization is rather facile and specious: those he killed were 'traitors,' by his convenient self-excusing definition.

WAKE OF THE RED WITCH

1949, 106 mins, ⊕   *Dir* Edward Ludwig   US

★ *Stars* John Wayne, Gail Russell, Gig Young, Luther Adler

Wake of the Red Witch, with its Polynesian locale, is replete with action, drama and adventure. Story is a gripping account of deadly rivalry between two men. Struggle between John Wayne, an impetuous sea captain, and his employer, shipping tycoon Luther Adler, should have been stressed more fully.

As master of the square rigger, *Red Witch*, Wayne has a score to settle with the ship's owner, Adler. He chooses to do it by scuttling the bullion-laden vessel on an uncharted reef. Gail Russell appears miscast among the South Pacific flora and fauna. Her romantic scenes with Wayne never achieve an aura of realism.

THE WARRIORS

1979, 90 mins, ◇ ⊕   *Dir* Walter Hill   US

★ *Stars* Michael Beck, James Remar, David Patrick Kelly, Deborah Van Valkenburgh

Theme of the pic, based on Sol Yurick's 1965 novel, is a variation on countless westerns and war films.

Update the setting to modern-day New York, and the avenues of escape to graffiti-emblazoned subway cars, and that's *The Warriors*.

The slaying of a hood (Roger Hill) is pinned on a Coney Island gang, the Warriors of the title, and the word soon goes out that the group's members are to be eliminated. It's a long subway ride to Coney Island, so for at least 70 of the film's 90 minutes, the boys in this band experience a variety of macho passage rites.

As with his previous pix, *Hard Times* and *The Driver*, director Walter Hill demonstrates an outstanding visual sense here, with the gaudy 'colors' of the gang members, the desolation of night-time NY, and the cavernous subway platforms where much of the action takes place.

WATERLOO

1970, 132 mins, ◇ ⑰ *Dir* Sergei Bondarchuk ITALY, USSR

★ *Stars* Rod Steiger, Christopher Plummer, Orson Welles, Jack Hawkins, Virginia McKenna, Dan O'Herlihy

Directed by Russia's Sergei Bondarchuk, who made *War and Peace*, and filmed on location in Italy and Russia, with interiors at De Laurentiis's Rome studios, the long-nursed Dino De Laurentiis project has an international flavor. Despite the fact that the battle is the focal point, and a striking din-laden affair it is, the film is raised from being just another historical war epic by the performances of Rod Steiger as Napoleon and Christopher Plummer as Wellington.

The story begins with Europe entirely opposed to the ambitious, flamboyant Napoleon and the French, scared of overwhelming odds, forcing him to abdicate and retire to the island of Elba. But barely has the film started than he's back again. The emotional French rally again to Napoleon, defy Louis XVIII, and follow him as he marches into Paris. But his overwhelming lust for France's power sets the allies of England, Austria, Prussia and Russia against him.

Steiger gives a remarkably powerful portrayal of Napoleon. It's a Method performance, with his sudden blazes of rage highlighting his moody introspection.

Others stand out as well. Dan O'Herlihy as Marshal Ney, devoted, loyalist to Napoleon, and Orson Welles, making much of two minor but memorable moments as Louis XVIII.

WEST OF ZANZIBAR

1928, 70 mins, *Dir* Tod Browning US

★ *Stars* Lon Chaney, Lionel Barrymore, Warner Baxter, Mary Nolan, Jane Daly, Roscoe Ward

West of Zanzibar will satisfy Lon Chaney fans who like their color regardless of the way it is daubed. Lionel Barrymore captures the magician's bride, just after Chaney has subtitled his affection for her. The latter part is dully played and given scant meaning. She passes out of the picture too soon thereafter for the magician to believe that the competition is the kid's dad.

Then, for no particular reason, the action is transferred to another world. Chaney, too hurriedly, is shown as an ivory robber and just as mysteriously Barrymore suddenly develops to have quit the stage and become a white trader in Africa. With the same unexplainable rapidity, Chaney is revealed to have started his revenge by training the babe in the ways of tropical fleshpots.

Mary Nolan as the grown daughter does not make the matriculation of a prostitute any too vivid. Rather, a blonde saint in Chaney's eerie jungle den is the reaction. Jungle scenes with crocodiles oozing through slime and a score or so of vaselined black extras doing their dances and attending to their funeral pyres are what get this by.

WHERE NO VULTURES FLY

1951, 106 mins, ◇ *Dir* Harry Watt UK

★ *Stars* Anthony Steel, Dinah Sheridan, Harold Warrender, Meredith Edwards, William Simons, Orlando Martins

Excellent Technicolor photography and a few thrilling wild animal sequences are the highlights of *Where No Vultures Fly*. On the whole, it's a soundly made film, lensed in the attractive East African setting of the Kenya National Park.

Merely as a peg for the fine location work, there is tagged on an insignificant though basically true story of a game warden who starts the National Park after fighting local prejudice, hunters and ivory poachers. Plot is of little consequence. Main entertainment is derived from some of the exciting animal sequences.

Harry Watt's direction of the game sequences is top grade, but he tends to flounder when handling human characters. Notwithstanding this, Anthony Steel, does an excellent and spirited job as the warden, but Dinah Sheridan is never anything but demure as his wife.

WHITE LINE FEVER

1975, 89 mins, ◇ *Dir* Jonathan Kaplan US, CANADA

★ *Stars* Jan-Michael Vincent, Kay Lenz, Slim Pickens, L.Q. Jones, Don Porter, Sam Laws

White Line Fever is a good action drama starring Jan-Michael Vincent as a young truck driver fighting corruption.

Air Force vet Vincent returns home to marriage with Kay Lenz and starting in as an independent trucker. He soon finds smuggling to be endemic to the career, and is repeatedly and violently hassled when he refuses to go along.

What seems missing from the film is more depth and logical transition: Vincent passes too rapidly from a stubborn honest lone wolf to practically a union leader.

With stunt experts Carey Loftin, Nate Long and Joe Hooker creating some powerful action footage, Vincent and Lenz experience assaults, fires, beatings and other troubles sent their way by L.Q. Jones and others, all under orders from Don Porter.

Timothy Bottoms, Lou Gossett and Warren Oates are white intruders in an Eskimo village in **The White Dawn.**

THE WHITE DAWN

1974, 109 mins, ◇ ⓥ *Dir* Philip Kaufman   US

★ *Stars* Warren Oates, Timothy Bottoms, Lou Gossett, Simonie Kopapik, Joanasie Salamone, Pilitak

James Houston's 1971 book, subtitled *An Eskimo Saga*, is the springboard for this production. Both limn the tale of how a trio of whaleboaters, stranded in the late 1890s near the North Pole, interact with and nearly destroy the band of Eskimos who saved their lives. But while the book had a logic and sensitivity of its own, the film version emerges as a static narrative.

Essentially, the three whalers bring familiar baggage to the pristine setting of the Eskimo village - they find ways of making booze, they gamble, they take advantage of village women, they steal, etc. Although each member of the trio is by no means uniform in his misconduct - Billy (Warren Oates) is easily the most nefarious - collective behaviour is at first accepted by the Eskimos, then tolerated and then viewed with a deepseated displeasure. Oates is properly blustery as the roistering older sea hand.

THE WHITE TOWER

1950, 98 mins, ◇ ⓥ *Dir* Ted Tetzlaff   US

★ *Stars* Glenn Ford, Alida Valli, Claude Rains, Oscar Homolka, Cedric Hardwicke, Lloyd Bridges

Magnificent scenic Swiss backgrounds and a gripping yarn are welded together in *The White Tower* for a powerful emotional impact. Out of James Ramsey Ullman's novel, scripter Paul Jarring has fashioned a pictorial theme with elemental appeal – the struggle of man to conquer nature. Plot opens in a peasant village, where a small group of Europeans and one American (Glenn Ford) have gathered.

The dominating passion of the group is to lick the forbidding heights of a nearby summit.

The pic may be resented for its attempt to define various national characteristics. In the case of the German member of the party (Lloyd Bridges), the pic frankly exploits the opportunity to blast the cold brutality and superman pretensions of the Herrenvolk.

WHO DARES WINS

1982, 125 mins, ◇ ⓥ *Dir* Ian Sharp   UK

★ *Stars* Lewis Collins, Judy Davis, Richard Widmark, Edward Woodward, Robert Webber, Tony Doyle

Who Dares Wins is pulp fare about the politics of terrorism in which the anti-war movement is discredited as prone to reckless murder in the ironic name of peace. In this case, provocative premise is no substitute for classy drama.

The simple-minded plot [from an original story by George Markstein] has a militant anti-nuclear organization take over a United States diplomatic facility in London with its glitzy bunch of hostages and demanding the wipeout of a US submarine base in Scotland by a nuclear missile. Wiped out instead, by a crack British commando team, are the peaceniks when the building is stormed. All the characters are stereotyped rather than cliched.

Performing standout is Judy Davis as the 'terrorist' leader. Lewis Collins offers pleasing virile projection as an undercover agent who shacks up with Davis.

The SAS storm a US diplomatic facility where anti-nuke terrorists are holding hostages in **Who Dares Wins.**

Richard Burton in **Wild Geese**, *an actioner about mercenaries in Africa.*

THE WILD GEESE

1978, 132 mins, ◇ Ⓥ *Dir* Andrew V. McLaglen   UK

★ **Stars** Richard Burton, Roger Moore, Richard Harris, Hardy Kruger, Stewart Granger, Jack Watson

Euan Lloyd's uppercase actioner, centered on a caper by mercenaries in Africa, attempts to be a cornucopia of tried boxoffice hooks but ultimately fails to meld its comedy, adventure, pathos, violence, heroics into a credible whole.

Reginald Rose's adaptation of Daniel Carney's story – about mercenary toughguys who parachute into the African bush to snatch a deposed African president for reinstatement to suit British business interests – is routinely predictable and, in the end, cornily incredible.

Roger Moore's shootouts with the Mafia in London and Hardy Kruger's neat killing of three sentries with cyanide-tipped arrows is good 'traditional' escapism. Then, as if to contemporize the film, Peckinpah-fashion, the screen's suddenly filled with bloody graphics and four-letter words.

Winston Ntshona is well cast as the deposed president Limbani though much of his 'message' dialog is unnecessarily and unpalatably heavy for what's presumably designed as a riproaring blood and guts actioner.

WILD GEESE II

1985, 125 mins, ◇ Ⓥ *Dir* Peter Hunt   UK

★ **Stars** Scott Glenn, Barbara Carrera, Edward Fox, Laurence Olivier, Robert Webber, Robert Freitag

Script [from the book *The Square Circle* by Reginald Rose] has a promising basic premise. An American TV station commissions mercenary John Haddad (Scott Glenn) to kidnap the nonagenarian Nazi leader Rudolf Hess from the impregnable Spandau prison in Berlin, but the follow-through never arrives. A routine car ambush is substituted for the impossible jailbreak. The liberated Hess just doesn't want to play games with history by revealing the Watergate-style story supposedly underlying Hitler's rise to power.

Despite these structural problems, film contains a wealth of incident. Haddad is the object of numerous assassination attempts organized by the German Heinrich Stroebling (Robert Freitag), who is in league with the Russians and Palestinian terrorists. The British are after Hess too. There's also a supporting role for members of the Irish Republican Army and the kidnap of yank journalist Kathy Lukas (Barbara Carrera) occasions a major shootout.

Edward Fox plays Colonel Faulkner with comic zest. Unintentionally, perhaps, Laurence Olivier also extracts laughs from his Hess cameo. By contrast, Glenn and Carrera take their parts more seriously than the script merits.

THE WIND AND THE LION

1975, 119 mins, ◇ *Dir* John Milius   US

★ **Stars** Sean Connery, Candice Bergman, Brian Keith, John Huston, Geoffrey Lewis, Steve Kanaly

Sean Connery stars as an upstart independent Berber chieftain who in 1904 kidnaps Candice Bergen and children, provoking Brian Keith (as Theodore Roosevelt) into dramatic power politics, which confound European moves into North Africa.

The quasi-fictional story gives full exposition to the black, white and gray personal and political elements involved, providing focal points of empathy and criticism for all concerned.

Connery scores one of his major screen impressions, while Bergen handles with assured excellence the subtleties of a woman first outraged at her captor, later his benefactor after a multinational doublecross.

Milius, armed with an expert crew of action specialists, has crafted a superior film, enhanced even further by Jerry Goldsmith's outstanding score.

WINDOM'S WAY

1957, 108 mins, ◇ ⓥ *Dir* Ronald Neame   UK

★ **Stars** Peter Finch, Mary Ure, Natasha Parry, Robert Flemyng, Michael Hordern, Marne Maitland

Peter Finch is a dedicated doctor working in the village of Selim, on a Far East island. He is loved and trusted by the villagers and finds himself involved in their political problems. Mary Ure is his estranged wife who comes out for a trial reconciliation at a time when the locality is in a state of unrest. Finch's ideals are such that he tries to prevent the villagers from getting up in arms against the local police and plantation manager.

The acting throughout this drama is first class, with Finch particularly convincing. Ure has little chance in the

colorless role of his wife, but Natasha Parry as a native nursing sister, in love with Finch, is warm, sensitive and technically very sound.

Screenwriter Jill Craigie has provided a slow moving, but literate script, from a novel by James Ramsay Ullman. Ronald Neame's direction brings out qualities of dignity and credibility.

THE WRATH OF GOD

1972, 111 mins, ◇ *Dir* Ralph Nelson US

★ **Stars** Robert Mitchum, Frank Langella, Rita Hayworth, John Colicos, Victor Buono, Ken Hutchison

The Wrath of God is a good solid action-adventure film, starring Robert Mitchum as a renegade priest who frees a Latin-American town of fear and terror during a rebellion of the 1920 era. Ralph Nelson's film has hard action, offsetting character-comedy relief, excellent production, and an outstanding cast of principals. James Graham's novel has been adapted by Nelson into a screenplay which, apart from some sporadic dialog cliche, neatly establishes and steadily develops a set of constantly-interesting characters.

With Victor Buono and Ken Hutchison, both outstanding as likeable freebooters and soldiers of fortune, Mitchum is forced by army colonel John Colicos to attempt the assassination of Langella, who rules his mountain retreat with vicious authority, largely implemented by Gregory Sierra.

THE WRECK OF THE MARY DEARE

1959, 105 mins, ◇ *Dir* Michael Anderson US

★ **Stars** Gary Cooper, Charlton Heston, Michael Redgrave, Emlyn Williams, Richard Harris, Ben Wright

The mystery of a 'ghost' ship looming suddenly out of the night, with only a crazed captain aboard, is solved skilfully and with a good deal of suspense in *The Wreck of the Mary Deare*, from the Hammond Innes novel originally published in the Saturday Evening Post in 1956. It's the kind of adventure yarn which, thanks to intelligent treatment and topnotch photography, comes off with a bang.

Gary Cooper is Gideon Patch, the captain who's been the victim of foul play but stands accused himself of negligence. And Charlton Heston plays the skipper of a salvage boat who becomes innocently involved in the mystery of the *Mary Deare* and, in the end, helps solve it. Both men are perfectly cast in rugged roles and Cooper particularly conveys a surprising range of emotion and reaction.

In the smaller (almost bit) parts, Michael Redgrave and Emlyn Williams are very British as they participate in the London Court of Inquiry. Richard Harris is the snarling villain. Ben Wright is comfortable as Heston's partner.

There's a letdown in pace at the middle of the film when the Court of Inquiry appears stacked against Cooper. But the climax comes off with bangup effects.

THE YEAR OF LIVING DANGEROUSLY

1982, 114 mins, ◇ Ⓥ *Dir* Peter Weir AUSTRALIA, US

★ **Stars** Mel Gibson, Sigourney Weaver, Linda Hunt, Michael Murphy, Bill Kerr, Noel Ferrier

Peter Weir's *The Year of Living Dangerously*, is a $6 million adaptation of Christopher Koch's novel, set in Indonesia in 1965 in the turbulent months leading to the fall of the Sukarno government.

Mel Gibson limns a young Australian journalist on his first posting as a foreign correspondent. Wide-eyed and innocent, he is befriended by an astute Chinese-Australian cameraman, a dwarf who seeks to manipulate people as deftly as he handles shadow puppets.

Here is an astonishing feat of acting by New Yorker Linda Hunt, cast by Weir because he could not locate a short male actor to fit the bill. A bizarre, yet touching, romantic triangle develops between Gibson, Hunt, and Sigourney Weaver as a British Embassy official.

Having laid the groundwork, Weir hits the action button. Gibson learns that the Communists are bringing in arms for a coup against Sukarno and in broadcasting the story blows a confidence from Weaver, who rejects him.

Filming in the Philippines, and then Sydney, where the crew was forced to repair after receiving threats from the Islamic community, Weir and his crew expertly recreate the squalor, poverty, noise, heat and emotion of the pressure cooker that was Indonesia in 1965.

Mel Gibson, with Linda Hunt, covers a political rally in Jakarta in The Year of Living Dangerously.

YOU ONLY LIVE TWICE

1967, 117 mins, ◇ Ⓥ *Dir* Lewis Gilbert   UK

★ *Stars* Sean Connery, Akiko Wakabayashi, Tetsuro Tamba, Lois Maxwell, Bernard Lee, Donald Pleasence

Film begins with a prolog in which a US astronaut's spacewalk is interrupted by another spacecraft that, crocodile-style, opens its jaws and swallows the capsule. US government is peeved at what it assumes to be a Russian attempt to foil space exploration, and 007 is assigned by helpful British intelligence to locate the missing rocket before full-scale war breaks out.

Film's title refers to Bond's 'murder', which precedes the credits. Ensconced with the first in a long line of Japanese beauties he is abruptly gunned down and pronounced dead in her bed by officials.

Sean Connery plays 007 with his usual finesse. Rest of cast in the $9.5 million film is strictly secondary, although Akiko Wakabayashi and Tetsuro Tamba register well as Bond's Japanese cohorts. Donald Pleasence makes a suitably menacing German heavy who appears in film's final scenes.

YOUNG SHERLOCK HOLMES

1985, 109 mins, ◇ Ⓥ *Dir* Barry Levinson   US

★ *Stars* Nicholas Rowe, Alan Cox, Sophie Ward, Anthony Higgins, Susan Fleetwood, Freddie Jones

Young Sherlock Holmes is another Steven Spielberg film corresponding to those lamps made from driftwood and coffee tables from redwood burl and hatchcovers. It's not art but they all serve their purpose and sell by the millions.

The formula this time is applied to the question of what might have happened had Sherlock Holmes and John Watson first met as teenage students.

As usual, Speilberg's team – this time led by director Barry Levinson – isn't really as interested in the answer as it is in fooling around with the visual effects possibilities conjured by George Lucas' Industrial Light & Magic shop.

Nicholas Rowe as Holmes and Alan Cox as Watson maturely carry off their roles, assisted by Sophie Ward as the necessary female accomplice. The adults are just there to fill in the spaces.

YOUNG WINSTON

1972, 157 mins, ◇ ▼ *Dir* Richard Attenborough   UK

★ *Stars* Simon Ward, Robert Shaw, Anne Bancroft, Jack Hawkins, Ian Holm, Anthony Hopkins

Rate this biopic of Winston Churchill's early years as both a brilliant artistic achievement and a fascinating, highly enjoyable film – a combination not always obtained.

It's a richly multi-faced scrapbook [from Churchill's book *My Early Life*] which is unfolded, touching on his lonely childhood and only occasional contact with his politician father and a socially much-involved American mother, early school experience, first combat and war correspondent stints in India and the Sudan and on to first political defeat and ultimate vindication as – after a headline-grabbing Boer War exploit – he makes an early political mark in an impassioned House of Commons speech.

Far from a sycophantic paean to a great man in the bud, pic manages a believable portrait of an ambitious and sometimes arrogant young man.

ZEPPELIN

1971, 97 mins, ◇ *Dir* Etienne Perier   UK

★ *Stars* Michael York, Elke Sommer, Peter Carsten, Marius Goring, Anton Diffring, Andrew Keir

Zeppelin settles for being just another wartime action melodrama, with some good aerial sequences and a powerful, brisk raid sequence in the finale .

Pic deals with Britain's concern about Germany's new World War I weapon, the Zeppelin, the monstrous, looming aircraft that made Britain vulnerable. Indication that the Germans have perfected a new and even more effective Zeppelin jerks the British high-ups into swift action.

A young Scottish lieutenant, of Anglo-German parentage, who had left Germany and eventually joined the British Army (Michael York) looks the perfect spy. Worked on by an attractive German Mata Hari (Alexandra Stewart), he is softened up and when called on to `volunteer' to 'defect' and dig out the secrets of the new Zeppelin he reluctantly agrees.

Many Germans are suspicious of his sudden switch back to the homeland. But only one appears to be convinced that he's a spy. She (Elke Sommer) is the wife of the aircraft designer (Marius Goring) and she's more concerned with helping to prepare the Zeppelin for its final trial run than in exposing York.

ZULU

1964, 135 mins, ◇ ▼ *Dir* Cy Endfield   UK

★ *Stars* Stanley Baker, Jack Hawkins, Ulla Jacobsson, James Booth, Michael Caine, Nigel Green

Joseph E. Levine makes an impressive debut in British film production with *Zulu*, a picture that allows ample scope for his flamboyant approach to showmanship.

Zeppelin, *an action melodrama about the development of the German's secret weapon - an airship.*

Based on a famous heroic exploit, when a handful of British soldiers withstood an onslaught by 4,000 Zulu warriors, the production is distinguished by its notable onscreen values, which are enhanced by top-quality lensing by Stephen Dade. It also has an intelligent screenplay which avoids most of the obvious cliches. It keeps the traditional British stiff upper-lip attitudes down to the barest minimum.

The defense of the garrison at Rorke's Drift took place on 22 January 1879. At the time the garrison heard the news

The British soldiers stand up to another attack in Zulu, *epic portrayal of the true story of Battle for Rorke's Drift.*

that the 4,000 Zulu braves were on the way, reports had just come in that a far larger garrison had been wiped out, and there was no prospect of help from any other source.

One of the more obvious cliches in this type of yarn is apt to be the malingerer who displays great heroism in a moment of crisis. There is such a situation in *Zulu*, but the cliche is avoided, largely because of the excellent performance by James Booth. Indeed, the high allround standard of acting is one of the notable plus features. Stanley Baker, a solid and reliable performer, turns in a thoroughly convincing portrayal as the resolute Royal Engineers officer, with an effective contrasting study by Michael Caine as a supercilious lieutenant. Richard Burton contributes a brief and dignified narration.

ZULU DAWN

1979, 117 mins, ◇ Ⓥ   *Dir* Douglas Hickox   UK

★ *Stars* Burt Lancaster, Peter O'Toole, Simon Ward, John Mills, Nigel Davenport, Denholm Elliott

The subject of *Zulu Dawn* is the Battle of Isandlhwana wherein some 1,500 redcoats were slaughtered by 16 times their number of Zulu warriors led by legendary chief Cetshwayo.

The film is, in fact, a sort of 'prequel' to the 1964 picture *Zulu*, which dealt with an heroic stand at Rorke's Drift by a small band of British soldiers in 1879.

The action sequences are superbly handled, as are the scenes in which the men and material are assembled and manoeuvered. For sheer scope and numbers of people being manipulated for the cameras, *Zulu Dawn* is positively DeMillesque in scale.

Such banality as there is is, thankfully, confined to the expositional sequences which are quickly gotten out of the way to allow the army to get on the march.